D0872803

'... a moving and sadly accurate description of
Australia's greatest river system.'
The Age

'Timely and revealing ... an immensely readable travelogue,
reveling in the rich heritage and character of the Australian bush.'
Australian Bookseller & Publisher

'[Hammer's] clear-eyed analysis of the environmental issues is
matched by compelling and often poignant storytelling.'
G Magazine

'This is an important book ... Hammer has brought us the
humanity of the people and families so badly affected.'
Good Reading

'A disturbing and though-provoking account for all Australians.'
Sun Herald

'[Hammer's new work] ... deserves a place among
the Australian classics'
Tony Wright, *The Age*

'Poignant, urgent environmental writing at it's best.'
Better Homes and Gardens

'*The River* should be required reading for all politicians ... because
it is a true and honest account of a great Australian icon in crisis.'
The Canberra Times

Chris Hammer has been a journalist for over twenty-five years. He has been an international correspondent for SBS TV's flagship current affairs program *Dateline*, the chief political correspondent for *The Bulletin* and a senior political journalist for *The Age*.

The Coast

Chris Hammer

MELBOURNE
UNIVERSITY
PRESS

MELBOURNE UNIVERSITY PRESS
An imprint of Melbourne University Publishing Limited
187 Grattan Street, Carlton, Victoria 3053, Australia
mup-info@unimelb.edu.au
www.mup.com.au

First published 2012
Text © Chris Hammer, 2012
Design and typography © Melbourne University Publishing Limited, 2012

Text design by Phil Campbell
Cover design by Nada Backovic
Typeset by Mike Kuszla, J&M Typesetting
Printed by Griffin Press, South Australia
Cover photograph ©iStockphoto / Benjamin Goode

National Library of Australia Cataloguing-in-Publication entry
Hammer, Chris.
The coast / Chris Hammer.

9780522858723 (pbk.)
9780522862171 (ebook)

Coasts—Australia.
Coastal biodiversity—Australia.
Coastal zone management—Australia.
Coastal settlements—Australia.
Environmental protection—Australia.
Conservation of natural resources—Australia.
Australia—social life and customs.

551.4570994

Australian Government

Australia Council for the Arts

Contents

Prologue   ix

1   The Reef   1
2   Torres Strait   36
3   The Cyclone Coast   65
4   The Gold Coast   97
5   Towards Sydney   126
6   Bermagui   168
7   Bass Strait   205

Acknowledgements   238

Prologue

Broulee Island, currently joined to the mainland.

Another summer has come to the coast, another La Niña summer. For the second year in a row, the weather has been cool and wet, at least compared with the baking hot drought years of the past decade. Once again there are floods in Queensland and parts of northern New South Wales. So far the rising waters have been less widespread and less destructive than last summer, although it's only January 2012 and the Bureau of Meteorology is predicting at least another month of rain and warning that more floods may be on their way.

La Niña is distinguished by a large mass of warm surface water gathering in the western Pacific Ocean. This puts more moisture into the atmosphere, helps drive the Asian monsoon, and pushes clouds down across northern Australia. Newspapers report that 2011, while relatively wet and cool, was nevertheless the warmest La Niña year on record. That's not good news; the warmer the water in the western Pacific, the greater the chance of more frequent and more powerful cyclones heading towards the east coast of Australia. But so far this summer, no cyclones, nothing remotely like the devastation wrought by Cyclone Yasi. Fingers crossed.

It's almost a year to the day since I set off to explore Australia's east coast, ostensibly to catalogue the myriad threats posed by climate change, but also just to see it, in all its unspoilt grandeur and seaside kitsch. As I write I'm at Broulee on the New South Wales South Coast, at the holiday house shared by my family, wallowing in the traditional post-Christmas beach holiday. Today I took my kids, Cameron and Elena, down to the small beach formed by the spit that stretches between Broulee's headland and the nearby island. For, at this time, the island is no longer an island; it's joined to the mainland by a seemingly substantial dune system stabilised by low-lying scrub. The south-facing beach is typically sheltered from the swell by the island and shallow reefs, bestowing it with a type of Mediterranean calm. My daughter, like my mother, loves swimming here, away from the surf and swell. But today there was a strong southerly blowing, inciting white caps and whipping sand into our faces. So we crossed the sandy isthmus, all 15 metres of it, to North Broulee Beach. It's a long beach, kilometres long, but up near the island it curls into a shallow, north-facing bay, completely sheltered from the southerly. It was only when we climbed the dunes that I realised that the tide was out. Back on the windward side, the southerly had pushed the sea well up the beach, but on the leeward side the sea had retreated further out than I had ever seen it. It was, I realised, the day of the summer king tide, when the sea advances further and retreats more dramatically than on any other day of the year.

After swimming and a bit of horseplay, the kids and I walked off towards the northerly side of the island. On this day we could simply walk across the sand where the water had retreated. The tide was so low that for a panicked moment I wondered if we had stumbled across the beginnings of a tsunami. Rounding the point of the island, we came across the most ephemeral of rock pools, the size of several backyard swimming pools, separated from the ocean for a few hours by this infrequent phenomenon. Sea grass lay limp in the shallows and surprisingly large fish zipped this way and that while small zebra-striped fingerlings clouded curiously around our legs as we waded in. A wet slapping alerted us to a stranded ray, marooned by the retreating tide on the still-wet sand near the pool. It was the size of a large dinner plate. 'Poor Mr Ray', entreated my daughter, looking at me with her puppy-dog eyes. So I climbed up into the bush and found a couple of sticks. Carefully, I dug them into the sand beneath the ray and half carried it, half flung it flapping back into the pool; Elena clapped her hands with approval. Once back in the safety of the water, Mr Ray displayed his gratitude by immediately beaching himself again. This time, at least, he was still partially in the water, and the tide wasn't about to fall any lower. I was explaining this to Elena when movement caught my eye in the seagrass: an octopus insinuating its way through the weeds, perfectly camouflaged save for its liquid creep. The kids gathered round and we watched its slithering progress. Warning them not to get too close, I pointed out the brown rings around its tentacles, explaining that if the octopus was provoked the rings could turn an iridescent blue and its bite could kill. They looked on with suitable awe, eyes wide. I have no idea if it was indeed a blue-ringed octopus, but the rock pools of southern New South Wales are one of its primary habitats: a lesson well dispensed.

Later, after more swimming and ball games, we packed up and headed for the car, back across the spit towards the south-facing beach. I stood for a while atop the dune and, squinting into the sand-laden wind, surveyed the two beaches separated by this narrow isthmus of dune. The water level on the southern beach was at least a metre higher than its northern neighbour. I wondered what sort of pressure was being exerted on the dune. It seemed quite a fragile thing, that dune. And I knew there had been times when it had failed in holding back the Pacific. When I was a teenager, the island was indeed an island, and the strait between it and the shore a treacherous channel of rapidly flowing water. Later, as sand built up, it was possible to walk to the island, but only at low tide. Now the dune feels permanent, sheltering the twin beaches between the island and the headland. Then again, the same impression of permanence had once fooled the early settlers. Walk around the island, close by where the kids and I found our rock pool, and rusted remnants of rail lines protrude from the scrub, the last indication there was a small port here back in the nineteenth century. The settlers made the mistake of creating a track along the top of the dunes to connect the island jetty with the headland. The track helped erode the sand, and in 1873 a wild storm carved its way through the spit, separating the island from the shore. The roar of the sea as it passed through the breach was reportedly heard many kilometres away. Since then, the dune has periodically reformed and dissolved, with six breaches between 1966 and 1988 alone, before a more stable formation asserted itself.

The fragility of the Broulee spit is instructive. The shoreline of eastern Australia advances and retreats unpredictably, obeying the commands of tide and current. Some climate change forecasts predict more accentuated El Niño and La Niña events, bringing greater pressure to bear upon the shifting sands. We have now encrusted much of the coast with harbours, breakwaters, groynes, seawalls, marinas and multi-storeyed edifices boasting absolute water frontage. We have tried to make permanent the ephemeral, like the early settlers of Broulee. The Pacific Ocean is a mighty thing, sands are by nature shifting, and the capacity of our concrete reinforcements to resist that reality may prove illusory.

A few years ago I set out to explore the impact of the millennial drought on the environment and river communities of Australia's major river system. The result was a book: *The River: A Journey through the Murray-Darling Basin*. While I learnt a lot about rivers and those that live by them, I also came to appreciate just how important the notion of the bush has been to the formulation of an Australian identity. And if the bush is important to Australians, the beach is without a doubt equally so. So this book suggested itself. It is, after all, the great Australian dichotomy, our essential yin and yang: the bush and the beach. Most of us live in suburbia, but our hearts are elsewhere.

I travelled to the Torres Strait, and learnt of the threat posed by rising sea levels, staying on an island where the beach has been lost and storm surges push waves through people's living rooms. At Heron Island, a green gem on the Great Barrier Reef 70 kilometres off the coast of Queensland, I was told of the twin threats of coral bleaching and ocean acidification. In Far North Queensland I journeyed through the wreckage wrought by Cyclone Yasi, humbled by the resilience and optimism of its survivors. At the Gold Coast I lost my way in a city built on sand and found myself wondering what its self-perpetuating spiral of population growth and wealth accumulation might mean for the future. At Manly, Bondi and Cronulla I watched the surf lifesavers and considered their iconic status. Further south, I found myself growing more optimistic. In beautiful Bermagui, a fishing village reinvented, I found evidence that addressing environmental challenges is not beyond the will or wit of our governments. And finally, in Tasmania, I met with people on both sides of the Tamar Valley pulp mill development.

At times along the way, I felt depressed, the predicted climatic shift too huge to contemplate, its effects too complex to safely predict. At other times I was exhilarated by the awesome grandeur of the Australian seascape and by the quirky individualism of its inhabitants. I finished my journey convinced that climate change is real, but just what it means for the future, the environment and Australian identity remains to be seen. No doubt others undertaking the same journey, or reading this book, will come to different conclusions. The trip is over, but the journey of discovery continues.

THE REEF

The reef flat joins the beach on Heron Island, 70 kilometres off the Queensland coast.

The talk at Brisbane airport is of cyclones. A weather map has engulfed the front page of the *Courier Mail*: the land is brown, the sea is blue, the clouds are a lurid yellow-and-red spiral—the unmistakeable shape of a cyclone bearing down upon the northern coastline. The headline warns: 'HERE WE GO AGAIN'. I sit near the gate awaiting my connecting flight north to Gladstone, reading the copy:

> Queensland is on alert for a week of cyclones. Cyclone Anthony, shown approaching the coast, is forecast to hit between Bowen and Cairns as a possible category 3 storm on Monday. But of more concern is a low-pressure system off Fiji which could form into a category 4 cyclone and threaten the state late next week.

It's late January and Queensland is still recovering from devastating floods. Between late December and mid-January, the rain came in wave after wave, inundating an area the size of New South Wales, more than twice the size of Germany. At least thirty-five people died, with a further nine missing. In the Lockyer Valley, an 'inland tsunami' swept cars, houses and people to their destruction. The body of one victim was found 80 kilometres downstream. In Brisbane, a young man wading through floodwaters stepped into a storm-water drain, was sucked under and drowned. Three-quarters of the state has been declared a disaster zone. Now, just two weeks after the Brisbane floods hit their peak, the city's newspaper shouts: 'HERE WE GO AGAIN'.

Not just Queensland is affected. There has been flooding in northern New South Wales and catastrophe in Victoria. In the same week that the Brisbane River burst its banks, leaving 20 000 homes sodden and sullied, the rivers of western Victoria rose up and broke their banks. After the driest decade in Australia's history, the rains have returned with a vengeance to eastern Australia. The El Niño of the dry, which has taunted and tormented this last dozen years, has finally made way for the La Niña of the wet. The contrast is unnerving. Two summers ago I travelled the inland rivers, through the parched dustbowl of the Murray–Darling, where entire communities shrivelled under the relentless sun, and drought ate at the faith of farmers: the worst drought in living memory, in a hundred years. Rivers hadn't just stopped flowing; some were empty, bone dry. Everywhere, people longed for, prayed for, the return of La Niña and her sweeping skirts of rain. Now the prodigal has returned, not dancing lightly across the landscape, but throwing lightning bolts and thunder, storming across the countryside, as if in anger at being excluded for so long by her brother. It's the most intense La Niña since the summer of 1973–74, the last time Brisbane flooded and Queensland found itself so thoroughly awash. Such ill-mannered children are these, such petulant twins, not mellowing with age, but growing more careless and destructive like a couple of delinquent teenagers. Perhaps it's their diet: like toddlers downing red cordial, maybe they're being fed too much carbon and have become hyperactive. The climate itself has ADHD.

The announcement comes: 'Flight QF 2308 for Gladstone now boarding'. I drop the *Courier Mail* and its speculation of cyclones in the bin, my musings in there with it, and walk out across the tarmac. The sun is beating down under an untroubled sky; rain, storms, cyclones and tempest seem remote.

⟶

'Gladstone is an industrial city', the bus driver states proudly as she takes us into town from the airport. She's not wrong. There's not one, but two alumina refineries, Australia's largest aluminium smelter, the country's largest cement kiln, the state's largest coal-burning power station and the world's largest ammonium-nitrate plant, all gathered round the port, the biggest coal exporter in Queensland, fed by a constant stream of kilometre-long trains wheeling in from nearby mines. 'At present we're exporting approximately 60 million tonnes of coal through Gladstone annually. At this rate of exploitation, it's estimated that there's enough coal to last for three hundred years,' the driver declares cheerfully. 'We have at least three different companies planning to export coal-seam gas. So, we have plenty of people coming into Gladstone now. You'll notice a number of new apartment buildings.' Indeed I do. The place reeks of optimism.

Later, I stand atop Auckland Point lookout over Gladstone Harbour. Laid out before me is an industrial panorama that wraps around the foreshore, as neat and easily defined as a feature from *SimCity*: the cement works, the fuel tanks, the alumina refinery and the power station chain-smoking in the distance. This is a city built on cheap and abundant energy, the coal that's there for the taking. With a population of just 30 000, Gladstone may well be the most carbon-intensive community in Australia. Look out across Gladstone and you look out across Australia itself, the most carbon-intensive economy per capita on earth. Here is the prosperity that pays for our wide-screen televisions, SUVs, reverse-cycle air conditioners, hospitals, schools and roads. Here are the mines, the cheap power, the smelters and the ports. Here is the house that coal built.

But I haven't come here to admire the industry. Or to condemn it, for that matter. I've come for the Great Barrier Reef. The other face of Australia: natural, unspoilt and enduring. Our great marine wilderness, guarded by statute and protected by affection. One of the great natural wonders of the world. That it lies off the coast of Gladstone is an irony that can be lost on no one.

⌒

Selina Ward and Jez Roff, Queensland University research scientists, are waiting for me at the Gladstone marina. Selina is blessed with a natural generosity. I met her by chance last year, and as soon as she learnt I was planning to write about the coast, she insisted on helping any way she could. Now she's invited me along to the university's research station at Heron Island, 70 kilometres off the coast of Gladstone. It's a famous place, Heron Island. Arthur C Clarke used the research station as the setting for his submarine thriller *Deep Range*; David Attenborough shouted over-emphatic observations from the beach alongside the station in the BBC's *First Life;* and NASA put an image of Heron Island aboard the *Voyager 1* and *Voyager 2* spacecraft before sending the probes tumbling off through the void beyond the solar system. And now I'm going to see it for myself.

The morning is warm and the skies are clear. I'm bubbling with enthusiasm at the thought of travelling to Heron, but Selina and Jez are more circumspect. There's a two-hour boat trip ahead of us, and it may be rough. Belatedly, I recall the *Courier Mail*'s front page and its predictions of a 3.6-metre swell. Selina sets out our tactics. The secret, she says, is to get on board first, claim the 'sleeping seats' on the lower deck, and then try to sleep through the trip. I act nonchalant, even as I surreptitiously down a seasickness tablet. Selina, behaving more like a platoon leader than a marine biologist, leads Jez and me back around the queuing tourists, so we get in first when the gate opens. Her timing is immaculate: the three of us board first, storm down the internal stairs and lay claim to the sleeping benches, one each.

I've had a mixed record on seasickness over the years. One night I crossed the heaving seas of the English Channel amid a heaving mob of football louts, mysteriously unaffected. On other occasions, I've miserably succumbed. Back in the land before children, I went fishing on successive summers aboard a charter boat, the *Red Fin*, out of Batemans Bay with my good mate Brisso. The first time out, Brisso spent his time hauling fish; I spent mine hurling breakfast. Taking refuge below, I encountered an elderly man, in even worse state than myself. 'This is very embarrassing', he whispered.

'Why?' I groaned. 'I'm as sick as you are.'

'Yeah, but you weren't a professional fisherman for twenty years.' Seasickness, it seems, can be as unpredictable as the sea itself.

The next summer, I boarded *The Red Fin* determined to conquer the malady and catch some fish: I'd had an early night, with no drinking, and swallowed motion-sickness tablets the recommended half an hour ahead of time. And yet, as we headed out past the Tollgate Islands and hit the swell of the open sea, the nausea again began to rise. I kept my eyes fixed on the horizon, as I had been advised to do, trying to compensate for the rise and fall of the boat. It didn't work. But then, before the swirling misery could entirely engulf me, I observed those around me, particularly the crewmember handing out fishing lines and buckets of bait. He wasn't looking at the horizon. He seemed oblivious to what was happening outside the boat. That's when the penny dropped. The trick was not to compensate for the yaw and pitch, but to roll with it. I forgot about the horizon, and tried to go along with the movement of the boat, not attempting to predict it. It worked a treat. In a short while the encroaching nausea had receded, and I was able to man a line and catch some fish. Brisso still caught more fish, but I was every bit as happy.

The memory is only partially reassuring; it all happened a long time ago on a relatively placid sea unruffled by newspaper reports and rumours of cyclones. Now I find myself in the company of sea-tempered scientists. I think of the supposed importance of first impressions; I don't want to introduce myself as a spewing neophyte. So, even as the *Heron Islander* powers through the calm waters of Gladstone Harbour, I stretch out, put on some airline eyeshades and close my eyes. Seasickness, I have read somewhere, is caused by the conflict between what you see and your sense of movement. This makes sense given my experience on the *Red Fin*. My kids never get car sick when they're sleeping, or dozing with their eyes shut. So I lie on my back, with my eyes closed, and try to enjoy the movement of the boat. I hear the squeals of delight from the deck above as the boat leaves the relative calm of the harbour and starts smashing into the first waves of the open sea. With my eyes shut, I go with the flow, trying to enjoy the haphazard gyrations of the boat as it's knocked first from one side and then another. It shivers as one hull and then the other ploughs into the crest of a wave. Below me, there are bangs and more shivers as the swell slaps up under the boat. The movement is erratic, as the catamaran pivots on one ephemeral fulcrum before lurching to find another. The squeals subside as those above retreat, perhaps soaked through or no longer exhilarated. The sea grows rougher. I'm forced, eyes still closed, to extend an arm and cling to a table to avoid being thrown bodily from the bench. Babies and young children are crying—a chorus of distress—but I'm feeling warm and secure in my dark cocoon: lifting, swaying and shifting. Riding the swell, enjoying the moment. Eyes shut, ears open. I hear a few telltale coughs and the sound of someone vomiting, but I will get to the research station without embarrassing myself.

⌣

Heron Island, a coral cay, sits glowing gem-green on the wide and shallow reef. It's a tiny thing, this piece of land, just 800 metres long and 300 metres wide and less than 4 metres above sea level at its highest point, insubstantial amid uninterrupted horizons. The northwest corner of the island houses a tourist resort, the southwest the University of Queensland research station. The eastern half is a national park. The catamaran sweeps into the small harbour, past the rusting hulk of a strategically placed wreck, and is tied up to the wharf.

At the end of the jetty, the passengers split into two groups, the tourists heading left towards the resort, and the scientists turning right towards the research station. The station itself is large, more like a small village, hidden from the beach by a thin strip of tropical forest. There's a narrow compacted-sand road down the middle, flanked by accommodation, offices, equipment sheds, classrooms, a library and computer room, and a self-catering kitchen and dining room. And at its heart, there's a two-storey laboratory complex. On the deck outside, huge tanks of seawater house coral and other reef life, the raw material for dozens of experiments. Much of the station was burned to the ground in 2007, and the buildings that greet us are new and well designed. I'd been expecting share accommodation; instead, I get a room to myself, with its own small balcony and glass-louvre windows, in an apartment I share with Selina and Jez. The station can house more than a hundred people at any one time, but in January there are no undergraduates, just a dozen or so researchers with their graduate students, getting their fieldwork completed before the teaching year begins. Downstairs from our apartment is the kitchen-dining area, the social hub of the research station. There are researchers here from the University of Queensland in Brisbane and from James Cook University in Townsville, and various foreigners on exchange. As we unpack our food, I hear American accents, French accents, hybrid accents.

Selina and Jez go to the lab almost immediately to start setting up their experiment. Their first job is to scavenge pieces of equipment. It's one of the limitations of island research: bring critical elements with you, then make do with what's here—there's no hardware store round the corner to pick up extra widgets. The scientists are going to be occupied for a few hours, which is fine by me. The lab is modern and sterile; the island is timeless, natural and teeming with life. There's a track behind the lab that takes me to the south-facing beach. It's another world. The research station is deliberately screened from the beach, not just for aesthetic reasons, but because lights can disorientate giant sea turtles as they come ashore at night to lay their eggs. So the beach is left undisturbed. And right now, I seem to have it to myself. To the west I can see the wreck guarding the harbour, so I walk the other way, towards the east. Before me stretches the beach, flanked by reef on one side and a low forest on the other. Curiously, there are no palm trees. Coconuts have floated all round the pacific, colonising coral cays, atolls and volcanic islands alike. But not here. Later I learn that the resort owners planted palms several years ago, keen that Heron should conform to preconceptions of paradise; the national parks service ordered them ripped out to preserve the natural environment. Heron Island hosts the resort and the research station, but it's the parks service that calls the shots.

The beach is made of sand, surprisingly fine for a coral cay, and littered with lumps of dead coral. A ridge of dark rock a few metres wide, an uplifted layer of reef flat, separates the beach from the sea. And it's the sea that demands my attention. The wind is whipping in hard from the east, churning the water into a petulant chop, white caps suggesting worse weather to come. But it can't change the colour of the water: a light aquamarine, a turquoise that seems to glow of its own accord. The reef is shallow here; at low tide you can walk for hundreds of metres out to sea. To the east, the direction I'm walking, the reef extends for 11 kilometres. Heron Island is just a speck by comparison, a small accumulation of sand and coral at one end, and the reef is just one part of a much larger system: almost 3000 reefs stretching more than 2600 kilometres down the coast from the Torres Strait to 100 kilometres south of where I'm walking. And here I am, right in the middle of it. I breathe deep the wonder of it, of this island in the middle of nowhere, formed by a conspiracy of wind and tide and time—that, and the industry of billions of tiny coral polyps.

The Great Barrier Reef is a massive interconnected ecosystem, host to a bewildering range of life, the aquatic equivalent of the Amazon rainforest. Here's the curious thing: like the South American jungle, the reef thrives in spite of a lack of nutrients. Just as Brazilian farmers find the Amazonian soil poor and leached, so too it is with the reef. That crystal-clear, 'desert island' water you see in the tourist brochures is just that: a marine desert. Indeed, if there were more nutrients in the water, plants would grow readily in the warm shallow waters, and seaweed and algae would choke the coral. This is what happens all too frequently on inshore reefs: heavy rain falls on land cleared of forests, washing silt and fertiliser and God knows what else into the waterways. Brown rivers flush into crystalline seas, subverting the natural balance and degrading reefs. But that's not a problem here, not this far from land.

For all its complexity, biodiversity and interdependence, the reef is built around a single organism: coral. Coral underpin everything. Some 400 distinct species form the base of the food chain and build the massive structures that support an estimated 1500 species of fish and 5000 species of mollusc. Coral are simple creatures: little more than bags of protoplasm. Like a bag, they have a hole at one end: in comes some food, out goes some waste. No brains, no guts, no mobility—like a superannuated senator. And yet, from these creatures grows such grandeur. So insignificant as individuals, they form colonies of millions of genetically identical polyps that behave at times like some far more complex creation. Touch one polyp and a frisson of reaction sweeps across the colony, like a shivering beast. As colonies, the coral form intricate shapes, some branching like trees, others forming immense brain-like domes, others yet folding around themselves like scrolls. Some rest on the ocean floor as solid as rocks; others branch brittle and exposed; others yet sway soft and supple back and forth with the movement of the water. Here, there are reds and oranges; there, there are blues and greens, a kaleidoscope of complexity. Beneath the veneer of life, the thin layer of living cells, lie the skeletons deposited over centuries by previous generations. The polyps extract calcium carbonate from the seawater and build their protective shells so they can withdraw at times of danger, and as the coral grow outwards, the skeletons are left behind. This is the freshly grown bedrock of the reef, the superstructure upon which one of the planet's most extensive ecosystems is built. It's an interrelated universe, home to everything from single-cell exotica to dolphins, whales, porpoises, turtles, dugongs, sharks and rays. It's an evolutionary explosion, where every possible location and every possible niche is identified, fought over and occupied.

Yet the coral do not work alone. The tiny animals have a silent partner, minute and unpublicised: zooxanthella. I had not heard of it until Selina explained its role. Zooxanthella is a microorganism that lives inside the coral. Not just inside the coral polyps, but within their very cells, so close is the relationship. Like plants, the tiny organisms photosynthesise, producing sugars, fats and proteins. It's the same alchemy that lies at the heart of the Amazon, the combination of water, carbon dioxide and sunlight that powers life itself. It's this process that turns a marine desert into one of the densest and most intense ecosystems on the planet. Zooxanthellae provide coral with up to 95 per cent of their energy, including glucose, glycerol and amino acids, which is why many coral, including all of those reliant on this symbiotic relationship with zooxanthellae, live in shallow, clear water, where they can pick up enough sunlight for photosynthesis. It's why coral reefs are so like an underwater garden: branching coral are reaching out, competing for sunlight, just like terrestrial plants. In return for the energy, the coral provide the zooxanthellae with carbon dioxide, nitrogen and phosphorous. So tight is the relationship, these waste products don't even leave the coral's cells; they are consumed there and then by the zooxanthellae. Coral can live without zooxanthellae, and zooxanthellae can live without coral, but the great reefs of the world could not exist without this symbiotic relationship.

In the old textbooks, zooxanthellae were often referred to as algae, but they are not. The assumption was not unreasonable; zooxanthellae are single-celled organisms dependent on photo-synthesis. But it seems the little critters have more in common with animals than with plants. When a University of Queensland grad student set out to sequence its genome, his initial findings attracted the wrath of his supervisor, who believed the sample must have been contaminated by the student's own skin. Double-checking confirmed that zooxanthellae have DNA remarkably similar to our own. Such a tiny animal, such a mighty genome. One theory is that somewhere back in the mists of evolutionary time, some single-celled organisms ingested plant material and somehow incorporated the genetic material into their own DNA, giving them the ability to photosynthesise. It's a humbling thought: that a single-celled organism, so small it can live within the cells of a coral polyp, is some sort of cousin of ours. It's also inspiring: the same single-celled organism has helped construct a reef complex stretching 2600 kilometres up the coast of Queensland. What have you achieved lately?

I ponder the enormity of this industry as I sit under a casuarina tree 70 kilometres off the Australian coast on an island built by coral and its silent partner, zooxanthella. Gladstone, with all its engineering wonders, pales by comparison. I stand at the sandy eastern point of Heron Island, looking across kilometre after kilometre of reef. I wonder how long Heron Island has been here. Not long at all, not in geological time. The Great Barrier Reef didn't even exist just 10 000 years ago. Yet now it's an ecosystem as visible from space as the Amazon rainforest. This mind-boggling platform of life, built in such a short time on such a narrow base, is the precarious combination of an organism that can turn sunlight into food, and a minute, immobile polyp that can extract calcium carbonate from seawater to build reefs the size of a conurbation.

Talk is of cyclones as we prepare dinner that night. There is no mobile phone reception on Heron, but the research station has the internet, and we've all been following the progress of Cyclone Anthony as it swings in from the Coral Sea towards the Queensland coast. The latest predictions have it making landfall somewhere between Townsville and Mackay, well to the north. The consensus is that it will be too far away and too weak to have much affect on us. But the depression off Fiji is another matter. It's still there, lurking with menace, growing ominous. Heron Island has experienced its fair share of cyclone damage over the years. The reef might be mighty, but it's not impervious.

Selina is still in the lab, so Jez and I get on with the cooking. Jez is a striking looking guy, tall and muscly with clear blue eyes. But that's not what makes him striking. It's his hair: dreadlocks, woven and wilful, some piled high atop his head, the rest hanging low down his back. It's the hair and the metal: the shiny silver jewellery piercing his skin at every opportunity. There's a ring through his lower lip and studs in each cheek that glint when he smiles like robotic dimples. He wears something akin to a bolt through one ear, and an oversized ring is inserted in the other, so heavy that it creates a hole through the centre of the earlobe, into which Jez has inserted a hand-rolled cigarette, storing it for later.

'Isn't it a hassle at airports?' I ask. 'The metal detector must light up like a Christmas tree.'

'Nup. Not really,' says Jez. 'Although, there was one time in Mexico. This girl had one of those hand-held wand detectors. She passed it over my nipples and it went off, and she just smiled. Then she went lower, and it went off again. "That's not your belt buckle, is it?" she said. "Nope," I said. And she just smiled and let me through.'

I like Jez; everybody likes Jez. He has an open, laid-back style and an intriguing accent: soft, English Midlands mixed with Dutch and Scottish, all modified by a dozen years in Australia. The 28-year-old reckons he is often mistaken for a Canadian. He's a refugee of sorts; he doesn't think much of Britain. He recalls Glasgow in particular as a dangerous place, where you had to cross the road to avoid a fight. At university he quickly decided he wanted to study either rainforest ecology or coral reef biology; both offered a ticket out of England.

That night I sleep amid a cacophony: mutton-birds with their strange hooping cries, the noddies and other seabirds competing to fill any small moment of silence. The natural world seems so strong here, so dominant, the research station and resort ephemera sitting on the surface of something much grander and more profound.

⌒

Selina is deeply concerned. She's a warm woman, ready with a laugh, quick with a smile. Generous. But right now the smile has been put away and she's deadly serious. She's scared the reef may not survive, or not as we know it, that the process of millennia that has created it and islands like Heron may be thrown into reverse. She believes that climate change threatens to attack the very foundation of the ecosystem: the symbiotic relation between the coral and the zooxanthellae. She's not alone. There's widespread concern that increasing sea surface temperatures will lead to widespread coral bleaching and the decline of the world's great reefs, Australia's among them.

Coral bleaching occurs when coral polyps expel their zooxanthellae. This happens when the polyps become stressed or when the zooxanthellae, losing their ability to photosynthesise, become a liability rather than an asset. The precise mechanisms remain elusive; a tidal wave of science is trying to establish what is happening. Selina explains it's the zooxanthellae that give the coral their colour. Without the microorganisms, the polyps are left colourless and translucent. Deprived of its major source of food, the coral weakens and can die in huge swathes unless conditions stabilise and they once again take on zooxanthellae.

Upstairs, in lab number three, Selina and Jez have got their experiment up and running. They've commandeered a steel-framed desk from somewhere, upended it and placed it on top of one of the lab benches. They've secured a couple of steel shafts to the metal frame of the table to act as brackets, and then clamped a large lamp to these makeshift brackets. The lamp is there to simulate sunshine. Resting on the upturned tabletop, they have set out Petrie dishes containing young coral polyps growing on ceramic tiles. These coral have yet to acquire their own zooxanthellae. Selina is keen to see if they can survive without zooxanthellae for any length of time by gaining energy from marine algae living on the tiles. 'It probably sounds very trivial to you, but to show, fundamentally, that zooxanthellae aren't the only way for the coral to survive is very important', she explains.

With the experiment up and running, Selina has time to explain why bleaching poses such a threat. She says it can be caused by many things, including pollution, disease and cyanide fishing, but these are mostly localised phenomena. Widespread bleaching, the sort that may threaten entire reefs, is caused by rising temperatures. In other words, global warming. If sea surface temperatures increase by too much for too long, the symbiotic relationship breaks down and coral eject their zooxanthellae. In 1998, a devastating bleaching event caused by high sea surface temperatures killed an estimated 16 per cent of reefs worldwide.

'Reefs have a really narrow threshold for temperature', Selina tells me. 'You can lift your summer maximum one degree above the average for long enough and you can get a bleaching event. So, it doesn't have to be five degrees or anything.'

For Selina, the link between climate change and bleaching is both obvious and irrefutable. She says there are no records of widespread temperature-related bleaching events before 1979. None. Thirty years later, they are becoming increasingly commonplace. What's more, they are following the expected pattern of climate change, with warming happening first and most intensely in higher latitudes and moving inwards towards the equator. Bleaching is starting to encroach on the most extensive reef structures of all: the coral triangle of Southeast Asia.

'The intensity is increasing. My colleagues in the coral triangle have been saying, "What are you fussed about? We don't get bleaching." Closer to the equator changes in temperature are smaller, but in the last year there have been incredible bleaching events throughout Thailand, Indonesia and Malaysia. It's the same in the Caribbean. In 2005–06 there was a shocking bleaching event. Mortality was incredibly high. So, there is no safe place really.'

Selina was on hand to witness the bleaching event of 1998, the biggest the world has experienced. The Great Barrier Reef was by no means the worst affected. Most of its damage occurred on the inshore reefs, which were affected by warm water trapped close to the coast. The impact was still felt on Heron, as the entire food chain was disrupted, and everything from the bait fish to the seabirds that prey upon them suffered the consequences. 'That year the noddies died in enormous numbers. Everywhere we walked, there were dead noddies on the ground. If it wasn't so awful it would have been funny. You'd see them flying along and then just drop, and they'd die. They'd be sitting on a branch and just fall off and die. We were all wondering, is this a neurotoxin? What could possibly cause them to die so quickly like that? But it seems that year, they were simply just starving to death.'

That terrible El Niño year of 1998 saw sea surface temperatures only one or two degrees above average. But the temperature remained elevated for many weeks; still water combined with the lack of wind and clouds left the coral stewing under the tropical sun. Water temperature in the ocean globally is already 0.7°C above pre-industrial times. Even if greenhouse gases were stabilised at year 2000 levels, the models show a further 0.5°C temperature rise. The CSIRO and the Bureau of Meteorology estimate that sea surface temperatures off the Queensland coast could increase by 2°C by 2070 with just a moderate level of carbon dioxide emissions. Scientists like Selina fear such a dramatic spike in temperature would inevitably cause frequent and widespread coral bleaching, and coral death.

This year there is little danger of bleaching on the Great Barrier Reef. La Niña has arrived, with her cooling winds, her dramatic storms and her cloud-filled skies. But what happens when she inevitably makes way for her sunny brother, El Niño?

⌒

I'm off exploring again. The scientists are back in the lab: lights calibrated, Geiger counters clicking, microscopes focused. I'm free to roam, restricted by no such exactitudes. I've already circumnavigated the island twice: once clockwise, once counter. I've already had a look around the resort, low-rise and laid-back. The paths between apartments are pockmarked with plywood sheets stencilled 'MUTTON BIRD NEST BELOW'. Humans have settled here, built the resort and the research station, but nature is not surrendering an inch without a struggle.

I've also waded out onto the reef at low tide. The wind was up, rain falling intermittently, the water ruffled and visibility distorted. Nevertheless, with the coral almost brushing the surface, I could see the structure clearly, growing in outcrops. I waded past, stepping on the sandy bottom, careful not to tread on coral. It was branching, brown and orange, with hints of red and blue. The tips were white: not bleached, but new polyps yet to adopt zooxanthellae. It's a sign that even in the shallowest waters of the island, this coral is growing. There'll be no bleaching events this year, not with all the clouds and cooling rain. I splashed around happily at the thought, a big kid in a wading pool. I donned a pair of swimming goggles and plunged my head underwater. Small tropical fish darted about, black and white stripes with yellow accents. Later, everyone told me it was a lousy day for it, questioned why I had bothered. But for a southerner like me, there was something to be said for walking off the side of an island in the middle of an ocean, supported by a reef flat made of coral past and gazing in wonder at coral present, no matter the weather.

Now, having walked the beach and waded the reef, I wander the forest, which is awash with the sickly sweet smell of bird shit. Everywhere there are birds' nests: in the trees and under the ground. A sign warns me to stay on the pathways to avoid stepping on the burrows of nesting shearwaters, the proper name for mutton-birds. 'BURROWS ARE EASILY COLLAPSED, KILLING YOUNG AND TRAPPING ADULTS', the sign warns. The tracks are of soft, dark soil, almost volcanic in appearance, but it's sand enriched by rotting vegetation, eons of bird shit and the bodies of dead birds. The dominant vegetation, pisonia trees, has a nasty habit of feeding on the birds. Not literally, not like a Venus flytrap, but devouring just the same. The pisonia's wide-leafed canopy provides shelter for noddies and their nests. It seems that every available fork supports a nest. But the trees exact a deadly rent. A sign on the trail tells me all about it. 'CRUEL BUT NECESSARY', asserts the parks service. 'Pisonia seeds, covered in sticky resin, trap some noddies … Trapped birds ultimately die; their bodies help fertilise the soil for growing Pisonia. This benefits future noddies and other wildlife dependant on Pisonia. We should not interfere even though this is a disturbing sight.' I take a furtive look around. I'm hoping I won't encounter any entrapped noddies and face the moral dilemma. I'm told that, in fact, it's not so much the Pisonia seed's sticky resin but rather its microscopic claws, somewhat like velcro, that attach the seeds to the birds, and that an expert bird cleaner can clear a noddy, commuting its death sentence, in little more than thirty seconds with very little stickiness involved. I wonder if the parks service may be engaging in a little misinformation.

The track winds this way and that, but I soon emerge on the beach again near the island's eastern point. Even the most twisted forest walk isn't going to take long to traverse this small, dead-flat island. I'm glad to be out of the forest, with its overpowering stink of bird shit and the hazards of collapsed burrows and pisonia-ensnared noddies. By contrast, the air on the beach is fresh and uncomplicated.

I watch as a Scandinavian documentary team wades ponderously past, weighed down with camera gear. It's late in the day, and they'll be off to capture the sunset, mandatory footage for any tropical-island exposition. I've done it myself, reporting from the tropics. Yet sunsets don't last nearly as long near the equator as they do during summer in higher latitudes. It's just one of those things we are preconditioned to expect. No doubt the camera crew is bemoaning the lack of coconut palms. They pass round the point and I have the beach to myself. Well, almost. I recognise a scientist from the research station standing down at the water's edge, looking out to sea. I wander down and join him. We exchange greetings and introductions; his name is Darren, a good-looking young bloke down from James Cook University. We turn to watch the teeming seas. Right in close to the water's edge are schools of huge rays, hovering in the shallows like lily pads, so thick you could walk on them. And just beyond, bobbing up and down in the chop, are sea turtles, their necks extending out of the water every now and then like periscopes.

'Are they coming ashore?' I ask.

'Not now, not with us standing here. They'll wait a bit longer, till it's dark and the tide's a bit higher,' Darren advises. I watch fascinated as they bob up and down. 'You see them?' asks Darren pointing along further to the left. 'See the fins?' I can indeed. They slice the water, like props from a bad movie. Sharks, some dark, some a greenish yellow. 'Lemon sharks', says Darren. 'They've come in for the turtles.'

'Not those ones?' I ask, pointing to one of the large turtles sharing the sea with the sharks.

'No. You're here at a good time of year. The big girls are still laying, but the first of the hatchlings are coming out as well. Come back later tonight. You might be lucky and see some hatching.' Darren wanders away, and I make a note to return later on in the evening.

I'm still standing there when I hear a shout. Darren is a little further along the beach, waving at me to come. I can already see why; gulls are circling, squawking. One flies over, chased by two others, with something dark and struggling in its beak. A nest of baby turtles high in the dunes has exploded out into the open and the small turtles are flapping their way seaward. They're maybe 10 centimetres long and cute as all hell, flippers energetically brushing them forward down the slope of the beach. They've emerged en masse from their sandy nest, all the better to increase their chance of survival. But the odds aren't great. In the light of the setting sun they stand out clearly against the sand, making easy pickings for the gulls. I watch one bird land next to a baby turtle and examine it for a moment with a quizzical turn of the head before scooping it up and carrying it off, its flippers still gyrating against the emptiness of the air. This is nature at its cruellest, and the parks service has issued another of its edicts: visitors to Heron are not to interfere. This doesn't deter Darren, who chases off a couple of gulls, then turns and gives me a conspiratorial grin. Soon, I'm in among the baby turtles as well. I stop short of carrying any to the water's edge, but being up close and taking photographs deters the gulls. Even so, very few make it to the water's edge. I watch one little hero make the water, only to be taken in one awful gulp by a passing lemon shark.

'Here!' calls Darren.

Another nest has opened, baby turtles scurrying over the top like soldiers on the Somme. This nest is closer to the sea and the gulls are still preoccupied by the stragglers from the first nest. Darren and I are joined by Melinda, a pretty French researcher from the station. The sun has set; the twilight is falling. We don't pick up the baby turtles, except for photographs, but again our presence deters the gulls and more of the turtles make the water, though there's nothing we can do about the sharks and their meticulous appetite. How many of the hatchlings make it through to deeper water is impossible to know.

Those that prosper may have a long life ahead of them. Perhaps eighty years. They ride the currents south down the coast and way out across the expanse of the Pacific, growing and fattening in the rich seas off the coast of Chile. They'll disappear for years, maybe decades, before returning to breed and lay their eggs. As adults they ride the currents again: north along the coast of South America, west across equatorial waters, before arriving back at Heron and the same beach they struggled down years before.

The last of the hatchlings are now struggling towards the uncertain water in the gathering gloom. Behind them, a huge shape is lumbering its way up onto the beach, untroubled by sharks and gulls. A green turtle is coming ashore to lay her eggs, returning home to begin the cycle again.

Later that night, as we cook dinner, Selina and Jez are bright eyed and attentive as I recount my turtle experience. They've been coming here for years, but there is no sign of boredom or jaundice. They're coral experts, but the charisma of the turtles is undeniable. It's hard to believe that Heron Island was first settled as a turtling station, expressly to massacre the beasts and send their meat off to fill the tureens of empire.

Talk of the turtles is eclipsed soon enough by talk of the weather. Cyclone Anthony has stepped up a level to a category 2 and is about 280 kilometres off the coast of Townsville. It's expected to cross the coast later this evening. Winds of 130 kilometres per hour are predicted, with rainfall of 200 millimetres expected during the day. But Anthony, even before entering the stage, is being cast as a bit player. The tropical depression off Fiji has consolidated closer to Vanuatu, and is already classified as a category 1 cyclone. It's been given a name: Yasi. And it absolutely dwarfs Anthony. Experts say it is destined to become at least a category 3 cyclone, and that its size and energy will give it the impetus to penetrate far inland and dump even more water into the flood-ravaged interior. 'We are not battle weary; we are battle ready', says Queensland premier Anna Bligh, detecting a hitherto undiscovered link between barometric pressure and opinion polls.

Outside, the wind is still up but the sky is cloud-free and ablaze with stars. I make my way along the track towards the dock, in search of turtles. Once away from the research station, I try turning off my torch. There's no moon, no man-made light, but the luminous swathe of the Milky Way allows me to pick my way along the sandy path between the darkness of the pisonia trees and their swarms of hooting noddies. By the wharf, I stand on the invisible concrete circle of the island's helipad and look to the heavens. Six hundred kilometres up the coast, Hamilton Island is already being hit by the gale-force winds of Anthony, but here the sky is clear. How good is this—walking on a coral cay out of sight of the mainland, guided by nothing more than starlight?

I think of my dad. He's lying in a hospice in Canberra, dying of cancer, preparing himself as much as he can for what cannot now be far away. I look at the spread of the universe, trying to memorise its beauty so I can tell him about it when I return to his bedside. My mind swims with the stars, and my eyes swim with tears.

I walk through the resort. It's a low-impact kind of place, not designed for party animals and desperate singles. It doesn't need any of that, not when it offers such a window into the natural world. I pass the near-deserted bar, and make my way onto the resort beach, hoping that I may be able to spot a turtle. Selina has filled me in on turtle-watching etiquette. Don't stand between them and the dunes; don't pass in front of them, and no lights. I'm not sure about no lights—how will I be able to see anything?—so I've slunk over to the resort to see if I can tag along with someone with a bit more experience. But the beach is empty. No tourists, no staff, no turtles.

I head back to the research station, down the track to the helipad and the wharf. I flick off my torch again, enjoying the game of seeing by starlight alone. So it is I almost fall headlong over a turtle. I hear it just in time, its flippers slapping the hard sand near the wharf. I back away, allowing my eyes more time to adjust. It's a large, dark mound, moving slowly away from the sea. A little further down, on the shallow beach by the wharf, I spot a second turtle coming ashore. For long minutes I stand with senses turned up high: the sound of the slapping flippers, the background hooting of birds, the gentle wash of the sea and the dark shapes moving in front of me against the starlit sand. Then something hits me with a soft thud on the left side of my chest, not hard but surprising, startling me from my reverie. A noddy, not one of the most astute birds in creation, has flown straight into me in the darkness, and is now wobbling along the ground, stunned by the impact. Selina has warned me about this, recounting how one of her students was once left bloody faced by the impact of a bird's bill. It's time to return to the research station.

I'm in luck. Jez is sitting by the payphone at the admin block, smoking a rollie, having called his partner. I tell him of the turtles by the dock. 'Fantastic', he says. 'Wait here. I'll get a red light.' He's back in a minute or two. It seems the great turtles of the Pacific are not able to see light at the red end of the spectrum. I guess there's not a lot of it to be seen in the ocean. We locate my turtle soon enough, and the other following not far behind. But Jez is not optimistic. The earth here is compacted from the construction of the wharf and the impact of passengers walking to and from the dock. 'No good', he says. 'The ground here is too hard. She won't be able to dig a nest.'

'So what will happen?'

'She'll probably give up and head back into the sea and then try again somewhere further along. But come on, we're bound to find some others.' And sure enough, as we head along the beach on the research side of the island, the tractor tracks of turtles are evident in the sand. Two, three, four sets. We spot one easing its way seaward, its eggs laid, biological imperative fulfilled.

We follow some other tracks, up towards the casuarina trees, and our luck is in. We come across an old girl, her nest almost complete. In silence we kneel beside her. She must know we are there, but with no visible light and little noise, her need drives her on and we are permitted to stay and bear witness. The red light from Jez's torch is familiar, reminiscent of all those years I spent in pre-digital darkrooms watching photographs emerge as if by magic from their alchemist's swamp of chemical. But those images were still, mere imitations of life. What reveals itself before me now is alive and vital. We are right up close, mere centimetres away. The turtle has scooped out a shallow depression in the sand and filled it with her body. She steadies herself with her front flippers, while her back flippers excavate a smaller, much deeper hole beneath her egg duct. The flippers curl, prehensile, as they carve into the moist sand and lift it to the side of the hole. First she braces her weight with one flipper against the side of the hole and digs with the other, and then she swaps over. A small root from a nearby tree is interfering with her quarrying, but she expertly circumvents it as she lifts more sand clear of the nest and slaps it down by the lip of the hole. Finally she is satisfied, and with quiet effort and dignity, she lowers herself down a touch further and the glistening white softness of the table-tennis-ball eggs start dropping silently, gently into the nest.

Jez gives me the nod. Once the turtles begin laying, they go into a kind of trance, oblivious to what is occurring around them, unable to move until they have deposited their eggs. Quickly I take some flash photos—Jez close up behind the turtle, his face alight with wonder.

The experiment is going well, and Selina and I sit at a table down by the admin offices. Cyclone Anthony crossed the coast in the early hours and is already little more than a large grey dampness. There's been next to no damage, but plenty of rain. It's raining here too, but it's just as likely to be caused by localised squalls as by the larger storm system. Still, there's a portentous gloominess to the day, and it's reflected in our conversation. Selina is expanding on her fears for the reef.

She tells me acidification is potentially a bigger threat to the reef than bleaching. Coral skeletons, the building blocks of the Great Barrier Reef and all coral reefs around the world, are made from calcium carbonate. But calcium carbonate can dissolve in seawater; the more acidic the water, the more easily it dissolves. The more carbon dioxide is pumped into the atmosphere, the more it's taken up by the ocean, creating carbonic acid. The oceans of the world are becoming more acidic. Acidity is measured on the fourteen-point pH scale. Pure water, neither acid nor alkaline, is rated at 7 on the scale. The further below 7 a liquid is, the more acidic it is; the higher above 7 a liquid is, the more alkaline it is. The pH of seawater varies depending on local variations, such as temperature, depth and salinity, but the global average is about 8.07. So, seawater is alkaline, which is what allows not just coral, but anything with a calcium-carbonate shell, from krill to lobster, clams and crabs, to survive and prosper. Place them in acidic water, and their shells will dissolve. 'I had a student who did a short-term project with me on pteropods', Selina explains. 'Pteropods are little tiny crustaceans. They're actually the most abundant animals in the world. She put them in low pH treatments for four days and found they started to fall apart.'

But here's the thing: calcium carbonate can dissolve not just in acidic water, but also in alkaline water. The deciding factor is how much calcium carbonate is already in the surrounding seawater. If the water is saturated with the compound, then it's easy for animals to metabolise it and build shells, but if the level of calcium carbonate in the water falls below saturation, then the water will start dissolving the shells of the animals. The more carbon dioxide is in the atmosphere, the more acidic the oceans become, and the lower the levels of dissolved calcium carbonate.

There's no doubt the oceans are becoming less alkaline, more acidic. In pre-industrial times the pH is thought to have been about 8.179. By the last decade of the twentieth century, this had fallen to 8.104. This might not sound like much, but don't be fooled. The pH scale, like the Richter scale, is logarithmic. So, just as an earthquake of 7 on the Richter scale is ten times as strong as an earthquake measuring 6 on the scale, a solution with a pH of 7 is ten times more acidic than a solution with a value of 8. Put another way: the oceans of today are already 29 per cent more acidic than the oceans of the eighteenth century.

As the pH of seawater continues to fall, the first to go will be coral and those marine animals like the pteropods that have skeletons and shells made of a form of calcium carbonate called aragonite. Other marine animals use a different form of calcium carbonate called calcite. Calcite is more resilient to acidification and won't begin to dissolve until pH levels fall further. Levels of calcium carbonate differ greatly throughout the oceans. The colder and deeper the water, the less calcium carbonate is held in solution. Indeed, below a certain depth, the conditions already exist where seawater dissolves aragonite shells. Deeper yet, and it dissolves calcite. The depth where it's turns from being conducive to growing calcium carbonate shells and skeletons to where it starts dissolving those shells and skeletons is known as the saturation horizon. Already, it's thought that saturation horizon is somewhere between 50 and 200 metres closer to the surface than it was in pre-industrial times.

What I want to know is how acidic the ocean has to become for the saturation horizon to reach the surface. Because when that happens, I will no longer be able to wade out onto the reef flat and admire the coral: it will be dead and melting away into the water. Given enough time, the whole reef, living and dead, will disappear, and Heron Island itself will fall beneath the waves. The answer is sobering: some scientists fear the saturation horizon could reach the surface with a fall in pH of just 0.2 from pre-industrial times. In other words, we're already half way there. Now it's not just Selina who is sounding concerned. I'm finding myself growing more and more anxious as I ask more questions; her answers are not reassuring. Carbon dioxide levels in the atmosphere are currently about 390 parts per million (ppm), up from 280 ppm before the industrial revolution. International efforts are focused on stabilising them at about 550 ppm. But Selina tells me that the saturation horizon could reach the surface with carbon dioxide levels in the atmosphere as low as 450 ppm. The scary thing is that, more and more, it's becoming accepted that atmospheric levels won't be kept under that level. Think about that: no more coral, no more reef.

But surely, I posit desperately, there have been times in the earth's distant past when there was even more carbon dioxide in the atmosphere than now. Wasn't there coral then? Won't the reefs adapt?

'I don't think you could ever call it adapting', says Selina, shaking her head. 'They've come and gone. They've disappeared for millions of years, and then come back, but in different forms. You could say that 60 million years ago that CO_2 levels were much higher than they are now, but the coral existing on the reefs back then were completely different; they were based on calcite not aragonite.'

I understand what she is saying. The coral of today haven't so much evolved from the calcite-based reefs of the distant past, as evolved from scratch to fill a similar ecological niche. And it could be millions of years before calcite reefs could evolve anew.

The loss of the Great Barrier Reef would be devastating for Australia. Devastating for tourism, for fishing and for our national identity. But Selina makes the point that for people in other countries it would be far worse. Reefs feed millions and millions of people, providing their major source of protein. And for some island nations, like Tuvalu and Kiribati and the Maldives, the reef provides not just protection from storms and swell, but the very foundations on which the islands are built. So much has been written about the threat of rising sea levels, but the threat from acidification may be so much greater.

The trouble with reefs is that they are always in a delicate balance between erosion and growth, between erosion and calcification', Selina explains. 'So, you have all these things like coral and molluscs and crustaceans, etcetera, that add to calcification. Then you have cyclones and storms and every-day wave action, as well as this huge array of animals that bio-erode as well. The ones like parrot fish that eat the coral, and the ones that get inside and burrow. So, we only get growth because the rate of calcification is beating erosion by 10 per cent. But the call is that by 450 ppm, it will have turned so erosion will beat calcification. The reefs will begin to collapse.

We had a winter storm here in 2008. You don't expect big storms in winter, but it was so severe the cat didn't run for two days. I came over the day after, the first day the cat ran. I was telling students about this particularly beautiful place we would go to later in the week. We went there, on the other side of the island, and it was catastrophic. It was as if a bulldozer had gone through, and all that remained was this layer of dead coral. That was just one winter storm. The devastation was extreme. I was in tears ... I guess my biggest fear is that the reef won't be with us for that much longer. Unfortunately, with the problems that climate change causes—increases in temperature and acidification, storm damage and sea level rise—I just don't see a way for the reef to survive.

It's an apocalyptic vision. For the first time, I consider the possibility that the threat posed by climate change to the oceans may be far greater and more imminent than any of the threats posed to land. Like everyone else, I've been thinking about what climate change means to people and where we live, the impact on farmers, and the effects of drought and flood. We could be preoccupied with reticulating the Murray-Darling even as the Great Barrier Reef moves into irreversible decline.

It's not just the reef, either. Consider all those little pteropods floating around the Antarctic, little snails with wing-like fins. Sea butterflies, they're called. They're the most abundant animals on earth with a biomass estimated at hundreds of thousands of tonnes, the bottom of a food chain that includes everything from fish, penguins and whales to seals, sea birds and humans. Their shells are aragonite, not the more resilient calcite. The aragonite horizon in the cold waters of the Antarctic, already relatively high in the water column, is climbing ever closer to the surface. Some projections predict the horizon will reach the surface within a decade. So, no more pteropods. Starving fish, starving penguins, starving whales. Maybe Sea Shepherd should give up harassing Japanese whalers and send a flotilla instead to blockade Gladstone harbour and protest against the coal-burning power station, the aluminium smelter and the cement factory.

I think of the *Voyager* spacecraft, hurtling through space, carrying their photos of Heron Island, like some overly ambitious tourist promotion. 'I'll put another calcium-carbonate covered shrimp on the barbie.' Will that be the final wave of tourists, after the Japanese and Chinese and Arabs have all moved on: aliens, beaming in to visit the glowing green jewel on the reef? Will it still be here, with coral gardens and seabird choirs and hovering turtles to greet them, or will Heron Island and its reef have been eaten away by acidification and bleaching and sea level rise and cyclones and neglect? Will our interstellar guests have to make do with Gladstone, still spewing energy from its near-inexhaustible supplies of coal?

Just to cheer me up, the news of Cyclone Yasi isn't good. Out in the Coral Sea (what will we call it if all the coral die?), the storm is gathering strength and is predicted to hit the coast the day after tomorrow. Queensland premier Anna Bligh is telling residents in low-lying parts of Townsville, Mackay and Innisfail, a 750-kilometre stretch of coastline, to evacuate and move to higher ground. Authorities fear the cyclone could wield winds of up to 260 kilometres an hour, that it could wreak as much damage as Larry, the 2006 category 4 cyclone that devastated Innisfail and destroyed the nation's banana crop. Yet it's the size of the storm that sets minds to thinking, as much as its intensity. The satellite images reveal it to be bigger than Queensland itself: a third of the size of the entire continent, three or four times larger than Anthony—the cyclone that had the *Courier Mail* hitting the panic button just a couple of days ago.

The worst-case scenario, now being openly considered, is that it could make a direct hit on Cairns, population 150 000, and hit the city at high tide. With the tide expected to peak at 7 metres, a storm surge of up to 5 metres on top of that would inundate the city. Thirty thousand people are being evacuated. So too are the two bayside hospitals, one public, the other private, the patients being airlifted 1700 kilometres to Brisbane.

It's our last full day on Heron Island. We were going to stay for four nights, but the experiment has progressed so well, Selina and Jez are confident of wrapping it up today, freeing us to leave on tomorrow's lunchtime catamaran to Gladstone. I, for one, am reluctant to leave, but none of us wants to endure a two-hour boat trip through cyclone-excited waters. If we can get off before Yasi reaches Heron, so much the better.

I sit down in the air-conditioned coolness of the lab and have a good chat with Jez, gleaning his views. He offered me a brief insight last night, after our turtle hunt. He warned me not to be too black and white in my views; that the science was complicated and not as straightforward as I might first think. He reminded me that apocalyptic predictions had proved to be wrong in the past. We'd discussed the great crown-of-thorns starfish scare that had many predicting the demise of the reef back in the 1960s and 1970s. What had happened was this: in the early 1960s a large outbreak of these starfish was discovered near the tourist magnet of Green Island, off Cairns. By all accounts, an outbreak of the starfish is a terrible thing to witness. They march en masse across a reef, devouring everything in their path, leaving nothing behind but a skeleton-clogged wasteland. It was not the first outbreak of the starfish on the reef, but it was the first witnessed up close and personal by humans. The location was easily accessible, and the recent popularisation of scuba equipment and underwater photography allowed scientists to witness the destruction first hand and for the media to magnify their concerns. There were wild predictions that the starfish would devour the entire reef—that it would be gone by now. 'It may seem funny to outsiders, but that prediction of catastrophe has left some scientists' careers in tatters', Jez tells me as we revisit the subject in the clinical fluorescent lights of the lab. He's worried that more scientific reputations, and the credibility of climate-change science, may be endangered by over-enthusiastic extrapolation.

'The classic example was the 1998 bleaching event. People predicted there would be bleaching, and massive bleaching occurred. Then people were saying by 2020, or even by 2015, that we would see the reef impacted by significant bleaching events every single year because of increases in sea surface temperatures. It's 2011, and the last major bleaching event we saw here was 2002 and, before that, 1998. Every year that goes by is a year where some scientist has put his career on the line. So, you need to get across the message that it is serious, that we will see more and more bleaching, but if that doesn't happen and time goes on, people will think, "My reef looks great. You're just scare mongering."'

This is an interesting line of thought. Could it be that despite his youth, his radical Rasta locks and his metal-pierced face, Jez is a sceptic, here in the very bosom of coral research? It's an intriguing thought, but not an accurate one. Jez is no climate-change sceptic, let alone a denier; he's simply cautious. His real name, which I learn only by asking, is George Roff, and despite his youth, his research has spread across an impressive variety of areas. His honours research was into coral disease; his PhD examined the geological history of coral reefs, and his current research focuses on coral-reef ecology.

Jez doesn't doubt that the reef is being affected by climate change, but he says it's impossible to say to what degree. 'The situation is probably quite serious. There's no question climate change and acidification impact on coral health and on coral growth, on calcification and reproduction,' he says. 'So, the sky is falling, but the degree to which it is falling is the thing people really need to start figuring out.'

Jez confides that he has witnessed what he describes as 'bad science', with researchers falling over themselves to predict the ultimate impacts of climate change before the basic scientific foundations have been established.

> I think what most scientists at the moment are doing is jumping on the bandwagon of ocean acidification. And they're rushing through experiments. I think that regardless, it will never be the case that the reef will die. It's not mass extinction. Coral are a bit like cockroaches. Some of them will survive through almost anything. They are incredibly robust creatures.
>
> So, the question then becomes: what will the reef look like in 2030 or 2050 or 2080? What's going to happen? You'll lose certain species and certain groups. Sensitive coral like branching coral will die out. In other groups, they'll still be there, but they won't reproduce or grow at the same level, so instead of having these amazingly diverse reefs like you do at the moment that bring all the tourism, you'll end up seeing reefs that look impoverished—high macro-algal cover, dominated by very few species, and they will take longer to come back from disturbances like floods and cyclone damage.

Jez may look like a Rastafarian who has come off second best to a nail gun, but he's not spouting thought bubbles; they're considered conclusions. He's frustrated with bad science and the bad journalism that feeds from it. But he is no friend of the sceptics and climate-change deniers; after all, he is a scientist and can analyse the data for himself. He knows that climate change is real and the impact on the reef is tangible; he just believes that apocalyptic claims and over-extrapolation of findings can be as damaging as denial.

His analysis leaves me somewhat more hopeful, but not a lot. The fact that the sky is falling more slowly than I might have previously thought, that the reef won't be replaced by a marine wasteland but by some pale, less vibrant, less diverse imitation, is far from comforting. He may well be right. Individual species may come and go, but life itself is pervasive, with some new adaptation ready to fill whatever evolutionary niche may open up. Perhaps the future looks more like purgatory than apocalypse.

The experiment complete, Selina, Jez and I go snorkelling in the deep channel of the harbour where decades ago a passage was blasted through the reef flat to allow boats access to the island. Selina explains the channel has had an unintended impact. As the ebb tide withdraws, water streams off the reef flat and into the channel, carrying sand with it. Over the years, this has reduced the amount of sand on the beaches on each side of the harbour. Nevertheless, the channel is still one of the best places on the island to swim, although not until after 4:30 in the afternoon, when boating is finished for the day. We move into the water from the dock, and swim out towards the wreck that sits near the entry to the channel. The wind is still up, and the water is not at its clearest, with visibility less than 10 metres. For the others, adept scuba divers both of them, it must be a very average swim. But I am thrilled by the promise of turtles. I'm hoping I might stumble across one of the charismatic creatures. In the meantime, I enjoy the coral. There is branching coral, brown with pale-blue tips; soft coral, pink and orange, swaying in the current; and large boulder-like specimens, adorned with various anemones and outgrowths. Small fish, glowing blue or striped with yellow, dart about, urgently going nowhere. The coral has grown dense and profuse on the side of the channel, recolonising with vigour where the reef was once dynamited. I see a couple of large wrasse, rainbow flecked, moving quickly below a somnambulant snapper. A school of large, silver fish idle by, built for speed but cruising in low gear.

And then I see it, hovering beneath me, deep down near the sandy bottom, hazy and grey, the unmistakeable silhouette of a turtle. I feel exhilarated. I float on the surface breathing through my snorkel, watching the shape, deciding whether I should dive down for a closer look. I look up to find the others, and there, so close I can almost touch it, a huge green turtle is hovering right in front of me. I check it out; it checks me out. We hold our positions for a while, and then begin to circle each other. I examine its shell, its flippers, admire its hydrodynamic lines, so perfect for the sea, wondering at its relaxed buoyancy and unhurried mastery. It keeps looking me directly in the eye, as curious of me as I am of it. It displays no fear, no trepidation. We are in its domain and I am the interloper. These are ancient creatures, older than the dinosaurs, evolving first on land, and then returning to the sea 150 million years ago. The old reptile gives me one last look over, grows bored and, with a couple of desultory pulls of its front flippers, leaves me floundering in its wake.

I paddle back towards Selina to recount my experience, but before I can speak she points down. We dive down 2 or 3 metres, and find a turtle resting beneath a ledge of coral. It appears to be dozing, as comfortable under its ledge as under a doona. They may be air breathers, but they can remain under water, often sleeping there, for a couple of hours at a time.

On the surface Selina says she's not sure what species the turtle is. 'Did you see the markings?' she asks. I am, of course, of absolutely no use whatsoever. She's a scientist, curious and categorising; I'm just a child in wonderland. Another turtle shunts across my path, and I follow it. It humours me for a moment, as I swim admiring, holding my breath, before it puts on a most amazing turn of speed and disappears off into the haze in a second, leaving me to surface, gasping for air. Selina and Jez have headed in the opposite direction and are rounding the wreck. I swim over to join them. They point out a new find. On the bottom, in a sandy patch, a black shark lurks, almost 2 metres in length, its very shape exuding menace and intent. It's said that sharks must keep moving to survive, to keep the water flowing through their gills. Not this one. It just floats stationary, almost on the bottom. Fish swim lazily by, not too close, but not distressed either. Selina and Jez are the same. After years of swimming, snorkelling and scuba diving on the reef, they're not perturbed at all by the shark. But for me, it's visceral. I don't like them. It's not a phobia—I'm not struck by panic at the sight—but I'm not about to dive down and test its patience. It occurs to me how inconsistent I am, full of wonder at the turtles and antipathy towards the shark. I would, I fear, make a lousy scientist.

Next morning we are packed and waiting for the catamaran. The experimental equipment is back in its place, the table that supported the lamp returned to its upright position. The specimens are packed, ready for transit. Selina, Jez and I are in the kitchen-dining area, eating what we can of our food, giving the rest away. There are four or five other researchers there, work complete, drinking beers and killing time before departure. We talk about Yasi, upgraded to a category 5 cyclone, even more powerful than Larry or Tracy, the cyclone that levelled Darwin in 1974. The storm is so big, villagers in coastal Papua New Guinea are being told to move to higher ground even though its eye is predicted to cross the Queensland coastline south of Cairns. Tens of thousands of people are on the move, from Cooktown in the north to Townsville in the south, as authorities urge those in low-lying areas to evacuate while there is still time. The deputy police commissioner is already calling it a deadly event, thirty-six hours before it's scheduled to make landfall. The premier warns it may be the biggest storm Queensland has ever seen. And to make it all the worse, the Bureau of Meteorology is saying there's a good chance the cyclone's landfall may indeed coincide with the high tide, creating a devastating storm surge.

On Heron it all seems a bit remote. Outside, the day is clear and sunny, the best weather of our stay. The sporadic rain of the previous days seems to have cleared for good. But Yasi doesn't remain remote for long; a staff member rushes in the door, out of breath and face flushed.

'Where are the others? The other researchers?' she gasps. She's told some are snorkelling, others are out in a boat.

'Well, we've got to get them back in. The order has come through from Brisbane. We're evacuating the station in forty-five minutes!'

Outside, chaotic urgency has descended. In a place where no one runs, where the tropical dawdle has been perfected, the nonchalant slappity-slap of thongs a mark of the weathered researcher, staff are running this way and that, hauling material indoors, tying down equipment. Some researches are rushing to pack equipment and fetch their belongings, but others are paralysed by disbelief.

'You can't do this', protests one researcher, a likeable blond guy called Alastair. 'I've been working on this for months. I can't just leave it now. It'll all be for nothing.'

He's told he can't stay: the decision has been taken at the highest levels of the university in Brisbane; local staff have no authority to grant dispensations. To me, it has the smell of bureaucrats covering their backs. The University of Queensland has already been stretched by the Brisbane floods; the powers that be are eliminating all possible risks, ensuring they are beyond reproach should anything go pear-shaped. It is no concern of theirs that dedicated scientists, people far better equipped to read a weather map, far more knowledgeable of the marine and island environments, are the ones who will suffer.

An American researcher runs up, still wearing a rash shirt and swimmers. 'Is this real? They radioed us in.'

'Yes', I say. 'It's real.' I can hardly believe it myself, standing in the hot sun under clear skies. No one believes we are under threat this far south; we've all seen the weather maps.

All around me there is commotion, but there's not much I can do. Selina and Jez, their equipment already packed, are helping colleagues. Selina says she'll see me at the dock. As I walk towards the harbour, Alastair runs past, still dressed in shorts and T-shirt, clasping his wallet in one hand.

'Where you going?' I shout.

'The resort. I'll get a room there,' he replies over his shoulder.

The dock is like a stage where two plays are being enacted simultaneously. In the first, scientists arrive higgledy-piggledly, still dazed by the rapid unfolding of events, shaking their heads and muttering dissent. In the other play, tourists amble along, taking the last of their happy snaps, blissfully unaware of any cyclonic threats or bureaucratic duck shoving. The catamaran arrives from Gladstone. One researcher disembarks, only to be told he has to return to the boat immediately. He looks in disbelief, first at the person imparting the message, then at the clear blue sky, and then at the tourists blithely walking past him off towards the resort. For the resort, unimpaired by bureaucracy, is writing its own script: it's open for business and welcoming new customers.

The tourists have left the dock by the time we cast off, perhaps already imbibing their first piña coladas. Only Alastair is left standing there, giving us a stilted wave and wondering if he has made the right decision.

⌒

Cyclone Yasi spares Heron Island, and the research station reopens the next day; Alastair is vindicated. But those further north are not so lucky. Yasi passes directly over Willis Island, 450 kilometres off the coast, registering winds of 185 kilometres per hour before demolishing the meteorological equipment piece by piece. The storm hits the mainland around midnight on Tuesday 2 February, crossing the coast south of Innisfail. The eye passes over Mission Beach and Tully Heads, with winds gusting upwards of 290 kilometres per hour.

Like all cyclones, it begins to lose energy passing over land. Yet such is Yasi's size and intensity that it careers on, well inland, for another 900 kilometres before being downgraded to a tropical low. A week later, its remnants are still dumping rain, causing widespread flooding as far south as Victoria and South Australia.

There will be only the one death: a young man asphyxiated by a generator. The authorities in Brisbane won't say so, but they must be relieved, even with 150 000 houses without electricity and thousands of people homeless. Yasi crossed the coast in a relatively unpopulated area, not at Cairns, not at Townsville. More importantly, the tides were out of synch: the storm surge was much lower than if Yasi had arrived a few hours earlier.

But I wonder what the impact has been out on the reef. I'm reminded of Selina's description of it being engaged in a constant struggle between the forces of growth and those of erosion. By definition, the reefs live and grow in shallow water, dangerously exposed to the full force of cyclonic winds and surging seas. Under the surface, huge wounds will have been carved into the living reef. I search the papers, but there is no word on the damage to the great coral edifice and its thin veneer of life; the impact on land has been too large and too dramatic. Human-interest stories abound. The damage to the reef is out of sight and out of mind.

2

TORRES STRAIT

High tide on Yam Island, marooning outlying mangroves.

T he water is rising. Unnoticed at first, it starts to creep up the edge of the reef flat, 150 metres offshore. It's a placid invasion, unhurried and unperturbed, meeting no resistance; nothing is more inevitable than the tides. The early morning low has been

36

remarkably low, just as today's noontide will be remarkably high. And so, with quiet persistence, the water rises to become level with the reef flat and starts to penetrate towards the shore, progressing gently through well-worn grooves and gullies. I sit on the beach under the shade of a spreading almond tree, nursing a cup of tea, and watch the sea climb towards me. There is no to-and-fro about it this morning; there are no waves. Beyond the reef, the sea sits like glass under the tropical sun, making this tidal encroachment, this implacable swelling, all the more mesmerising. Elsewhere on the coast of Australia, the tidal shift will be masked by the swell, by foaming breakers and the rushing of water through estuarine necks, but here in the Torres Strait, halfway between Cape York and Papua New Guinea, the encircling reefs and lack of wind have eliminated any subterfuge. The movement of the water is driven by the tide alone, and the tide by the moon. And today the moon will swing closer to the earth than at any other time during the month. And now, at the height of the Australian summer, the elliptical orbit of the earth has swung it closer to the sun than at any other time during the year. The sun and moon are coming into alignment, combining their gravitational pull and invoking their celestial authority. Today the water will climb higher up the shores of this island, wind and waves notwithstanding, than on any other day of the year.

Crossing the reef flat, the water moves stealthily, reconnecting rock pools with the sea, covering dead coral, honouring the promise of life renewed to the molluscs and crabs sheltering in the rocks. Motorboats and runabouts that not long ago were marooned on the sparse mud are now floating free, bobbing ever so slightly atop the encroaching glass, their shapes reflected faithfully in the still water. The reef flat conquered, the sea begins its polite assault on the beach itself. Its manners are impeccable, its intentions implacable. It's a narrow beach, a metre or two of elevation, no more. And beyond the lip of the beach, not worthy of the description of dune, the houses of Yam Island lie exposed. By 9.30 a.m., roughly halfway between low and high tide, the sea level has already risen by more than a metre. Even with no wind and no swell, it will still be a close-run thing.

This is why I'm here, what I've come to witness: the summer king tide. This is the day when I may see firsthand the impact of climate change in action.

⌒

Getting to Yam Island is not difficult, but it's not straightforward either. I fly from Canberra to Sydney, and then to Cairns. From 30 000 feet, the Queensland interior is dressed in camouflage. Two weeks after it crossed the coast, the violence of Cyclone Yasi has left the land resembling jungle fatigues: swathes of khaki where old growth endures, blocks of bright green where flood waters have receded and new growth has sprouted, and the flat browns of water still trapped in shallow lakes, as if the landscape itself is dressed for battle. At Cairns airport, the real uniforms of the crisis are everywhere: SES personnel in their bright orange jumpsuits exchange tired banter and flick through thought-free magazines as they await repatriation to southern states. The emergency phase is coming to an end; the long, slow rebuilding is just beginning.

From Cairns, the most northerly city on Australia's east coast, it's a further two-hour flight north to Horn Island, nestled in a group of six or seven islands just off the tip of Cape York. Horn Island is the airport; the main settlement is across a thin strait on Thursday Island. Waiting for the ferry to take me across to TI, as it's known hereabouts, I regard the signs on the wharf. One warns of crocodiles. It says they can grow to 7 metres long, weigh 1000 kilograms and eat people. 'Never provoke or interfere with crocodiles', the sign states, somewhat superfluously. A few steps from the crocodile sign, less permanent A4 pages have been taped to the wharf's piles: 'SUSPECTED IRUKANDJI. ENTER WATER AT OWN RISK.' Irukandji are the small box jellyfish whose sting can kill in minutes. Welcome to far north Queensland.

Thursday Island was so named by Captain James Cook on his epic voyage of discovery in 1770. He found it on a Thursday. Nearby, in the same group, can be found Wednesday Island and Friday Island. I guess that by the time he had reached the tip of Australia, having travelled some 3500 kilometres up the coastline over a period of four months, naming everything in sight as he went, the venerable captain must have been running short of names. It's surprising he didn't name something after Joseph Banks's two greyhounds, or the ship's goat. Who knows: perhaps he did.

At Thursday Island I am dropped at the Grand Hotel, which is grand no longer. Once it was a colonial institution, whitewashed weatherboards and wide verandahs, slow-moving fans and gin slings. Somerset Maugham stayed here in the 1920s, writing as he looked out over the bay, dressed, you might imagine, in a crumpled linen suit. It is after all the sort of thing Somerset did: swan about the tropics, traversing what the English still insist on calling 'the Far East', documenting the fading days of empire. 'I do not think that many people have been to Thursday Island', he wrote. 'I went there since they told me in Sydney that it was the last place God ever made. They said there was nothing to see and warned me that I should probably get my throat cut.' The great man survived, throat intact, yet his ghost would be sorely disappointed if it were to revisit his old haunt today. The Grand Hotel he knew burnt down in 1993 and the one that stands before me is a reinforced-concrete edifice, painted a pastel orange growing motley in the tropical humidity, and exuding all the charm of a multi-storey car park. In the downstairs bar, tiled for coolness and easy hosing, a Lady Gaga video blasts out at ear-ringing volume, exorcising any residual charm, and driving all but the deaf and the drunk from the air conditioning out into the moist heat. But from the upstairs verandah the view across the bay, with its azure water and jangled islands, is much the same as in Maugham's day, taking in Horn Island, Prince of Wales Island and, away in the distance, the smudge of Cape York itself. You can understand how well the old boy might have liked the place.

The receptionist, bottle blond and blue-eyed, is from Berlin. Her boyfriend, residual Mohawk cut short, is from Manchester. He tells me the couple have been here for three months, refloating their bank balances. 'The money is awesome', he says. 'Plus food and accommodation [is included]. You save a heap. You have to: there's nothing to spend it on.' Before Thursday Island, the couple worked in Ayr in Far North Queensland, picking squash, backbreaking work.

They have no complaints about the Grand, which appears to be staffed entirely by backpackers. In the breakfast room, a handwritten sign by the cornflakes reads: 'If you mess upstairs—clear it! I'm not a slave to staff—I serve customers. Catie.' And the fish and chips I'll pick at that evening must surely have been cooked by a Scotsman, for no one can deep-fry with the passion and conviction of a Scot. The once-tasty morsel of local mackerel emerges from the kitchen looking like it has been dipped in road tar and plunged into a nuclear reactor.

I walk across the road to Mairu Beach. 'FOR YOUR CARE AND ENJOYMENT!' suggests one sign, its welcome diminished by a second, more temporary notice: 'WARNING', it screams in garish capitals, 'RECENT CROCODILE SIGHTING IN THIS AREA'. And to make sure the message gets through: 'ACHTUNG'. There's no French, no Italian, only a smaller, more subdued exclamation in Japanese. What is it about the Germans, I wonder, that makes their flesh taste so sweet to our native fauna? Am I wrong? Is it my imagination, or are a disproportionate number of Germans taken by crocodiles?

Further along the waterfront there are dark letters stencilled onto the paving, spelling out a potted history of Thursday Island. '1606—Luis Vaes De Torres was the first to navigate the Torres Strait.' A telltale smudge reveals that Luis was originally inscribed as Louis. Never mind. I wonder what local Islanders think of the greater mistake, the assertion that Torres was the first to navigate the strait. '1871—Coming of Light: First London Missionaries arrive on Darnley Island.' And towards the end: '3 June 1992—Historic High Court Mabo decision was made on Native Title.' I remember the day well; I was in court when the decision was handed down. Not that the judges said much: we journalists had to line up for the printed decision and work out for ourselves how momentous it was. Now, almost twenty years later, I've finally made it to the Torres Strait, resting place of Eddie Mabo, to see what all the fuss was about. The inscription is a timely reminder that, despite their remoteness, the islands of the Torres Strait are an integral part of Australia.

Across the road from the beachside esplanade, real estate advertisements alert me to the state of the local economy. There are houses for sale, up on the ridge with sweeping views across the harbour, for $1.3 million. It seems a lot of money for a town of fewer than 3000 in the middle of nowhere. Later, the captain of the ferry to Horn Island will tell me such houses are bought by governments, state and federal, to house employees on secondment from Canberra or Brisbane or Cairns. He says that just 15 per cent of the island's economy is private sector; the rest, either through employment or welfare, is government. The island floats above the Arafura Sea on a cushion of taxpayers' money. I wonder if the largesse can float it above the growing threat of higher seas and bigger storms.

I climb the hill to see the million-dollar views for myself, and find myself making my way to the Green Hill Fort, looking out across the approaches to Thursday Island from Battery Point. The fort was built in 1892 to guard against marauding Russians. The Russians, perhaps unaware that they were expected, failed to turn up. Neither did anyone else. A 1902 photo of the fort's long-gone Victoria Barracks reveals a series of elegant two-storey wooden buildings, erected high off the ground for ventilation and boasting verandahs of considerable width, enough to put the old Grand Hotel to shame. The wooden structures would have been disastrous should the Russians ever have got around to lobbing a shell over the ramparts, but perhaps by the time the buildings went up the military was well aware of what an untroubled idyll they had stumbled across. The Australian officer class has a fondness for water views.

The barracks would have been a good place to see out World War I—better than the alternative offered by the Western Front. Life at the fort during World War II, with the Japanese in Papua New Guinea and bombing Darwin, wouldn't have been quite so carefree. Thursday Island was evacuated (well, at least the whites were evacuated) and the local Japanese, of whom there were many, incarcerated. A small garrison manned the fort as a signals station. The fort was abandoned decades ago, then restored as a bicentennial project, its three massive six-inch guns still pointing out over the island approaches. It recalls a simpler era, when threats were tangible. You can't use artillery against climate change.

I continue over the ridge of the hill down to the far side of the island, the side that used to be the Islander side in the bad old days of segregation. Nowadays, it's looking pretty natty, and no different from the harbour side. I rejoin the coastal ring road, walk past a high school and come across the cemetery, stretching up from the shoreline, on the opposite side of the island from the main town. It's an old cemetery, with many of the older graves so covered in tropical growth they've become inaccessible. Closer to the dirt track that winds through the graveyard, a floral arms race has broken out between a couple of adjacent plots. Family members have so bedecked them with artificial flowers that the graves themselves are submerged between explosions of plastic flowers: carnations, lilies, chrysanthemums, roses—reds, whites, pinks, blues and yellows. It's the sort of grave to which Carmen Miranda may have aspired. Nearby, a smaller interment, decked in white tiles and blue dolphins, still exudes sadness seven years after a 2-day-old baby was laid to rest. Its tidiness and a sodden teddy bear speak of ongoing grief. Nearby lies another grave, marked only by a weathered and unmarked cross, its diminutive size alone testimony to early death. Among the crosses and headstones stand shoulder-high termite mounds, as if in sympathy with the loss of locals.

Down in one corner, close to the road, and to the sea, are the graves of Japanese pearl divers, many dozens of them. Traditionally, the Japanese revere their ancestors, setting aside a day each year to honour them and tend the family graves, a difficult undertaking if they're buried on some foreign shore. But these graves are not forgotten. Amid them stands a rather striking polished granite obelisk, mounted on a matching grey plinth. The characters are Japanese, but the relief sculpture of an old-fashioned diving helmet indicates what it commemorates. Nearby, a translation, dated 1979, is inscribed in stone:

> This monument has been erected in memory of the cen-
> tenary of the Japanese people who worked, lived and died
> here in the Torres Strait area. From 1878 till 1941 thousands
> of Japanese were employed in the gathering of pearl shells,
> and this constituted the principal enterprise of Northern
> Australia. They worked hard together with the islanders, con-

tributing to the development of the fishing industry. During this period, approximately 700 of the Japanese people died in the Torres Strait area.

What the monument does not say is that many of those hundreds died on one day: 4 March 1899, when Mahina, a category 5 cyclone long held to be the most intense storm ever recorded on Australia's east coast, bore down on Cape York and the Torres Strait. More than 400 people died in what remains Australia's worst natural disaster—more than in any flood, more than in any bushfire. The Thursday Island pearling fleet, sheltering in Bathurst Bay on nearby Cape York, was decimated. Sixty-six pearling luggers were sunk. The storm surge was reported to be more than 14 metres high and swept more than 5 kilometres inland. According to one report, dolphins were found marooned 15 metres up a cliff face on Flinders Island.

Mahina, with a central pressure of 914 hectopascals, remained the most intense and powerful cyclone recorded in Australia for ninety years, not eclipsed until 1988. Now, however, it rates ninth. There have been eight more powerful storms since 1988, four in the last decade. Neither Larry nor Yasi are among them. I contemplate the Japanese graves and wonder what it must have been like, back in the days before weather maps, satellite photographs and radio warnings, to find such a massive storm bearing down, without time to prepare or a place to escape. How fortunate we are, in this era of larger and more potent storms, to have forewarnings of such disasters. Provided, of course, that we heed the warnings.

⌒

The Torres Strait is some 150 kilometres wide, separating mainland Australia from Papua New Guinea. I had imagined a vast, uninterrupted expanse of water, an undisturbed horizon, but as I head off across it in a single-engine Cessna, those 150 kilometres take on a different perspective. There are islands ahead, islands behind, islands flanking us on either side. Some are no more than sandy beaches atop the reef, covered with a shallow smattering of green, or a sandbar topped with a lone coconut palm, like a cartoon from *Punch*. Some are coral cays:

dense green pancakes of jungle, ringed with white sand, surrounded by their own shining blue-green lagoons. Many islands though are substantial, not flat to the sea, but hilly, standing high, dry and rocky, their reefs and lagoons afterthoughts. I look at them with respect. They're not like the mountainous islands found out in the mid-Pacific—Hawaii, Fiji, Tahiti—spawned by plate tectonics and thrust, new minted, out of the volcanic depths. Those of the Torres Strait are quite different: old mountains, not thrusting upwards, but sinking slowly into a rising ocean. They are the final peaks of Australia's Great Dividing Range, which begins in Victoria thousands of kilometres south and continues north until it peters out on the very shores of Papua New Guinea.

From the plane, all this is set out beneath us. The pilot has the latest instruments, GPS and Sat Nav to complement navigation beacons and radio contact, but on a fine day like today he really doesn't need any of them. He could steer by the islands—we are never out of sight of three or four, often more. There are around 250 significant islands in the strait, many more insignificant ones.

Where there isn't land, there is shallow sea, with reefs swirling and bending just below the surface, a canvas of light blues and greens, soft yellows and subtle whites. Even in the deeper water the ocean isn't dark or blue; it's a pastel aquamarine, milky with sand, white blotches rising and swirling beneath the surface, as if some giant has been dabbing at it with a sponge. It looks like Lake Eyre in flood, except the land around Lake Eyre is much flatter. It's not a bad comparison nevertheless: the deepest channel through Torres Strait, connecting the Pacific and Indian oceans, is just 11 metres at its shallowest; Lake Eyre lies 15 metres below sea level.

Jules Verne knew all about the shallow waters of the strait. In *20,000 Leagues under the Sea*, published in 1869, he described Torres Strait as 'the world's most dangerous strait, a passageway that even the boldest navigators hesitated to clear'. Indeed, his hero, Captain Nemo, is forced to manoeuvre his submersible, the *Nautilus*, along the surface in an attempt to traverse the treacherous waterway. But the master seaman miscalculates, running the *Nautilus* aground on a coral reef. It is wedged fast for several days. Nemo isn't perturbed;

he knows the time of year and the phases of the moon. With just minutes to spare, the vessel is refloated by, of all things, the summer king tide. I stare out the window of the Cessna, enchanted by this new and unexpected seascape. I must be traversing the strait south-to-north at precisely the same time of year that Nemo attempted his fictional west-to-east traverse.

After less than an hour in the air, the horizon begins to fill with another colour, low and dark and olive green. Papua New Guinea. A much larger island at the end of the chain of smaller ones. We cross into PNG airspace as the pilot swings the plane around and down onto the tarmac at Sabai Island, the northernmost part of Queensland. This is yet another species of island, lying so close to PNG that it is formed from silt washed down rivers from the highlands. Large sheets of muddy water are covering much of Sabai's interior as the plane touches down. Even from the tarmac, I can see across to Australia's nearest neighbour. You don't need a plane or even a motorboat to cross the narrow strait between the two countries: you could row across, or even paddle a surfboard if you don't mind the crocodiles. I've been warned not to leave my boots outside on Sabai: PNG villagers are liable to sneak across the channel and knock them off.

But I'm not getting off at Sabai. I wait aboard the nine-seater as a mother and her two kids disembark and a couple of locals arrive with their luggage in a wheelbarrow. The loadmaster greets them with a set of bathroom scales, ensuring neither passengers nor luggage exceed the plane's capacity. Airborne again we thread our way across more islands before arriving at Yam. Yam, or Iama in the local language, is a tiny place, maybe 2 square kilometres, sitting roughly halfway between the Australian mainland and Papua New Guinea. As we circle to land, I can make out the island's geography. Roughly circular, it's defined by the east–west runway that divides it in half. North and east of the airstrip are mangrove swamps, flooded much of the time with seawater. To the south of the runway the land rises steeply, granite boulders smothered with jungle, rough and inaccessible, another outcrop of our sunken mountain range. That leaves a small triangle of habitable land in the west, its apex touching the runway and its base along the island's only permanent beach. Within this small triangle are dotted some fifty or sixty houses, accommodating about four hundred people. It's not exactly crowded, but with the population growing, it won't be long. There's a school, two churches, a cultural centre, the council offices and a supermarket, but no hotels, no restaurants and certainly no bars.

The airports have been getting smaller the further north I've travelled: Sydney's Central-station bustle, Cairns's shopping-mall hum, Horn Island's corner-store chat. Yam is more like a bus stop in the middle of nowhere, a small shed sitting outside the perimeter fence with a bench outside. I disembark and get my luggage, while two people are weighed on the bathroom scales and board. The plane takes off, and I am left alone in the silence of the bus stop. A notice pinned to the wall warns outsiders against 'sly grogging'. I take my bag and walk the 50 metres or so to where the wedge of houses begins. I've arranged a place to stay through the local council: a room at the self-catering Sun Downer Lodge, where the council puts up visiting bureaucrats and tradesmen. At the first of the houses, I ask directions.

'Oh, the lodge. That's way down there. As far as you can go, near the dock.' I don't like the sound of 'way down there', but it's a five-minute walk. Nowhere on Yam is very far. I call in at the council office, and a kind and chatty woman, Bethalia, escorts me to the lodge, where she works sporadically as a cleaner. It's not much of a place: fibro and lino, fluorescent tube lighting and cockroach cadavers. I check the kitchen: an old gas stove, a new fridge, a broken freezer with a pool of fetid water in the bottom. There's a tired collection of kitchen implements: predictably blunt knives, together with two saucepans and a fry pan, all three with dangerously loose handles. But there are ceiling fans throughout, and a functional, if noisy, air conditioner in my room. I'm not sure what Somerset Maugham would think, but I reckon it's just dandy.

The best thing about the Sun Downer Lodge is its location. Across the road, overlooking the end of the beach, there's an open space, an unofficial town square. Here, in the shade of spreading almond trees, seated on temporary benches or three huge tractor tyres, the village comes to gossip, sit by the cooling sea and watch the tides wash to and fro across the reef flat. Where the beach ends, a seawall has been constructed to protect a small artificial headland. Sitting on top of the seawall are four pergolas looking back at the town square and the beach. Next to the pergolas a slim wharf angles out to sea, just wide enough for two people to pass between its guide rails. Next to the wharf, at the end of the headland, a boat ramp runs down to the sea. Once a week a barge from Thursday Island unloads supplies here. Next to the ramp at the end of the headland, housed in what could be mistaken for a suburban garage, is the island's desalination plant. Between the desal plant and the Sun Downer lies the island's one and only store—a community-run supermarket.

I stand on the Sun Downer's small porch and watch Islanders drift to the supermarket and drift back again, stopping at the pergolas or in the beach clearing for a chat. The weather is warm to hot, rather humid in this, the wet season, but not uncomfortably so, with a light breeze coming off the sea. The people move with an unhurried ease, minimising effort under the tropical sun. Dogs meander with the same lack of haste; there seems to be as many dogs as there are people. The mood is languid and peaceful. Even the gulls are well behaved and unhurried.

I wander across to the clearing under the almond trees. A group of women are seated in the shade, their children bouncing around on the nearby tyres. Laid out in front of the women are a few small things for sale: dilly bags, some dried fruits and small brooms woven from native vegetation. They smile when I try to strike up a conversation, but despite much waving of arms and laughter, we don't get far: their English is all but non-existent. The women are from Papua New Guinea, on Yam for a family funeral. Now they're trying to sell a few items in order to buy fuel for the return journey.

I leave the clearing and continue along the beach. The tide is in far enough to cover the reef flat, but still leaving a generous swathe of coarse sand, dotted with lumps of dead coral. Looking out to sea, there are three large islands off past the desal plant, and to the west, the peaks of three more protrude above the horizon. It's not a long beach, but it's a beautiful beach, flanked as it is by the almond trees. They're not European almond trees, the type that produce the familiar nuts, but a species found throughout tropical Asia and the western Pacific. There are two types on Yam: yellow and red. The locals eat the flesh of the fruit, as well as the almond-like kernel. The trees grow in the sand just above the high-water mark, binding the dune. They grow high, 20 or 30 metres, and spread their branches wide, their broad green leaves providing a wide umbrella of shade. Beneath the canopy, the sand is bare; the trees must take up all available nutrients. If there is any finer tree under which to while away an hour or two, I'm yet to encounter it.

Walking along the beach, I stop to admire a picture postcard of a tree, standing proud just over the lip of the beach. Hanging from its lower branches like Chinese lanterns, in shades of orange, yellow and red, of brown, cream and caramel, bleached pastel by the sun and the sea, are two dozen or so fishing-net floats the size of soccer balls. I guess they hang from the tree to prevent them being floated off by a tropical downpour or a mischievous tide, but the effect is something like an oversized, tropical Christmas tree, an image from a child's picture book.

'Hello', says a rich baritone.

It takes me by surprise. I've been so enchanted by the tree, I've overlooked the middle-aged man dozing in a director's chair in its shelter. 'Hello', I say, and introduce myself. A large brown dog stirs, thinks better of it, offers a desultory sniff and then winds itself back down to doze in a hollow in the sand.

The man introduces himself as Patrick and we get talking. Patrick points out his runabout, *Lawrence*, with its purple trim and black Mercury outboard, bobbing a few metres away on the lifting tide. He says when the water is a bit higher, he'll take the boat over and moor it at the wharf. Then later, when the tide falls, he'll take it out to get some crayfish. The weather is good, the sea is flat, and there's money to be made. A kilo of cray tails are $24, and it's $30 a kilo for live lobsters. For the most part, the Islanders free dive for them, although some might use a simple air compressor, what they call a hooker. They either spear the lobsters or, increasingly, scoop them into a net for the live trade. They're taken down to Thursday Island and flown south to Sydney or north to Asia.

'It's good money', says Patrick. 'Most people who have a boat do a bit. If you need a bit of extra money, you know. A kid graduating from school down in Cairns, that sort of thing.'

'How often do you go out?'

'Me? Not much. Not here that much.'

'You don't live here?'

'Yeah, yeah. My house is just here. My wife is here. The kids are at school or working in Cairns. But I work in a mine. I'm a carpenter.'

'A mine. Whereabouts?' I ask.

'Karratha.'

'Are you kidding? Karratha, Western Australia? How do you get there?'

'Plane. Two days' travel. The boss rings me on the mobile, and off I go. Costs a fortune to get there.' Patrick works for a month or so at a time, then comes back to Yam for a week or two.

The conversation pauses, and I sit in the shade of the perfect tree, regarding the perfect view and wonder why anyone would give it up, especially when crayfish are there for the taking, to travel to the far side of the country to work in the baking red dust of the Pilbara. Money, I guess. Or boredom.

I ask whether I can come along when he goes fishing for crays, but he shakes his head. 'Love to mate, but it's not allowed. None of us can take you out on a commercial fish. I'd lose my permit.'

We talk a bit more, and then I continue along the rest of the beach. At the end, I reach the hilly part of the island. A sharp outcrop of granite boulders extending into the sea bars my way, not to be climbed, not to be circumvented. It's a small place, Yam; you can only walk so far.

⌒

The summer king tide continues to swell, and Yam Island, halfway between Cape York and Papua New Guinea, grows smaller by the minute. The sea has risen and is filling the mangrove swamps. By

10.15 a.m. the lower part of the wharf is submerged, and the higher section is only a metre or so clear. A small boy, aged three or four, is hanging over the side, his eyes wide at the life swirling below him. A company of sardines are practising parade-ground drills over by the rocks, moving in lockstep one way, then about-turning and returning in unison. Closer to the surface, practically on the surface, white bait form a circle so tight it looks like a grey frisbee revolving in the water. They circle slowly, then suddenly burst into the air, splashing back like silver confetti.

'Wow', says the boy, eyes wide against his dark skin. His name is Pedro, and we watch the fish together. A few itinerant black-and-white damselfish make their way beneath us, asserting their individualism alongside the regimented sardines. A garfish slides centimetres beneath the surface: long, thin and dart-like, its body clear, as if made of glass. And then Pedro exclaims, 'Look! Look there!' I see them, too. Two white fish, gliding effortlessly out from under the wharf. But they are not fish. Their tails are moving up and down, not side to side, and their white skin is matte, not shimmering with scales. There's something else: the way they turn to each other, regard each other, as if chatting before turning back to where they are going. Baby dugongs, perhaps only 20 centimetres long, swimming in accord, mammals perfectly adapted to life beneath the waves. 'Wow', says Pedro. 'Wow', I concur.

Yet I can't stay watching fish with Pedro much longer. The water is rising. Soon it will start to cover roads and threaten houses. The tide is coming in, and I leave the boy staring down into a see-through sea.

⌒

I have four days on Yam. On my second day, instead of heading south along the main beach again, I head north. There's another beach here, beyond the headland, or at least there used to be. Here a crude seawall has been constructed, granite boulders lifted into place and splashed here and there with concrete. The sea, flat and docile once again, is hard up against this wall, about 1 metre from its top. Sheltering behind the ramparts is a line of about ten houses. These are known as the tin sheds; most of them have walls of Colorbond steel, sitting on concrete slabs, looking more like shipping containers than tropical housing. Behind the houses, on the other side from the beach, runs a narrow dirt road, and behind that the mangroves begin. The tin sheds aren't located so much on a beach as on a narrow spit, a single dune curving away from the more substantial land of the island proper, separating the reef flat from the mangroves.

From the track, I walk around the side of the first tin shed to where it overlooks the water. It sits a few metres back from the seawall, the intervening sand swept hard and clean, shaded by an almond tree. 'Hello there', says a voice from within the gloom of the house. And then the voice has a face. And a smile. It's Bethalia, the cleaning woman who escorted me to the lodge. She confirms this is her house. I ask if she is worried about the imminent king tide. She nods vigorously, a line of concern creasing her forehead.

'We evacuate twice a year. Put all our furniture up. The sea comes through, washes through. From here to the mangroves.' She tells me she's already been flooded this summer, just a month ago, when the monthly spring tide combined with the aftermath of Cyclone Yasi to send waves across her lounge room floor. She says she has only just finished cleaning. I notice that her windows—glass louvres, she tells me—are shuttered away behind protective sheets of fibre cement. I ask if the waves get that high, up to the windows.

'No, no', she laughs. 'But look, here, and here.' She points to dents in the green steel wall of her house. 'Coral, pieces of coral. The waves pick them up and throw them. It makes such a sound, you wouldn't believe.' I survey the dents, imagine the harrowing timpani, and notice the bottom of the walls, where they meet the concrete slab. They're stained brown with rust.

'How can you live here? How can you put up with it?'

'It wasn't always like this. There was a good beach here. Big, like the front beach. It protected us. But the sea has washed away the sand. They put the wall in, but the sea is breaking that too.' She's right. I can see where the boulders have been moved, crumbling away the supporting concrete. A wooden pole shows the wall's original height, half a metre higher than it is now. 'And see this sand here?'

She shuffles her foot beneath the almond tree. 'That's not from the beach. That's where the sea broke the sand bags, gave us a little back.' She laughs again.

I ask Bethalia if she will evacuate in two days' time, when the king tide hits. She shrugs. If the weather holds, if the sea stays as glassy calm as it is right now, she might be lucky and get away with only one inundation this summer. Eventually, though, she knows she will have to move away. The council, having spent a fortune on the seawall, has reluctantly conceded that to spend more would be sending good money after bad. It's decided the tin sheds are untenable. They will be demolished and the residents moved to a new model village being built alongside the runway.

I thank Bethalia, and tell her I may see her on Friday, when the big sea is due.

It's not possible to walk alongside the seawall—the houses are pressed too hard against it—so I go back round to the track that runs behind the houses, continuing north. I paddle through the edge of a large puddle that stretches across the road, left over from the last cloudburst or the last high tide, I can't tell which. I pass the last house and a cold room storing frozen crayfish, and the track narrows, just wide enough for a vehicle, with the beach to the left and the water of the mangroves to the right. There is at least some sand here, a remnant of what the beach once was. I come across four men standing next to a boat, hands gory, gutting two huge sea turtles, each a metre in diameter. The intestines lie glistening grey-green in piles on the sand. I make a cursory attempt at conversation, but the men want to get their grim work over with and I don't much feel like hanging about. I like turtles, and I'm glad I wasn't here to witness their deaths. The animals are protected, but Islanders are allowed to hunt a few for cultural purposes. Selling the meat is prohibited.

A little further along, the wall of mangroves gives way to reveal a waterway winding off through the trees, through the inside of the island, like a scene from *African Queen* or the Florida Everglades. The spit of sand is narrow here, maybe 6 metres wide, the sea on one side, the mangrove channel on the other. It's not hard to image a storm driving waves across from the sea into the channel. A number of boats are pulled up on the mangrove side. Three are typical runabouts, modern aluminium and fibreglass. But the fourth is something old and beautiful, dwarfing its neighbours. It's 30 foot long, hand carved from a single log of wood. Carved, but not crude. Its lines are graceful: sculptured, elegant and hydrodynamic. The bow is sharp and vertical, a little thicker to cut the waves, yet shaped and contoured below the waterline for stability and flow. The hull is curved, strong and sinuous, and the stern is somehow a little broader, a little flatter at the waterline. The only addition is a couple of flat boards at the back, fitted into a purpose-carved groove to support an outboard motor.

Beside the boat a man is squatting, prising the lid from a can of bright orange paint. It's the same colour that workers have been painting the fence at the airport. It's possible the boat needs painting— the last of its original red paint is so faded and worn as to be barely recognisable, although the wood still seems solid enough under its weathering. It's a shame; the weathered wood and faded remnants of original paint conspire to give the vessel an antique beauty. I've seen nothing in Sydney's Maritime Museum to match it.

'Your boat?' I inquire.

'Yes. My boat.'

'How old is it?'

'Don't know. Very old. I found it.'

'Found it? Really? Where?'

'Back there', he says, gesturing at the mangroves behind him. 'Been there a long time, I think. Long time.'

'It must be from PNG', I suggest. 'No trees of that size here.'

'Yeah, sure. From PNG.' The man's name is Philip. We chat a bit more, but I leave him before he sets to work with his fluorescent paint.

I keep walking, following a track towards the end of the spit and pushing through casuarina trees to a small clearing. From nowhere, a light drizzle begins to fall, although, in the distance, I can see an island glistening in the sun. I think I am on my own, but suddenly I am confronted by a wild-looking man, his chest bare and eyes red. He's wielding a machete. He takes a step towards me, and some alarm goes off in my head. Surely not here, not now. But then he smiles, and lowers the machete. I notice he is standing beside a fire, which is sputtering in the drizzle. Next to the fire, folded up in a wheelbarrow, is a small boy, his T-shirt pulled over his knees, his eyes closed under a hat. Under the wheelbarrow is a small pile of freshly cut wood.

'He's sick', the man explains. 'I'm trying to get him a bit warm.'

'I amazed you can get a fire going in this', I say.

The man tells me his name, Dymock Samuel. I ask if he is from Yam, and he says no, from PNG. He is down visiting his girlfriend. She's along the beach somewhere, catching fish for the barbecue. Under a treaty negotiated in 1984, Torres Strait Islanders and PNG citizens from thirteen coastal villages are entitled to travel between the two areas without passports.

Dymock and I get talking, and I ask him about the trip from PNG. He tells me it's not difficult; even in a small boat it takes about two hours. You can steer by the islands or, if the weather is fine, follow the reef. He likes to follow the reef.

The rain intensifies, and Dymock and I lift the wheelbarrow, sleeping boy and all, up onto the picnic table and under its protective awning. The New Guinea villager thanks me, and I wish him well.

Returning to the beach, the rain stops as suddenly as it started, and I sit on an obliging rock under a casuarina tree, thinking of Dymock journeying back and forth between Yam and his coast village. Following the reef. It's entirely possible that he's been traversing a similar route to that followed by his forbears when they walked the land bridge between Papua New Guinea and Australia as recently as 8000 years ago. The sea level at the zenith of the last ice age, about 12000 years ago, was some 120 metres below where it sits today—this rise all in the geological blink of an eye, well after humankind had left Africa and made its way to this part of the world. Imagine what it must have been like to be here as the sea level rose, to be on hand the day of that mighty storm, when the narrow dam between Pacific and Indian oceans was finally breached, and water surged through, carving in hours a channel hundreds of metres wide. The sound would have been stupendous, a roaring heard for kilometres. The ground would have shaken with the power of the surge. Somerset Maugham couldn't have known how accurate the description was when he was told the strait was the last place that God ever made.

Now, after pausing for 1500 years, sea levels are gradually rising again: 20 centimetres during the twentieth century. The Intergovernmental Panel on Climate Change predicts sea levels will rise by another 18–59 centimetres by the end of this century. Other less-conservative models suggest it may be as much as 2 metres. Some of this will be due to thermal expansion; as the sea gets warmer, it takes up more space. The rest would be due to the melting of glaciers and land-based snow and ice. The geological record reveals one 500-year period during which the sea rose 4 metres each century, 20 metres in all. At one time, 120 000 years ago during the last inter-glacial period, the oceans were 6 metres higher than they are now. There is, after all, plenty of ice still lying on top of Greenland and Antarctica that could melt and run into the sea. If it did, sea levels would rise 70 metres, drowning cities and redrawing coastlines. No one is saying that a complete meltdown is going to happen, at least not this century, but considering what has happened in the past, a rise of half a metre seems entirely plausible. It baffles me that some people are so sceptical about sea-level rise; how could one be so determined to see permanence in a shoreline that has never been stable?

But sea-level rise isn't the big threat here. Not on Yam, not right now. It's not melting glaciers and thermal expansion that have ripped away the beach from in front of Bethalia's house and chewed at the boulders of the seawall. That's something altogether more quick-tempered and unpredictable.

⌒

The three community leaders sit in the council chairman's office and tell me how worried they are about climate change. The chairman himself is not on Yam; he's down at Thursday Island on council business. In his absence, the council's chief executive, an efficient 41-year-old woman named Lily David has arranged the meeting for me. I suspect Lily is the real power on Yam, but she lets the men do the talking. One of them is her husband Ned, a wiry man dressed in a khaki shirt and a ranger's shorts. He expresses their mutual concern:

'It started about ten years ago. It was a strange thing. The tides don't usually come up that high. When the king tide hits in the strong weather, it scoops all the sand away and the island goes under water. Probably, the tide gets bigger every year with the northwest wind. When it gets very strong, the wet comes in. It is spilling in the lounge room, in the kitchen. And every year, the water goes across the road. Every year it gets bigger.'

Next to me sits Fred Peters, the school principal. He's a chubby man with a toothy grin and an infectious laugh. But he doesn't laugh as he agrees with Ned's assessment. 'For the last ten years, it has just been a constant bashing of these enormous king tides and cyclonic weather. It's been constant for the last ten years.'

The third man is Samuel Kapa, sitting opposite me on the couch next to Ned. Sammy says he's sixty-eight, born in July 1932 (which would make him seventy-eight, but who's counting). He's been a big man, and he embodies a sense of stature, graced by stillness. His English is broken, lacking the polish of post-war education displayed by the other two. But his presence is instructive. Ned and Fred, community leaders in their own right, constantly defer to him, calling him 'Uncle'. I ask Samuel his opinion. 'The island used to grow bigger,' he says. 'Now it's getting smaller.' Sammy seems to be talking about more than physical size.

Ned lays some photographs from the 1960s and 1970s on the table between us, showing how the beach in front of the tin sheds used to extend many metres out across the rock of the reef flat. 'See how far the beach went? All the way to the point. Also, the south side of the island [used to be] high. I think this erosion started about ten years ago. Maybe caused by development on the side of the beach, I don't know. Maybe they disturbed nature.'

We discuss the possibility that the almost total erosion of the beach in front of the tin sheds has been caused by development. At some point, the headland was artificially extended and a channel blasted through the reef flat to allow boats into the wharf and the barge to land supplies. I recall Selina telling me that the Heron Island harbour channel had caused erosion as the ebbing tide swept sand through the channel and out to sea. But Ned doesn't think so, saying that for a time the beach grew larger, not smaller, after the changes were made. We discuss whether the harvesting of mangroves for firewood might have had an impact, even though the mangroves are located behind the beach, not in front of it.

The men tell me the erosion isn't just happening near the tin sheds; it's happening all around the island. Not just on this island. 'Have you been to Coconut Island?' asks Fred. 'They can't build any more houses on that place. It's just a thin strip of coral cay with coconuts and houses on it. And it's eroding.'

Ned asks whether I've heard of Tudu Island. I have. It's the ancestral home of the Yam people. Captain William Bligh, he of the mutiny on the *Bounty* and the rum rebellion, named it 'Warrior Island' after some of these men's forefathers attacked his ship. The people of Tudu gradually resettled on Yam after the London Missionary Society established a settlement here. Tudu became uninhabited, but it still looms large in the minds and spirituality of the Yam people, and they visit it frequently to fish along its reefs. With virtually no human activity, it makes for a brilliant case study. 'Tudu Island, that island, is getting smaller. It has rapidly eroded,' says Ned quietly, a sadness in his voice. 'It is like a bank to us. There are fish stocks, other things, and now it is getting smaller. We used to live there, now we live here, but it is very important to us, very spiritual. Now that island is being eaten away.' Ned is right. The erosion that's hurting Yam is hurting islands across the Torres Strait.

This is the real concern about climate change: rising sea levels are one thing; wild weather is another. Yam has a granite core, but where the people live is effectively a coral cay. Other populated islands in the Torres Strait, like Coconut, Sue and Yorke islands are coral cays, pure and simple. Cays form on top of shallow reefs where intersecting currents slow down the speed of water, slow enough for silt and other debris to precipitate and accumulate. Over time, the cays emerge from the sea, at first only at low tide, then more permanently as they continue to gather in deposits of dead coral and other material. Resting seabirds deposit guano. Seeds, carried by birds, by the wind or by the tide, germinate and the plants help bind the surface of the new island. Over time, coral cays can achieve some area, though rarely much height. But what the sea gives, the sea can take away. Coral cays are active, dynamic places. The forces of growth and those of erosion are in constant competition. The more benign the weather, the more silt and other material can build up; trees become established, and dunes grow permanent. The worse the weather, the more the waves chop and chew at the island's flanks. If the islands of the Torres Strait are eroding, it is not rising sea levels; it is the rising rate and intensity of tropical storms.

Just last night, checking my email at Yam's cultural centre, I came across a news report on the ABC website. 'STUDY LINKS EXTREME WEATHER TO CLIMATE CHANGE', read the headline. The report said that a study in the science journal *Nature* had found that extreme rain and floods had increased by 7 per cent in the second half of the twentieth century, closely matching the effects computer models had predicted from climate change. The study only covered the Northern Hemisphere; there wasn't enough data for south of the equator. But 7 per cent is significant. In the Torres Strait, a figure like that may start to tilt the balance away from coral cay formation to that of coral cay erosion.

Now the people of Yam Island want help to preserve their home. Ned is growing passionate. 'For things like this to happen is terrible. We don't want to leave. This is our home. Two years ago, we started to talk to the Prime Minister about it—what else can we do? Surveyors come here and they say the water will continue coming. They say it will come up here, under the council.' The council building is a long way back from the front beach, maybe 100 metres or more, but only a narrow concrete road separates it from the mangroves that dominate the northern part of the island. Ned says that once the seawall by the tin sheds began to fail, the state Environmental Protection Authority decreed that nature would be allowed to take its course, and plans were developed to permanently evacuate the sheds.

Beside me, Fred is beginning to anger at what he sees as the double standard.

'I don't want to be biased, but I will make a point about the aid to us and to those down there who were affected by Yasi and Larry. They flew our SES volunteers from here to go and help clean up down there. The last ten years we've been bombarded by the harsh weather, we didn't get no SES people here to help us restore the waterfront. To me that is unfair.

'One of my relatives down in Cairns, they got a payout, compensation. They got $3000 for Cyclone Yasi. We've been bombarded here by high tides, but we didn't get no $3000 for when it came into the houses and we had to move the families to higher ground. Our people have been suffering for the last ten years. The government should back pay us!'

After the meeting with Fred, Ned and Sammy, I walk back down past the lodge to the jetty, and from there around to the back of the desal plant. The tide is running out and I want to see where the water goes. I sit on the wall behind the desal plant and watch. In front of me, protecting the channel blasted through the reef, is a breakwater curving round towards the tin sheds. A few gulls stand there. In a land without takeaway fish and chips, there's not much else for a gull to do. As the water recedes further, it doesn't pour through the channel but seems to be slowly retreating from the reef flat towards the open sea. If the water isn't rushing into the channel, then it can't be taking sand with it. In fact, there is nothing in the movement of the water in this gentle sea to suggest any erosion, natural or not. I think the men are right: the erosion is caused by the weather and the waves, not the wharf and its channel.

The sun is starting to sink towards the sea, and I watch it fall. Western Australia isn't the only place in the country where you can see an ocean sunset. The weather is balmy, the wind light. I walk back round to the front of the desal plant, past the supermarket and onto the wharf. A school of cuttlefish hover in the water, their colour alternating between translucent and black-green. There's thirty or forty of them, and they're all looking right at me with their unblinking green eyes. I wave to them, but they pretend to ignore me.

Snubbed by the cephalopods, I leave the wharf and take a walk along the front beach instead. Large clouds are gathered on the horizon, floating white and backlit by the setting sun. It's meant to be the wet season, but it hasn't rained for two days, and the sea remains calm. It's the king tide tomorrow, and there is no sign of bad weather. I've been secretly hoping for some sort of typhonic storm, the old journo in me wanting to see nature at its worst, to witness the waves crashing through the living rooms of the tin sheds, so I can write it up in all its drama for the enlightenment and entertainment of readers ensconced in suburban armchairs, safe above the high-water mark.

I walk along thinking such thoughts, musing away, and before long I'm at the end of the beach. I'm about to turn back when I realise the barrier of the day before is insurmountable no longer. The huge granite boulders that fell sharply into the sea now terminate in the exposed reef flat. All I have to do is walk out and around the headland, weaving my way round shallow rock pools and taking care not to slip on the slick, wet rock.

I round the largest boulders, and a thin strip of sand extends in front of me, granite to my left and the reef to the right. Above the boulders the land rises steep, the jungle impassable. This is the core of the island, the old mountaintop from the submerged range. Some accident of the tides has marked out a path where the sand meets the hard flatness of the reef, as if by design. Darker rocks line one side of the path, and paler rocks the other. Ahead, one huge cream-coloured boulder sits on top of another, like a head on a pair of massive shoulders, a sentinel looking out to sea.

The air is growing quiet as I reach the outcrop, the mechanical hum of the desalination plant diminished by distance, the sounds of habitation receding. The light is growing golden, that perfect illumination that comes only in the hour after dawn and the hour before sunset.

I pause to photograph nature's sculpture and then continue on beneath its gaze and around the point. And there it is laid out before me, a beach from another world, from a world before time and men. It is like walking in a dream: the golden light, the absolute silence emphasised by the occasional splash from the reef pools or the call of a bird from the foliage. The sea, flat and gentle, lies a hundred metres away, caressing the outer edge of the reef flat. In fifty years, I have never known a silent beach. Even in the Mediterranean, even in the landlocked expanse of the Caspian, there has always been some wind, a gentle ripple of waves, aural evidence of water meeting land. Here there is nothing: no sound of the sea, no wind and no bustle of humanity.

I enter the cocoon holding my breath. The jungle beside the beach is rich, thick and glowing green in the polished sun. The beach is wider than the front beach, the sand finer and whiter. The reef flat is a covered in a sheet of water, a mirror reflecting the changing colours of the sunset clouds. Small clusters of mangroves have begun to build their own small islands out on the flat. A fish leaps from a deeper pool, its image momentarily burnt into my retinas, as it flashes silver in the sun. On the sand, my feet lay down a trail of solitary footprints. I come to a sole coconut palm, growing tall from the edge of the jungle, its stem curving out over the sand. Beneath the palm is an old shack, a corrugated-iron shelter rusted and beaten by the elements. It looks like something Robinson Crusoe might have lived in.

My dad died last week, from cancer, in a Canberra hospice: his life taken from him, and he from us. A small death, one of many in the greater tide of things, but it is monumental for his family, for those who loved him. Life since has been a blur, of organisation, of grief, of solidarity, of denial and the thousand-and-one small things that drive us from one day into the next. But now the stillness of the beach has me and takes me into introspection. I think of him, how he would have appreciated this magical place. I want to tell him of what I have found, to show him photographs and describe the golden light and the silence of the sea. But now I never can.

In the tranquillity of the beach, I consider what it might be like, to cast oneself away from the wider world, to disengage, to step off the relentless conveyor belt. To take up solitary residence on one of these uninhabited patches of paradise in the glorious blue sea, to live on fish and rainwater and watch the sun set and the moon rise. There once was such a hermit in the Torres Strait, living on Deliverance Island. Somerset Maugham wrote about him. German Harry, he was called. My own deliverance is but a short one. I watch the sun flow burning into the sea, breathe one last breath of the silence, then scramble back towards the Sun Downer Lodge before the tides and profound darkness of a Torres Strait night can claim me. I get back around the point as the tide is coming in.

I sit on the seawall in front of Bethalia's tin-shed home and splash my feet in the water. Out at sea, thunder clouds are rising and falling along the horizon, white and roiling. But their menace is negligible, there to admire rather than fear. Their undersides are a bewitching aquamarine, reflecting the colour of the sea. It's the day of the summer king tide, and the people of Yam are in luck: the sea is flat, rippled by nothing more than a playful breeze. I belatedly realise that luck is with me as well. Sure, there won't be the drama of water washing through the tin sheds, the panic of the people scurrying to lift valuables above the torrent, the spectacle of a wave breaking across the spit to meet the rising water of the mangroves. But like an amateur scientist instead of a deadline journalist, I'll be able to gain an insight into the truth of the matter, to establish a perfect baseline scenario, to see just how high the water can rise without being supplemented by waves and storm surges. From there it should be easy enough to visualise what impact half a metre or more would have.

It's 11 a.m., an hour before the expected peak, and the water has covered the reef flat to a depth of about a metre, just half a metre short of the top of the seawall. The smallest of waves slap at the rocks, playing with my feet. Along the way, the families of the tin sheds are fishing, sitting or standing on the rocks of the wall. A few young kids are swimming, laughing and splashing. Runabouts bob atop the tide. One cruises past, and I watch it as the helmsman swings it towards the open sea, opening up the throttle on the outboard. I find myself wondering where it might be headed on a day as calm and full of promise as this. And so I am caught unaware. The wash from the boat is enough to push a 30-centimetre wave up against the rocks. It soaks my shorts where I sit on top of the wall: the ripple from a slow-moving motorboat.

I stand up, balancing on the side of the wall, with my feet in a couple of centimetres of water, and turn to face Bethalia's home. The top of the seawall isn't even up to my hips and the house is perhaps only knee height above sea level. No storm would be needed, I realise, to push water across the wall and into the house: not the 7-metre storm surge of Cyclone Yasi, not the 14-metre surge of Cyclone Mahina, not even the everyday swell on an Australian beach. A windy day on Port Phillip Bay or Sydney Harbour would do the trick.

I leave the seawall, walk round to the front of Bethalia's house, and I'm greeted by the sea once again. The water has risen zombie-like from the mangrove swamp and completely covered the road. My guesstimate from the seawall is about right; the water has penetrated to within about half a metre of the lowest-lying houses. Wheelie bins beside the road are sitting in knee-deep water and threatening to float away. On the other side of the road, which by now has taken on the appearance of a shallow canal, one home is perched precariously on its own island hard up against the mangroves. The water is up to the concrete slab, mere centimetres from inundation. I check my watch. About twenty minutes to go, although the noon deadline is an estimation.

I walk back towards the supermarket. Mangrove Road, which runs perpendicular from the waterfront to the airport, is under water for a distance of more than a hundred metres. Cars sit stranded, the water up to their hub caps. An ad hoc mixture of concrete, coral debris and sandbags prevents the flood reaching into the yards and houses on the other side of the road. I watch a man emerge from the back of the council building and wade slowly through the water towards me, holding the hand of a young boy, in up to his knees.

'Not so bad', I say as they reach me.

He gives me a big grin. 'Yeah. Not so bad.'

⌣⟶

Gaurab Village, it's called. There's an elaborate sign at its entrance with the name in gilded letters and a painting of tropical greenery. There's a couple of large two-storey buildings, made from Hardie board and sporting solar hot-water systems on their pitched steel roofs and water tanks out the back. They're painted cream and pale green, sitting low to the ground, cutting off the possibility of a cooling under-floor breeze. By a door on a shallow porch, a pastel-blue life preserver hangs on the wall, giving the building a quaint nautical air, even though the village is as far from the sea as it's possible to get on Yam. There is nothing tropical about the buildings whatsoever. Indeed, nothing Australian. There's something Nordic about them, as if they have been flat-packed in from Ikea. With their utilitarian lines and colour coordination they remind me of another island, far away, in the archipelago stretching from Stockholm into the Baltic Sea. Further along there is another sign, made of all-purpose steel, the sort of sign that has spread like a plague across the Australian landscape, bearing the national coat of arms and, in this case, the Queensland government logo. 'Jointly funding the $30 million Major Infrastructure Program (Round 2) incorporating Iama Housing Subdivision.' Thirty million dollars to move ten families strikes me as rather a lot, so I have to assume there's more to it than that. I hope there is, because if it comes to relocating all the people in Australia who live low down along its shores, it will be an expensive exercise. For the first time, I am getting an inkling of what rising sea levels might actually mean.

3

THE CYCLONE COAST

A 'see-through' house at Tully Heads in the aftermath of Cyclone Yasi.

Appropriately enough, it's raining in Cairns. The tarmac is glistening, rippling with each new sweep of rain, as my plane pulls into the terminal. The Atherton Tablelands are there one moment, radiant in the sun, then gone the next, hidden by curtains of water and low-hung clouds. Six weeks ago Cyclone Yasi made landfall 140 kilometres south of here, and still the monsoon is dumping rain on the sodden landscape.

'Where are you heading?' asks the lady at the hire-car counter.

'South. Down past Innisfail.'

'Well, no further south than Cardwell then. The Bruce Highway is closed.'

'Still?' I ask.

'Again. Since 3 a.m. this morning.'

'More rain, then?'

She sighs, shakes her head. 'Hasn't stopped.'

After the wettest spring in Queensland's history, and the wettest December, the summer just past has been the sixth wettest on record. And March is looking to keep up with the trend. It's not just Queensland either. Victoria, collecting plenty of rain from the remnants of cyclones and monsoonal fronts, has experienced its wettest summer on record. La Niña isn't mucking about.

It's raining again as I load my bags into the small Toyota and drive from the airport. It's late afternoon, yet the sun, when it finds a break in the clouds, invokes its tropical strength. A kilometre or two down the road, it's out again, and the metal roof of the car complains audibly as it expands. For a moment, the road is impossibly dry. But ahead of me, a solid wall of rain, as dense and dark a grey as the cloud from which it hangs, is moving in quickly from the south. It hits with a roar, thundering on the roof, rebounding from the bonnet. It's like driving into a waterfall. The traffic slows, then stops. Two minutes later, the deluge has passed on, leaving the road awash under the glare of the sun.

I leave Cairns via the Bruce Highway, heading south towards Tully, towards where Yasi crossed the coast and wreaked its havoc. The rain clears a little, but the clouds hovering round the hills are a reminder that it may come and go on a whim. The road passes under the shadow of Mount Bellenden Ker—its peak hidden by cloud, its flanks awash with waterfalls. I like the mountains hereabouts; they rise abruptly from the plain, young and vigorous, not so old and careworn as the mountains in the south.

By the time I get to Innisfail, an hour or so later, the rain has returned, less boisterous but more persistent. I leave the highway and seek out a motel. It's not so easy. Yasi has put a hole in the tourist trade, but the motels are booked by reconstruction workers and families needing emergency accommodation. I'm directed from one place to another, before eventually finding a room.

Innisfail itself looks largely unaffected by Yasi. The city bore the impact of Cyclone Larry five years ago, which damaged some 10000 homes up and down the coast and destroyed 80 per cent of the country's banana crop. But Larry also seems to have weeded out many older, weaker buildings, those constructed before modern cyclone standards were introduced—the evolutionary impact of climate change. With Yasi having made landfall 50 kilometres to the south, this time around Innisfail appears to have had luck on its side.

I'm corrected the next morning as I have a coffee, watching the rain fall on the main street outside. The *Cairns Post* carries the headline 'YASI'S STING', above the subhead 'Jobless rate returns to nation-high 13 per cent'. The copy reads:

> Cyclone Yasi and a relentless wet season have cost the Far North more than 5,000 jobs with the unemployment rate skyrocketing to 13 per cent—the nation's highest.
>
> Australian Bureau of Statistics figures released yesterday showed in February there were 19,300 people without jobs in the region, up from 14,100 in January.
>
> The rise in unemployment, the highest since the peak of the economic downturn in September 2009, has been attributed to the impact of Cyclone Yasi, flooding in the southeast and above average rainfall in the far north.

Driving south from Innisfail, there is little sign of cyclone damage, at least not at first. Banana trees are erect and cane fields solid walls of green. I pass a highway billboard: 'Are YOU cyclone ready?' with an aerial photograph of a destroyed house. 'Don't think it won't happen to you.' Just down the road, I pass a house, an old Queenslander, a blue tarpaulin where its roof used to be. I'm surprised its inhabitants haven't dynamited the mocking billboard. I reach Silkwood, and cross a line. The fields and forest begin to look ragged and untidy, somehow askew. Cane fields are swampy and water logged and the road is barely elevated above swollen creeks. Pieces of corrugated iron lie here and there, as if some gigantic child has been playing 52 Pick Up. Further along the skyline to the west, the range of hills has lost its clearly defined edge of green, appearing frayed and scrappy. I'm moving into the cyclone zone.

I reach Tully, and immediately like the look of it. Instead of being spread far and wide along the highway like so many country towns, Tully is tight and compact, nestled up under the towering heights of an imposing mountain range, with a narrow one-way main street flanked by shops, their awnings providing protection from the heavens. It has stopped raining as I pull up, which is something, considering Tully lays claim to be the wettest town in Australia, with an average annual rainfall of 4.5 metres. I park next to the Golden Gumboot, the monument erected to cash in on the town's sodden fame. The concrete boot, more mildew yellow than golden, stands 7.9 metres tall, the amount of rain that fell here in 1950—an Australian record. That makes it a fairly sizeable gumboot, about as high as a two-storey Queenslander. Walking around the boot, past the sign 'THE GOLDEN GUMBOOT—DREAM BECOMES A REALITY', absent-mindedly wondering what the dream might be, I'm surprised to find an open door, which gives the boot instant nursery rhyme appeal. My 8-year-old daughter would love it. Inside, past the sign declaring 'MAXIMUM OF 6 PERSONS IN BOOT AT ANY TIME', I climb a spiral staircase, the walls covered with photographs of Tully's water-logged past: black-and-white shots of bogged cars, sepia renditions of children rowing down the Bruce Highway and Ektachrome prints of washed-out bridges. At the top, as if ascending a medieval tower, I emerge onto the boot's ramparts. Europe may have palaces and castles, forts and chateaux, but Tully has a concrete gumboot guarding the approaches to its main street, with a view to match. To the south, the sugar mill looks no worse for wear, but to the west, the roofs of the town are a patchwork of tarpaulins. Above the rooftops, the trees on the mountainside are stripped of leaves.

Tully lay directly in the path of Yasi. If the cyclone lost any power in the 7 kilometres from the coast, it was negligible. Winds in the town gusted upwards of 300 kilometres per hour. Now, six weeks on, tarpaulins mark out the roofless houses, some for repair, others to be demolished. But I'm not staying in Tully. The rain sweeps in, ending my respite, and I'm back in the hire car. I want to see where the cyclone crossed the coast, where it did its worst. Tully was hit by winds of enormous power, but cyclonic winds are nothing compared to cyclonic waves.

The road to the coast at Tully Heads is in reasonable condition, although at some points it's more like a causeway than a highway. Debris is scattered through the bush, and tarpaulins flag the few houses along the way. The sign outside one remarks: 'THANKS YASI, FOR LANDSCAPING MY GARDEN'.

I reach the turn off where the road divides: straight on for Hull Heads, right for Tully Heads. The Googarra Beach Caravan Park marks the intersection, its sign blown in half, a fibreglass marlin wrenched from its mounting, so its tail rests on the ground and its head obscures what's left of the sign. A chalkboard informs passers-by that the caravan park remains closed until further notice. A little further along I find the Tully Heads Tavern in good repair and open for lunch. A table of electricity linesmen sit outside, eating burgers and chips. Inside, it's quiet and cool. There are no signs of damage.

I order some fish and chips and a beer, and get talking to publican Kim Barnes. He and his wife Jane took over the business just last winter. They were here in the pub the night Yasi hit. Kim knew the building was only seven years old and built to withstand a category 4 cyclone, but it was none the less frightening.

'The worst was the morning of the day it was due to hit. They started talking about all this water. They were talking about a 7-metre surge on top of the high tide. Seven metres. Glad that didn't happen. Thank Christ it didn't.

'We'd decided we wouldn't leave unless the police made us. But when the police came to town, they didn't come to see us, so, I thought, we must be right. I knew they were evacuating everyone down on the coast. We have a room out the back, my office, with block walls, so, we thought, if anything really happened, we'd be safe in there.'

Kim and Jane were lucky. They had a builder staying with them, hired to do some maintenance on the pub. Instead, he helped reinforce outbuildings, bolted down the amenities block and battened down the cold-room motor on the roof of the tavern. They cleared space inside the open-plan pub, parking two four-wheel drives, a ute and a boat on a trailer inside the pub. 'We braced them all up against the roller doors, because we knew if anything was going to go, it was those doors.' The roller doors are storm shutters, pulled down to protect glass windows and doors.

'And what would you have done if the roller doors had gone?' I ask.

'Well, I don't know. Just duck for cover. The plan was if there was any trouble, we'd just go into the cold room or straight through to the office.'

As it was, the office bolthole was not an option. As the storm moved towards its zenith, the pressure on the door was so great that Kim and his companions were unable to push it open. Instead, they saw out the cyclone, with its shrieking winds and terrific noise, inside the pub. The cyclone windows stood up reasonably well, but one ordinary commercial window was bowing inwards alarmingly, threatening to shatter. The steel roller doors braced by the vehicles were holding up well, but another, braced by a heavy slate pool table, was threatening to give way. Kim reckons the table is too heavy for two men to lift, but they watched in horror as it was pushed in across the floor. They pushed it back, bracing it with furniture and anything else they could find.

And then the wind stopped. The eye of the cyclone was upon them.

'Yeah, we went outside and had a look. See what we could see. We'd been told about the eye. That once you're in it, it goes dead still.

And it was. It was just like this, I guess. Or even quieter, because there was no power.'

'But you knew it was coming back?'

'Oh yeah. We could hear it coming back. It was about half past twelve when we went through the eye. It quietened down about 3 a.m. We thought it was on its way out, so we went across to the house, and even at that stage we had trouble getting through the door. We had to wait, because it was coming in surges then, for the surges to drop.'

Kim, Jane and Bert the builder survived the night unscathed. The house suffered some damage. The wind ripped metal awnings off its side, and rainwater was blown up under the iron roof, raining down from the ceiling through an electric fan.

They were still cleaning up when they got their first customer.

'We had one bloke come in here, knocking on the door. I'd never seen him before. He said, "Oh, can I get some smokes?" And I said, "Yeah, you've had a hard night". And he said, "You would not believe what I have been through". He'd actually stayed down at the beach and he ended up in the toilet, with the seawater rushing in, and he had to push his way out the top of the toilet to get out through the roof. He was pretty badly shaken up, and all he wanted was a smoke.'

'Have you seen him again?'

'No, I haven't seen him since. I think he moved on.'

I thank Kim for his story, and head down towards the beach, to see the damage for myself. In the immediate aftermath of Yasi hitting, it was widely reported that the eye of the cyclone hit the popular tourist destination Mission Beach, about five kilometres up the coast, and that was the worst affected community. The eye may also have crossed Mission Beach—it was a big cyclone with a big eye—but there can be no doubt that Tully Heads suffered the worst damage. Cyclones in the Southern Hemisphere revolve in a clockwise direction, so as Yasi hit the coast, communities north of the eye faced terrifying winds coming off the land. South of the eye, the same winds were coming off the ocean, driving a wall of water, a storm surge, before them. If the authorities did nothing else right during the cyclone, without a doubt the decision to make compulsory the evacuation of the beach community at Tully Heads saved lives.

The scene that greets me as I reach the beach, some six weeks after Yasi, is one of devastation on a totally different scale than Tully. In Tully, roofs are missing and walls ripped, signs torn down and trees shredded. Damage done by wind and rain. Here, the damage has been done by seawater. Entire houses have vanished, either destroyed outright or removed later by demolition gangs. House after house along the beachfront simply is no more. At one point, I see nothing more than the foundations, a concrete slab with a few tiles still cemented into place, unnervingly similar to the beachfront scenes I'd witnessed in the aftermath of the Aceh tsunami.

Other houses, mainly made of cinder blocks, remain, or at least their shells do. Some have solid enough looking fronts, but their backs have been blown out by the weight of water. Others are what the locals call 'see-through houses', where the windows and doors front and back have been swept away and all the furniture washed out. I stop outside one cinder-block house, its shattered windows chipboarded up. An elderly man, wearing a blue worker's singlet, his eyes hidden behind aviator sunglasses, is pruning what's left of two ragged rose bushes. I introduce myself and state my purpose, inquiring if I can ask a few questions.

'Not today, mate. I'm just not up to it. Maybe another day, but not today.' The lines on his face are deep, the weariness in his voice profound. He and his wife look as if they're in their late sixties. Retirees. A tough time to be starting again.

The greeting at the next place I call in couldn't be more different. A middle-aged couple walk towards me smiling and holding out hands as I alight from my car. They are only a little less welcoming when they discover my true identity. 'We saw your camera and notebook. We thought you must be the insurance assessor. We've been waiting all day.'

The couple's names are Sibi and Jenny. They live in Innisfail and have been renting their Tully Heads house for eight years. It's sited one block back from the beach, on slightly higher land. If Yasi had hit on the high tide it would have been destroyed, but as it is, it's more than salvageable—broken windows and minor water damage, but the roof stayed on and the tidal surge only reached the top of the verandah. They had six-ply wooden storm shutters that held up reasonably well, although the steel cyclone door protecting the front entrance was ripped off, bolts and all. One side was found in the neighbour's yard, the other half was never seen again. The house next door, a pale green cinder-block box sitting on lower ground, hasn't fared so well. The surge has gutted it: taking all the contents and pushing them out the back and into the swamp that runs behind the settlement.

'You think it looks bad now, you should have seen it before. It's clean now. Pristine,' says Sibi. 'There was a big building there. That's all knocked down, cleaned up. Over there, there was a house once. Some of the houses—up next to the white one—all there was left were the stumps. The houses were washed down into the bush.' Standing on the couple's verandah, there's a clear view through to the waterfront some fifty metres away, a view once blocked by houses and trees and the local post office.

'We're some of the lucky ones, compared to these other poor people', says Jenny.

I ask about the spray paint I've seen on some of the houses spelling out 'no go' in large green letters.

'That means don't come in. The sparky has to go right through and approve it before you can go in. We had a "no go" here as well. It just means you can't move back in until it has been completely checked out,' explains Jenny, saying electricity and asbestos were the main problems. 'They had the army here and they had specialist people who could handle asbestos. They had a police check near the caravan park where you come in and were only letting residents and property owners through. There were a lot of people in protective suits.'

Jenny says they're a bit concerned about insurance. 'We're insured but who knows if they're going to pay up. No one is insured for tidal surge or storm surge. You can be insured for flood, but storm surge is different apparently, so it's just a waiting game. We've done all they wanted, got quotes and what have you, but we've got to wait and see what they pay for.'

I thank Sibi and Jenny and walk across the road towards the beach. The block has been bulldozed clean, except for an in-ground swimming pool fenced off with orange plastic mesh and a keep out sign. A fridge, a shopping trolley and other household detritus lie submerged in its fetid water. Beyond a low seawall, the beach is largely gone. It used to reach out many metres here, with trees and plants and other greenery. Larry took out so many metres, Yasi the rest. Now the beach butts up against the rock seawall.

The wall itself is made of cream-coloured boulders, most of them too large to be lifted manually. But they've been splayed backwards across the sand, metres back from where they were originally placed—testament to the power of the sea. A few coconut palms growing on the land behind what's left of the wall are the only trees still standing. These face the sea with all their fronds blown back behind them, like 1980s rock stars singing into a wind machine.

I find some demolition workers taking a break in the shade of one of the few houses that seems fully restored. They tell me they're from Cairns, and have been working here for five weeks, coming in through the floodwaters about a week after the cyclone hit. 'We put our utes on our low loader. There was a metre of water across the road from way back. We brought people in and ferried some back out. We brought food and stuff in. People were very emotional. To see their whole lives washed out and into the swamp at the back there,' says a talkative bloke with grey hair and a big bushy moustache. 'It brought the community together. They were giving us free lunches, looking after us. There were a lot of donations. Now the neighbours are talking to each other and helping each other.'

I ask them if they're worried about asbestos. 'No, mate, no', laughs my chatty friend. 'What they call ACM is only 3 per cent asbestos. It's no more dangerous than smoking a cigarette. It's when it's broken up that it's dangerous. We wet it down and wrap it in plastic. It's been through parliament so you've got to do what the rule book says.'

'People die from gas, they die from potting mix. It depends on the person. You could have a hundred of us exposed here, and one of us could get it. Know what I'm saying? We're not all going to get cancer.' Then he looks across at the red-headed bloke next to him, who is lighting up a cigarette. 'More likely to get it from passive smoking.'

'Stick it up your bum', says his mate.

The men are in an expansive mood, so I ask them what they think about climate change. Before any of the others can get a word in, the chat-master is already expounding his theories. 'No, I don't believe in that. Nature is nature, you know. Like this carbon thing. We are carbon. Without carbon, we wouldn't be here.'

'Volcanoes put more CFCs into the atmosphere than mankind has done', interjects one of the others before the interlocutor gathers his next thought. 'It's like these trees now', he says. 'Trees rot down naturally and give off gases, right, but they speed the process up by mulching. You've got a V12 machine down there—it drinks 2000 litres of fuel a day—putting out pollution and mulching it more quickly than it would break down naturally. And everyone is saying, "Beauty, we're making mulch", but actually you're making a lot more gas a lot more quickly. It's accelerating the process. Everybody thinks it's a good green thing, you know. But it's not.'

Equipped with this fresh insight into the true causes of global warming, I take another drive around what is left of Tully Heads. I pass one house, its steel front wall seemingly intact, but its windows, roof and most of its back wall gone—a see-through house, eviscerated by the storm surge. On the lawn outside, facing the sea, there's a sign, black paint scrawled on a scrap of white roofing, voicing the owner's defiance: 'IS THAT ALL YOU GOT, BITCH?' At least I hope it's a sign of defiance. Either that, or they're not happy with the $3000 offered by Queensland premier Anna Bligh.

Outside another home, one in seemingly better condition, another sign, this time of determination: 'BIT BY BIT, DAY BY DAY'. This, I learn, is a famous sign, the one that Julia Gillard was photographed standing next to, the one Anna Bligh chose. I learn, because when I stop to take a photograph, I notice some movement in the garage under the house, and soon I am talking with Lesley Porter, the daughter of the owners. The house itself is typical of many thousands of seaside dwellings around the country: the lower storey, consisting of a garage, a laundry and a storeroom, sits on a concrete slab and is made from concrete bricks; the upper story is weatherboard and the roof is corrugated iron. Lesley is working on her laptop in the garage, where it's cooler and the wireless reception is better. She shows me newspaper photographs of the Prime Minister and premier, as well as relief coordinator Major-General Mick Slater, all standing at different times next to the sign. She explains her son Cameron, a soldier, made the sign soon after he made it back into Tully Heads after the cyclone. 'He came up, he just had two days. It was funny, because Mick Slater and Anna were under here. It was pouring rain, so we said come under here. It was still all muddy with a bad fish smell, all through here. Mum and Dad lost everything under here.'

While we chat, Lesley's mother Rita comes downstairs and joins us. Rita describes the scene after the storm surge swept through the lower storey. 'We had a fridge there, a big freezer, a table, a washing machine and a dryer. All that ended up back there in the bush. We had a big camp freezer that Dad made, which he used to take up the bush, that knocked a chunk out of the wall there. The cupboards were full of clothes and some came out, but others were just covered in slop.' Yasi left a layer of sandy mud about ten centimetres deep, even thicker where it had banked up against the far wall.

'What about upstairs?' I ask. 'All right?'

'Not really. The house has to go.'

'You have to demolish it?'

'The top has to go.' Lesley explains that the upper storey has been pushed off the supporting beams and that electricity is being supplied through a series of extension cords strung high off the floor. The family is camping in the shell of their home.

'But can you use the bottom as a kind of foundation?'

'Well, we don't know yet. We're just waiting.'

'Waiting on what? The assessors?'

'We've seen the assessor. Now we're just waiting for his report. I rang up this morning, but they haven't got onto it yet.'

For this family there is something worse. Rita explains the terrible aftermath of Yasi. 'Well, my husband and granddaughter came back the next morning. Les was hoping to start the generator to keep the fridges going. My husband is a fisherman, so the fridges were full of bait, as well as our food,' Rita gives an ironic laugh. 'Of course, when he got here, there was nothing here, no generators, no fridges, no nothing. There was a neighbour's car in here. It had got squished around that corner. Les's Land Cruiser was here, and it was a wipe-out. When he told us everything was gone … well,' Rita gives a little shrug.

'On the way back, because of fallen trees and everything, he got an infection in his leg. He didn't know he had a cut, but it got infected walking through the water. And the next day he wasn't feeling real well. He went to bed, and when I woke him up at 4 p.m.—we were having tea early, because we didn't have any power or any lights—I said, "C'mon, we're going to have tea shortly". Well he was rolling around, and I couldn't get him up, so I called an ambulance and they took him to the hospital in Innisfail. The hospital here wasn't taking patients because they had lost some of their roof.'

'But he's okay now?' I ask

'No. They found out that he has a brain tumour and lung cancer, and he's still got a problem with his leg. Because he had a fall, they did a scan. Then they moved him to Townsville. He was down there for about ten days.'

'We had no power', Lesley interjects, before Rita continues.

She tells me the floorboards upstairs are swelling and warping because the rain comes in under the walls, where they no longer meet the floor.

I ask the women if they intend on staying here, rebuilding. Their reply is instant.

'Yep', says Lesley.

'Yep', says Rita. 'I don't see any point in going. Wouldn't you like to stay here? If you were up on my verandah and you sat up there and looked out over that? And went for a walk everyday on the beach?'

'For the grandchildren, this has always been their base when they were growing up', says Lesley. 'And I know my children; the first thing Cameron said was, "They can't leave". Mum is the matriarch and this has always been their place.'

At the mention of her grandson, Rita asks if I have seen their sign. I tell her yes, that it's the reason I stopped in the first place. Lesley explains that the sign has become something of a totem for the family. 'If you didn't have that attitude—bit by bit, day by day—then I don't think you could get through very well. A lot of people are still very, very angry; it's a reaction to the stress. But if you just go, "Look, there's nothing I can do about that today, I'll leave it until tomorrow", you can get through.'

Rita adds: 'We had a good day today. We got the robes back, the washing got dry.'

We walk out of the shade into the early afternoon glare of a perfect day. The clouds have gone, and for a moment I can see what Rita means, what a beautiful place it is, far from the madding crowd, with the blond sand stretching into the blue sea and the islands floating out in the bay. The two women pose next to their sign and I take their photograph.

Before I leave, I ask them about climate change, whether they are believers.

'No', says Rita. 'I'm not in favour of all that rubbish. You only have to look at the world and read books. You had the ice age, you had this age and you had that age. It's all part of the natural progression, or whatever you want to call it. It's mother nature.'

'Climate change is not the truth', says Lesley. 'It's just a load of rubbish. Now they're going to tax us again. And you know what? In 1918, a hundred years ago, they had exactly the same kind of extreme weather here.'

⌣⌐

I drive back towards Tully, past the pub and the caravan park with its fallen Marlin. I think of Les, the old fisherman, lying upstairs dying, helpless at a time when his family needs all the help it can get. I think of my father, his last days in the hospice, surrounded by family, all of us helpless in the face of his disease. Even as the cancer took hold, Dad had managed to sell the family house of fifty years and move himself and Mum into a retirement village between stints in hospital. The stress of the time returns—the empty hopes and unanswered prayers, the inevitability. I told Rita and Lesley how sorry I was to learn of Les's illness, but found myself unable to extend any real comfort, to offer any insights they didn't already have. You can't get much better than 'BIT BY BIT, DAY BY DAY'.

I know why Rita and the rest of her family want to stay. It's not just the perfect scenery and the glowing sea, the fishing and the location; they own this spot, it is part of them. I remember the bumper sticker on the back of Les's car: 'you can kiss my Yasi. Queenslanders won't be beaten.'

I admire their defiance, but wonder about their denial, the refusal to believe that climate change could contribute to storms like Yasi, or other threats. Two years ago when I travelled through the drought-stricken Murray-Darling Basin it was the same story. Inevitably, it was those worst affected by drought that found it most difficult to accept that climate change may be real. Faced with the threat of losing everything—homes, livelihoods, farms, inheritances—how much easier to move into denial. Perhaps it is the feeling of helplessness, that events are moving on a global scale, well and truly beyond the control of individuals. It's an affront to Australian individualism, our belief that we can look out for ourselves and ours. And, of course, those farmers who categorically refused to believe the severity of the drought was connected to climate change would now point to the rain flooding their properties as vindication. Maybe, just maybe, time will prove them right, but to dismiss anthropogenic climate change outright, when the weight of scientific opinion supports it, suggests a psychological response, not a rational one.

For me, the science suggesting there will be more frequent and more intense cyclones makes sense. Tropical cyclones don't form unless the sea-surface temperature is at 26.5 degrees or above. That means they don't form in winter, and that, even in summer, they don't form too far north or south of the equator. So the Australian cyclone season extends roughly from November through to the beginning of April, and cyclones on the eastern seaboard come ashore in Queensland, not further south. The distinctive spiral shape of cyclones is bestowed by the rotation of the earth, with the spirals moving clockwise in the Southern Hemisphere and counter-clockwise in the Northern. Cyclones rarely, if ever, form immediately above the equator, because the movement of air that kick starts their spirals is not present.

There are other factors involved. The more moisture in the atmosphere, the more likely cyclone formation becomes. And, of course, the warmer the air, the higher the rate of evaporation, and the more water vapour becomes airborne. Although sea–surface temperature is critical, the colder the air high up in the atmosphere, the more powerful the suction of the cyclone vortex becomes, like an almighty chimney. As there is less greenhouse gas at altitude, this temperature differential is also likely to increase.

Sea-surface temperatures in the western Pacific are warmer in La Niña years than in El Niño years, and warmer water increases the likelihood of cyclones. The CSIRO states: 'There are about twice as many cyclones off the east coast of Australia in La Niña years compared with El Niño years'. The research organisation also says that sea-surface temperatures off the coast have been at or near record highs in recent years. The fear must be that as sea-surface temperatures increase, the relatively cooler seas of El Niño will exhibit the temperatures and exude the energy of La Niña years, while the warmer seas of La Niña years will reach unprecedented temperatures and fuel cyclones with unprecedented energy.

I think of the destruction I have seen at Tully Heads and wonder if it's inevitable that we will see similar devastation in coming years. You can't help but admire the defiance behind a sign that challenges nature: 'IS THAT ALL YOU'VE GOT, BITCH?' Unfortunately, the answer may well be: 'No, not by a long shot'.

⌒

The three Black Hawk helicopters circle the cyclone-shredded ridges above Cardwell before swooping in low to land at the town's showground. Built with menace in mind, their jungle camouflage black against the sky, there is little menacing about them today. They carry a precious cargo, His Royal Majesty Prince William of Wales, second in line to the British throne, destined to become monarch of Australia. Young Will, Charles and Di's boy. The people of Cardwell and surrounds, perhaps one thousand of them, have turned out in supplication. They line the roped-off pathway leading from the landing site to the showground hall like some latter-day cargo cult, come to welcome their thin, white god. But they don't wait for material largesse; instead they hope the stardust of celebrity may prove a turning point, that their awful run of luck may finally be coming to an end. Tully Heads may have borne the brunt of Yasi, but Cardwell, a more substantial town on the Bruce Highway where it runs directly along the beach, has possibly had a worse time of it. Thirty-five kilometres south of Tully Heads, it too faced the tidal surge generated by Yasi. One of the first and most dramatic images of the cyclone's aftermath was of the leisure boats and yachts piled one against the other in Cardwell's Port Hinchinbrook. But the real heartbreaker has been the incessant rain in the six weeks since. No sooner have houses and businesses been scrubbed clean, no sooner has new carpet been laid, than more rain sweeps in from the Coral Sea, the flatlands flood and the buildings inundated again. Small disasters, not enough to make the news bulletins of southern capitals, but devastating for those affected. Today is different. The day has dawned hot and clear, with only the occasional white cloud puff high in the sky to emphasise the fineness of the day. Scrubbed clean by an overnight shower, the town has put on its best face for its royal visitor. Perhaps the prince's totemic magic is already at work.

He emerges from the chopper looking fit and purposeful, not waiting for the rotors to stop, striding towards the waiting crowds, smiling broadly. He's inherited his mother's good looks, but also his father's balding pate. With his helmet off, he rubs at his head, spreading some last-minute unction, protection against the tropical sun. In his wake comes an entourage of minders, security men, publicity flaks and hangers-on, leaping onto their mobile phones the moment they've cleared the choppers. Premier Anna Bligh is here, wearing a broad-brimmed Akubra, choosing protection over visibility. Wardrobe has dressed William perfectly for the set: sensible shoes, beige chinos, a pale-blue shirt, sleeves rolled up and top two buttons undone in a nod to both informality and fashion. His three security men, of similar age, wear the same uniform, but sport dark glasses, serious expressions and prominent white earpieces. One passes by, whispering something into his sleeve. The prince's own earpiece is far less obvious, flesh-coloured and unobtrusive. Who, I wonder, is on the other end? Who is the Prince Whisperer? Is it for emergencies only—'Gun at three o'clock! Go left, go fast!'—or do they impart more mundane information—'The lamingtons are spiffing, but steer clear of the pikelets'?

The prince approaches, and the crowd strains at the rope, hands outstretched for the blessing of a royal handshake, a word from on high. He works the crowd expertly, shaking hands, making eye contact, issuing quick-fire hellos, nice to meet yous and thanks so much for comings, then stopping for a longer exchange, listening in earnest to a story of hardship or personal struggle, before offering a reassuring word, a hand on a shoulder and the radiant smile of benediction. He is the eye of this new cyclone, calm and unruffled, while excitement spirals around him. He moves closer to where I'm loitering, and the winds of anticipation pick up speed and intensity. He moves quickly along a gaggle of teenage girls, smiling and shaking each hand, then engages two older women in conversation. Up close, the rosy English cheeks are turning a deeper shade of red, the designer shirt is beginning to cling and the sweat is dripping on the royal brow. The temperature is in the low thirties, but the air is humid and the weight of the noonday sun is tangible. 'Yes', says the prince to the two women, 'It's a bit much for a pasty face like me'. And then he's gone, into the shade of the showground hall, to meet carefully vetted locals and select members of the emergency services.

Outside, the buzzing crowd moves from the front of the hall to its side, where tents and marquees have been set up, providing shade, bottles of iced water and places to sit. Volunteers are staffing a huge barbecue, providing not loaves and fishes to the masses but sausage sangers, with or without onions, with or without the sacrament of Heinz Big Red tomato sauce. Any minute, the prince is expected to leave the confines of the hall, to move once again among the common people and to partake of the sanger with them. And what could be more appropriate? The sausage sandwich lies at the very heart of the Australian community. Forget Vegemite and Aeroplane jelly and Violet Crumble bars and all the other commercial pretenders; it is the sausage sandwich that has assumed the throne of national food. Outside every hardware store, at the centre of every school fete, in the aftermath of every disaster, the sausage barbecue brings the community together, raising money for sports teams, community groups and victims. There is comfort in its soft, white bread and generosity in the hearts of the volunteers. For days, the media have been reporting that the prince himself will share the sausage sacrament with his people. Over under the tent, I watch the media pack, the television crews, photographers and microphones, elbowing for position, settling themselves for the day's money shot: the prince, sausage in hand, at one with his people. I admire the nonchalant expertise of one cameraman, his camera balanced on his shoulder by one hand, while the other hand stuffs—one, two, three—sausage sandwiches down his throat. Very wise, I think. Who knows when he might eat again? Especially for free. I think for a moment of joining my erstwhile colleagues, to enjoy the circus atmosphere.

I was put on standby, as a cadet journalist back in the 1980s, to cover an official visit by William's parents to Australia. He'd come as a babe in arms a few years earlier, but on this occasion he remained in England and the attention was on his oh-so-glamorous mother, Princess Di. I was assigned as backup, in case something untoward happened to one of the more senior correspondents. As it was, all went to plan and my services weren't required. However, I recall there was a strict order given as part of the briefing: there were to be no photographs taken, or television images broadcast, of the royal personages eating. It would, after all, inevitably be an unflattering image: gob open, fillings exposed, saliva shining in the camera flashes. Eyes intense, food hovering. But now here is this modern prince, willing to risk the manicured image and share the mighty sausage with his people.

I resist the temptation to join the fray. Instead, I park myself under the shade of an awning erected by the Cardwell and District Community Bank. I stand behind a group of elderly women, two in wheelchairs, another sitting next to her walking frame. The prince may eat his sausage, but how could he resist these feeble women who have braved the midday sun to be here? I bide my time, confident in my strategy. But there is something wrong. The camera crews and photographers have abandoned the sausage sizzle and moved back towards the front door of the hall. I walk across to the building and peer through a window smudged by the faces of those who have already done the same. Inside the hall, the prince is still circling, still smiling and attentive. A cop inside the hall comes up to the window, opens it and talks to his young son, who is standing next to me. 'Sorry, mate. Change of plans. He's not coming out this way.'

I look back at my old ladies, still waiting expectantly, and then head round to the front where the crowds are re-forming around the retaining ropes. Right on schedule, the prince emerges, not rushing, shaking hands and joking with his worshippers. 'Not you', he grins as he chides a teenage girl, 'I've already shaken your hand. You can't fool me.' She glows with pleasure. No second handshake, but the prince remembered her! A story to wear thin in the schoolyard and at the dinner table. The crowd is in high spirits; people laugh and smile, hold their phones and cameras aloft, trying to capture a memento of the great day. I can't help smiling myself. This guy is a class act; none of the awkward cuff-tugging of his father and all of the crowd-pleasing charisma of his mother. I turn from the back of the crowd, intending to move to a new vantage point a little closer to the Black Hawks, and I see one of my old ladies a little further down the slope, a helper valiantly pushing her wheelchair, struggling to keep it upright on the uneven and boggy grass. It threatens to topple and I rush to help. 'Is he there? Can you see him?' she asks, oblivious to the precarious balance of the chair. He is indeed, but with the thrusting crowd in between, there is no way she is going to see him, nor he her. The rotors roar, the engines throttle up, and he has ascended once again.

With the royal personage gone, the crowd begins to dissolve away towards the parked cars, the blessed regaling the disappointed, holding out hands that mere minutes before were touched by royalty. Rather than get caught in perhaps the only traffic jam Cardwell has ever known, I leave my car and walk the three blocks back to the beach—to where the beach used to be. There are no dunes, no trees, and the sand drops away sharply from the bitumen roadway. A little further along, there is a sign above a gateway: 'Cardwell Lions Park', but there is no park. Cyclone Yasi has eaten most of it, taking a massive chunk of it out to sea. Bulldozers are doing their best to make good what's left, clearing away fallen trees and storm debris.

Back across the highway, a man is working in the doorway of a store. His name is Bert, and it's his place, a large warehouse with a shopfront of plate-glass windows, newly replaced after Yasi shattered their predecessors. Bert is decorating the new panes with an edging of plastic tape. He's a gregarious type, happy to chat while he goes about his work. He must be about fifty, but he has the ruffled bleached hair of a surfy youth and a relaxed manner. But times are tough; he tells me he's been stiffed by the insurance company.

'They mixed it up, confused the mailing address of my house in Brisbane with the street address of this place. So when I claimed, they said no, that I'd insured my place in Brisbane. Why would I do that? Why would I insure my house twice and not insure this place at all?'

Bert's shop isn't nearly as badly damaged as some, and he gives me a tour to demonstrate why. The floor is solid cement, the walls held up by huge steel piers, the roof made from thick hardwood beams. 'It was built for cyclones; it stood up well.'

Bert is setting up a furniture emporium, and he's confident he'll make a go of it. He says there's a lot of passing traffic, especially in the winter tourist season. I admire his optimism. He tells me he was overseas on a buying trip, Bali and California, and was in Los Angeles when Yasi struck. He was back within a day, but already someone had knocked off his generator. Then he got a dose of Ross River fever, the mosquito-borne disease that's having a bumper this year. 'It's not good mate. I've had it before. It sits you on your ear.' But he reckons he's bouncing back, and is now rushing to get his shop ready for the containers of furniture arriving from overseas. He says that despite the insurance bungle, the illness and the larceny, he's in a lot better shape than others. At least he hasn't had the experience of fixing his place up only to have it flooded out again, like the hardware shop and other local businesses.

He certainly has a good location, right across the road from what's left of the beach. I ask if he's worried about climate change, whether he feels vulnerable in this perfect location. 'Too right I am. Very worried. Especially sitting here.' This is something of a first. The Islanders of Yam were worried about climate change, so too the scientists of Heron Island, but here on the coast south of Cairns, Bert is the first person I've met who has expressed a view that in any way coincides with scientific opinion. At least it does until he confides in me the true cause of climate change.

'Tell me', he asks, 'what keeps your car cool, stops it from overheating?'

'The water in the radiator, I guess.'

'Yeah, yeah. Water. But before that, it's the oil. The oil lubricates the engine, stops the friction and keeps it cool. Right?'

'Right', I say, clueless to where this is heading.

'Right, but what have we been doing for the last hundred years? Pumping all the oil out of the earth. We've been taking the earth's lubrication out. So it's starting to rub together, heat up with the friction. That's global warming. And when it heats up enough, when it overheats, then you get an earthquake, like in Japan. That's what a tsunami is. The earth cracks under the heat, like a head gasket, and the seawater pours in to cool it down.'

⌣⟶

The traffic jam has melted away, and I drive back north, back towards the epicentre of Yasi's damage. I get to Tully, the next stop on the royal disaster tour, just as the Black Hawks take off. Yesterday Prince William visited earthquake-stricken New Zealand, today it's cyclone-shaken Queensland. He's is getting married in a month; maybe this is some sort of preparation. I hope he got to see the Golden Gumboot—something to tell Kate about when he gets back to London. On the radio, the ABC is accusing him of snubbing locals at the Cardwell sausage sizzle. As the black shapes reverberate over the roof of my car, following the Bruce Highway north towards Cairns, I think of the prince's official title: His Royal Highness Prince William of Wales, KG, FRS, according to Wikipedia. I wonder why those two groups of letters are chosen to follow his name. His military rank, Flight Lieutenant, doesn't get a mention, nor do any of the twenty or so other groups and societies of which he is patron, like the Football Association or Mountain Rescue or the Honourable Society of the Middle Temple. KG stands for Knight Companion of the Order of the Garter, which would have pleased his fashion-plate mother. And FRS stands for Fellow of the Royal Society, one of the world's pre-eminent scientific academies. It was one of the world's first, the oldest still in existence, founded around 1660, growing out of a kind of secret society known as the Invisible College. It won the support of Charles II, who formalised its existence under royal charter in 1663, explicitly naming himself as the founder. Charles also established the Royal Observatory and was the patron of architect Christopher Wren. This was important stuff, coming in the immediate aftermath of Oliver Cromwell's Christian puritanism. Charles is best remembered as something of a pants man, fathering at least twelve illegitimate children by a bevy of seven or more mistresses. Yet by founding the Royal Society, and thereby endorsing the emerging scientific method of theory informed by experimentation, he legitimised the place of science and rationalism at the centre of British modernisation and helped them to gain gradual ascendancy not just over superstition and common quackery but also over the institutionalised power of the church. So, 200 years later, when Charles Darwin published *On the Origin of Species*, he didn't share the persecution of Galileo or Copernicus. Nineteenth-century Britain was mature and rational enough to debate and ultimately accept Darwin's contentious theory of evolution.

Today, the Royal Society remains a pillar of rational, secular civilisation. Nevertheless, it couldn't be a royal society without a royal or two, so Prince William, his father Prince Charles, his grandfather, that well-known polymath Prince Phillip, and his aunt Princess Anne are royal fellows of the Royal Society. My question is whether, by attaching the letters of his fellowship so prominently to his name, the young heir is obliged in any way to accept the conclusions of science. Perhaps he's like his grandmother, the Queen, handing out royal warrants to all those manufacturers of marmalade, chutney and gin. They may have By Appointment on their labels, but that doesn't mean the Queen is obliged to consume them for breakfast. Is it the same with the Royal Society? Is there any obligation on the young prince to accept the scientific method and its conclusions?

And so I daydream as I drive northwards along the Bruce Highway. How marvellous might it be if Prince William were to say a word or two in support of science in return for the privilege of attaching those precious letters FRS to the back of his name. Throughout Britain and the remnants of empire, in the world of science and beyond, those three letters represent the acknowledgement of a career of groundbreaking research, discovery and contribution. Scores of Australians have worn those three letters with distinction over the years: Macfarlane Burnet, Howard Florey, John Eccles, Mark Oliphant and Douglas Mawson, to name a few. And the Royal Society itself is in no doubt about the seriousness of climate change. In December 2009, as world leaders prepared to meet in Copenhagen, the society issued a statement: 'It is certain that greenhouse gas emissions from the burning of fossil fuels and from land use change lead to a warming of climate', it said. 'As the temperature rises further, so will the risk of more widespread and dangerous climate impacts; from sea level rise, from increasing frequency and intensity of climate extremes such as heat waves, floods and droughts … There is no such thing as safe climate change.'

Charles II had no legitimate children; he was kept busy with his mistresses. So, as yet, none of his descendants have assumed the British throne, but Prince William is directly descended from Charles II through his mother's family. And here he is, the young scion, flying through the very lands of ignorance. He would be doing the planet a favour, and his future subjects, and, who knows, perhaps even the credibility and relevance of the monarchy, were he to reiterate the beliefs of his fellow society members and pay some lip-service to the science, rather than merely comforting the affected. I wonder whether it ever crosses his mind, when the earpiece is out and the prince whisperers are silent.

⤙⤚

Truss Biddlecombe-Sanders and her husband Patrick travelled the world before finding their own personal piece of paradise in Far North Queensland. I meet Truss in a cyclone recovery centre in Mission Beach, where she is working as a Red Cross volunteer. She is an engaging, dynamic woman in her fifties, a good talker. She says she isn't authorised to speak on behalf of the Red Cross, that she has gotten into trouble before for doing that, but that doesn't stop her talking of her own experiences—of riding out the storm at a friend's place right here in Mission Beach. She tells me how beautiful the beach was before the storm, how of an evening she and Patrick would take some chairs from their beachfront property and walk down onto the sand with a bottle of wine or two. There they would watch the waves, perhaps spotting a whale or a pod of dolphins or a passing crocodile, and chat with passers-by, inviting them to have a glass of wine. I say it sounds wonderful and as quickly as that, she invites me to dinner. It seems promising; Patrick has worked as a chef around the world.

It's a beautiful house, with the upper of two storeys open-plan, a light, airy space below a raked ceiling of stained wood, with windows and a balcony looking out through palm trees to the ocean. Mementos of a lifetime of travel are dotted tastefully around the room. It's a piece of paradise all right, and the couple are making the most of it. That's why, when I arrive, bottle in hand, we immediately head towards the beach. Twilight is coming, and there is the promise of a full moon rising out of the ocean. But we can't get down onto the beach. The storm surge, supposedly weaker here than further south, has been powerful enough to carve a steep gouge out of the dunes, a metre or two high, undercutting palm trees that now lie in a tangled mass between the end of the yard and the sand of the beach. There is no obvious way to surmount the tangle and the sharp drop to the sand, so we prop our chairs up on a slight rise, close to the beach but not on it. A neighbour joins us, bringing some nuts with him. The space on our little clearing is tight, and one leg of Patrick's chair slowly gives way, sinking into the sand, sending him backwards into a slow-motion somersault. Undeterred, he picks himself up, and I pour him another drink. A couple pass, walking along the beach, and we wave to them and they to us. There's a brief, shouted exchange, but they can't join us and we can't join them.

They are an interesting couple, Truss and Patrick. She's Dutch, he's English. They've been everywhere. They lived for a year in the Sudan, in Khartoum, where they worked in a big international hotel. They've seen a lot, and know that life isn't always kind. So, as we sit by the despoiled beach, above the tangle of palm trees, I ask them what they think of climate change. 'Oh, it's real', says Patrick, 'but we'll be okay here. We got through Yasi. What could be worse than that?' The moon rises from behind a bank of clouds, floodlighting the rippling sea. Paradise indeed.

Mission Beach, I am told, is the next big thing, the next Port Douglas, the next Noosa, the next haven for ageing southerners feeling the cold. I can't quite see it myself. The beach is beautiful enough, but the settlement is too stretched out; there is no natural centre like the marina at Port Douglas or Noosa's Hastings Street. But plenty of people think otherwise, and a steady stream of tourists venture north each winter, flying to Cairns and travelling another two hours down the Bruce Highway. There are a couple of low-key resorts, some impressive beachfront homes and a spanking new Woolworths airlifted in from suburbia. There are plans afoot to construct a marina here as well, in the shallows of Boat Bay in the lee of Clump Point, and then surround the marina with apartments. I drive round for a look. There's already a boat ramp here, and there was a pontoon wharf where locals and visiting yachties could tie up. Its remnants lie scattered about: one piece up on the side of the boat ramp, another washed up on the shore, another still tenuously attached to a pylon. More evidence of Yasi's power.

Not everyone is besotted with the developer's vision. A cyclone-battered sign up on the low point identifies this as hallowed ground for the local Djiru people. 'Clump Point is an important part of our tribal country that includes story places, hunting and fishing grounds, waterholes, ceremonial, camp and burial sites. These sites remain today as reminders of the long-term occupation of the area by our people.' Sounds like the developers might have a fight on their hands.

Other opponents, like Adrian Walker, are concerned with the seagrass fields. I find the local naturalist living in a house set in the rainforest on the lower slopes of Clump Mountain, about one kilometre from the beach. A long deck connects three structures, with holes cut in the decking and roofs to allow trees to continue growing. Dragonflies hover over the deck, and golden orb spiders, the size of my hand, hang from huge webs. It's a beautiful spot, even with the trees stripped of their foliage. The house escaped Yasi largely unscathed, except where a large tree snapped off halfway up its trunk and landed on the bathroom roof.

Adrian has a calm, jovial manner, with the look and demeanour of an ageing hippy. His long hair and profuse beard have moved through grey to a snow white, tinted yellow here and there by nicotine. He's the local snake man, called upon to remove and relocate between 130 and 150 of the reptiles a year from local houses, businesses and chicken coops. They include the deadly rough scales and taipans, but most are non-venomous. The biggest are the pythons; Adrian tells me the largest he's caught was 5.8 metres long. 'It weighed 35 kilos and had two chooks inside it', he says. 'I did one last Monday that had a cat inside it. It wasn't too hard to trace whose cat it was. We just asked around in town if anybody hadn't seen their cat for a couple of days. Pythons around here love cats. The local cat population is quite dramatically reduced by pythons,' Adrian enthuses. As a bird lover, he's on the side of the pythons.

He says some locals are concerned that developers may use Yasi and the destruction of the pontoon to resurrect plans for a marina. 'The previous plan was outrageous frankly, and it got no support from anywhere. Various government departments flattened it pretty quickly,' he says. 'It entailed dredging the entire bay to build an artificial island out there and put housing on it, as well as a marina. If you dredged the bay you would lose all the seagrass pretty quickly. Boat Bay is not a natural harbour; it's an important dugong habitat and there is some very extensive seagrass out there.'

Adrian says some upgrading of facilities is fine, but large-scale real estate developments are fanciful. 'The town has hundreds and hundreds of unsold blocks of land, very little is selling here. Since Larry the real estate market has been in the doldrums right through Mission Beach.'

Cyclones, it seems, aren't good for business. Real estate developers find finance more elusive, insurance more expensive and investors more tentative. But that doesn't mean cyclones are good for the environment. Here on the Cassowary Coast, the cassowaries are dying. Everywhere you drive, there are prominent yellow signs depicting a car coming off second best in a crash with a giant black bird; 'SPEEDING HAS KILLED CASSOWARIES', read the signs. There are other temporary signs attached to trees and roadside poles depicting the birds in silhouette, 'TAKE CARE. RECENT SIGHTING.' But in the three or four days I've been driving around the Cassowary Coast, I haven't caught so much as a glimpse of the famous birds.

Yasi has had a devastating and ongoing impact on the cassowaries. Many survived the storm itself, but with the fruit stripped from the forest, they're in danger of starving to death. Adrian reckons the Mission Beach area boasted 180 cassowaries before the cyclone. He says the parks service has decided to let that fall to a breeding population of about forty, letting younger birds die while setting up feeding stations for adults. Adrian thinks that some birds, in desperation, have been raiding local banana plantations and that some of the more ruthless operators, themselves struggling to recover from Yasi, have started baiting the protected animals with arsenic. Some locals, unhappy with the parks service plans, have started setting up private feeding stations. The new Woolworths, still struggling to win the hearts and minds of anti-development locals, is donating leftover fruit.

I farewell Adrian and return to the beach by Boat Bay. I can't go any further north; the road still hasn't been repaired from cyclone-induced land slips. So I park the car by the jetty. All that remains of a boatshed is a concrete slab surrounded by mangled tree stumps. The jetty itself is supposedly closed, orange plastic meshing blocking passage, but it looks in reasonable condition. I can see movement at the far end, so I climb over the meshing and walk out. It's longer than a footy field, and just wide enough to fit a car, its hardwood planks showing long-term weathering more than any dramatic cyclone damage. Out at the end I find two boys fishing, bikes cast casually aside. One has a hand line, the other is casting a small net. The tide is out, and the water is two or three metres below.

'What are you after?' I ask the boy casting the net.

'Just bait', he says. Later they will fish for barramundi.

From the end of the jetty, I look back at Mission Beach, the next big thing, the distance blurring the cyclone damage. The setting is striking: white sand, palm trees and the rainforest-clad mountains rising to form the perfect backdrop. Clump Mountain is bathed in sunlight, but close behind lurks the dark-grey promise of rain. Lightning arcs across the billowing greyness and the wet season prepares to honour its afternoon commitments.

⌒

Back from the coast, along a narrow, winding road that was once the Bruce Highway, through the sugarcane fields and remnant rainforest, through a village where the rails for the cane trains run down the main street like tram tracks in Melbourne, I reach the small town of Mena Creek. It's no accident. I've come here looking for a monument to Australian eccentricity called Paronella Park. I stop next to the town park, and there it is, across a suspension footbridge stretching above the waterfall. The falls are in full bellow, fed by this wettest of wet seasons, pouring off the granite edge, thundering brown and foaming down into a deep, wide pool. And there on the cliff top on the opposite bank, lichen-camouflaged and forest-bound, José Paronella's castle, with turrets and balustrades, balconies and staircases.

Paronella was a Spanish migrant who arrived in Innisfail in 1913 and found work as a canecutter, but driven by a ferocious work ethic and a quixotic vision, he amassed a fortune restoring derelict cane farms and onselling them for profit. From 1929 until his death in 1948, he combined the migrant's love of concrete and country to build his castle and much more amid the virgin rainforest beside the thundering waterfall. It was a theme park, a magical place, where people could come to shelter beneath the canopy, to swim in the pool beneath the falls and to imagine themselves somewhere entirely more magical than the cane fields of Far North Queensland. Paronella did much of the construction himself, assisted by two Aboriginal employees, shaping the concrete structures by hand, leaving his fingerprints behind and bestowing them with flowing, organic eccentricities. He installed a hydro-electric turbine in 1933, years before electricity came to the rest of the district, so when Paronella Park opened to the public in 1935 it glowed and shone in the night, with a cinema and tearooms, balconies and turrets, and a ballroom where dancers could swirl in the speckled magic of a giant mirror ball.

I make my way to the entrance, pay my money and take the tour. The guide shows us the shell of the castle, destroyed by fire, and explains that what remains is slowly crumbling away. Paronella, with homespun ingenuity, reinforced his concrete structure with old rail tracks scavenged from the cane farms he bought and sold. But this is the tropics, the rainforest, and the steel has corroded and bent, warped and expanded, softening the concrete till it falls away. The guide takes us down the three-storey-high grand staircase to the picnic tables by the water's edge. On some other day it would be a tranquil spot, the water inviting, but the level is up, and the concrete balustrades and picnic tables are half-submerged. Away from the water we come to an elegant two-storey pavilion, with turrets and the ubiquitous balustrades, the concrete turned green by moss, so that the pavilion, with its idiosyncratic style and exterior staircases, could be a Mayan relic. There's a long pond set before the pavilion, coated with lily pads and crimson lotus flowers, encircled by yet more balustrades. Dragonflies hover erratically above the surface. The guide turns a hidden handle and fountains spring, water arcing and catching the sunlight. There are other marvels: a tunnel José carved by hand through a hillside leading to more waterfalls, and a long glen of Kauri trees towering skywards, some of more than seven thousand trees the family planted on their estate. The guide winds up the tour and I'm left to wander the follies by myself.

At the Paronellas' own cottage, built of durable stone, not spun from concrete, rail lines and dreams, there's a small museum. Sepia photos reveal José as a young man, dark and intense, and later with grey hair playing a flamenco guitar. A poor man's Picasso, an untrained Gaudi. It's not how I imagined him. I had pictured him as Klaus Kinski in Werner Herzog's *Fitzcarraldo*, blond-haired and crazy, obsessively taking on the jungle.

At its height, Paronella Park must have been truly something, hosting weddings and balls, cinema nights and tennis matches, swimming parties and picnic days. But then came floods and fires, cyclones and storms. The Bruce Highway was rerouted down along the coast—a straighter, less-eccentric road—and the park fell into disrepair. By 1993 it was all but abandoned, decaying back into the rainforest, when a wealthy couple came upon it. They've spent a fortune preserving what they can, investing their hopes and money in a second-hand dream. But the cyclones and floods keep coming and, day by day, José Paronella's concrete crumbles away. The tennis courts have become lawns, the changing cubicles are disused shells, doors missing, and the suspension bridge is closed for repairs. Paronella Park is returning to the jungle, like some lost South American civilisation.

The Cairns waterfront is a happy place today. The sun is out for once, and tourists and locals alike are promenading along the esplanade. The boardwalk sits above the seawall, the mud flats stretching off towards the open ocean. I look out to sea, enjoying the view. Cairns sits low to the water, as low as any Australian city. Protected by the Great Barrier Reef from the swell of the Pacific, the CBD has been built on the flatlands, the only elevation found in the upper storeys of the high-rise hotels and office buildings. The council has built a large and inviting swimming pool right here on the waterfront, an open invitation to all comers. There are no fences, no entry fees, just an expanse of watery relief. It is well patronised, full of locals and backpackers. A lifeguard tells me it's supposedly closed at night, monitored by closed-circuit television and roving security guards, but that he himself used to go skinny dipping in the early hours when he had a skin full and the spirits were up. Nowadays, he arrives at work to discover revellers sleeping it off under the trees, still nursing empties. I like the pool, the symbolism of it. Big, open and free to all comers. It expresses an optimism and an emphasis on the enjoyment it can provide, rather than the problems it might cause.

I turn 180 degrees and consider the mudflats and the still water of the sea, lying calmly at low tide only a metre, at most, below the level of parkland. The authorities evacuated 30 000 people from low-lying parts of Cairns when they thought Yasi might hit the city. I can see why. There would be few places in Australia more vulnerable to cyclonic attack than Cairns. If Yasi had hit here, the flooding would have been massive and destructive. Someday, of course, a cyclone will hit Cairns. And imagine that the force of the cyclone, powered by hotter temperatures and warmer seas, is more powerful than Yasi, more powerful than Mahina, more powerful than any cyclone yet experienced. Now imagine if the Great Barrier Reef, that massive wall of coral that prevents the Pacific swell from striking the Far North Queensland coast, has succumbed to acidification and bleaching, and has collapsed into the depths, leaving Cairns totally exposed. Thoroughly, comprehensibly, catastrophically exposed.

4

THE GOLD COAST

Looking north along the wide straight beach towards Surfers Paradise.

I arrive at the Gold Coast in the middle of schoolies week. Teenagers are staggering zombie-like around Cavill Mall or are flopped comatose on the beach, as if hit by plague. And they're the active ones. An hour past noon, many of their confreres are still in bed. Graduating high school students from all over Queensland have massed at Surfers Paradise for a week-long orgy of alcohol, junk food and sleep deprivation, leavened by hopes of romance and ambitions of sex. Schoolies is into its third or fourth day, and the standard bearers of Queensland's future are looking the worse for wear. There is little talk, few smiles, barely a mobile phone in sight. No one is texting, a sure sign that serious fatigue has set in.

'Breakfast', nods a shaggy-haired youth, holding a dripping hamburger with one hand.

I ask him how schoolies is going.

'Terrific. I eat Maccas every meal.'

The November day is unseasonably cool, the high-rise towers cloaked in mist and low cloud. This is my first journey to the coast this spring. I'm yet to visit the Torres Strait or Heron Island; Cyclone Yasi is yet to plough its destructive furrow from Tully Heads to Mount Isa. It's been hard to get away, difficult to plan my coastal excursions. My father is ill and I'm worried. My parents came over for dinner the night before I left, helping to celebrate our daughter's eighth birthday. I cooked duck, one of the old boy's favourites. He put away the duck and a couple of glasses of wine, but he couldn't face his vegies, couldn't bear the taste of them. No doubt the chemotherapy is working its magic; the scans show him free of cancer.

Night time, and after finding my accommodation at Broad-beach, a few kilometres south and a few generations north, I return to Cavill Mall, the centre of Surfers Paradise and the epicentre of schoolies. I leave my car, walking into the party zone. The schoolies have thrown off their afternoon lethargy and are moving in waves through the cool evening air, voices rising and falling with excitement and expectation. The closer I get, the more youngsters are on the street, descending from their high-rise eyries, moving moth-like in the one direction, towards Cavill Mall, attracted by the prospect of partying and diving headlong into the hormonal soup. I feel like I'm in an episode of *Doctor Who*.

I pass two guys, obviously pissed, sitting on the pavement, their backs against a low wall.

'Hey mate, give us a cigarette?' slurs one.

'Sorry. Don't smoke.'

'Well, how 'bout you fuck off then.'

A security guard has witnessed the exchange. He smiles apologetically, shrugging his shoulders. We immediately have something in common: of the hundred or more people on this block, we're the only two older than twenty. He tells me he's hired just for schoolies, to keep an eye on the apartments, all of them booked by schoolkids.

'I'm here till 6 a.m. Been here the last few nights. No real problems. Always something to see, to have a laugh at,' he says. He has no issues with schoolies; his own daughter is here somewhere among the revellers.

I reach Cavill Mall. Party central. Thousands of teenagers are swarming, moving this way and that in tidal surges, driven by no discernible purpose. The boys are wearing board shorts, T-shirts and crocs; the more self-assured are barefoot and bare-chested. The girls wear skimpy singlet tops and cheeky cut-off jeans or short summer dresses. Nearly everyone, boys and girls, has dressed down, with the occasional set of high heels or a cocktail dress looking out of place. I stand and watch, fascinated, rendered invisible by my age, like some BBC naturalist hoisted into the rainforest canopy, observing primates. Over to one side of the mall there's a bar, Kitty O'Shea's, standing all but empty despite the swell of people immediately outside. A couple of middle-aged blokes sip beers silently and watch the passing parade, like merchant seamen stranded in some foreign port where they don't speak the language. Queenslanders graduate from high school at seventeen: still underage, the bars and nightclubs are forbidden territory. That doesn't mean there's no alcohol about, quite the opposite. A group of three giggly girls totter past, each of them protectively hugging a large bottle of Coca-Cola with unlikely affection.

With the bars and nightclubs out of bounds, a huge concert space, with high fences and floodlights, has been set up on the beach across the road from the mall. I climb some stairs at the end of the mall and look out over thousands of kids surging to the music, waves of them sparkling with camera flashes, arms in the air and fists pumping in the floodlights. The concert is on every night this week, but next week, New South Wales's schoolies, will be different. High school students from the southern states graduate at eighteen, and the bars and clubs will be swollen with them. It will be a rougher, wilder party, when the venues will make up for lost time and their forbearance in locking out Queensland's own youth.

A television news crew walks up the street and into the mall, the female camera operator stopping to film a young girl gyrating to the music blasting across the road from the beach party. The camera is like a magnet; in no time, there are a dozen youngsters dancing and whirling and jumping, yelling at the camera, hands indiscriminately flashing peace signs and devils horns and L-shapes, eager to show the world that they're here. Descending back to street level I watch a posse of four or five police move through the crowd, purposeful among the flittering teens. The cops wear day-glo vests and carry belts heavy with menace. They pause by some marginally older youths, maybe in their early twenties, who stand smoking cigarettes and looking tough with their tatts, close-cropped hair and naked torsos. They don't belong here: they look like workers, not school kids. But they're not breaking any laws, not harassing anyone. Still, the police get the message across that this party is not for them. A pretty young girl, high as a kite and struggling for balance, tugging to keep her skin-tight dress down around her thighs, totters up to the police and, with a beatific smile, extends a hand and thanks a middle-aged cop profusely 'for just being here'. For a split second, the cop smiles back, before reassuming his professional scowl. Two of his colleagues move away, stopping a guy and demanding ID, writing down his details. The guy is a bit pissed but his crime appears to be that he is in his twenties.

There are other adults here as well, moving in small groups through the crowd: volunteers, unmistakeable in fluoro orange. 'We're just here to help, not to pass judgement', explains a volunteer named Brett. He says there are about three hundred orange vests roaming the precinct offering assistance to anyone who needs it. They pick up those who have fallen down, offer a patient ear to tales of teenage angst and walk girls who have become separated from their friends back to their apartments. Inside the apartment blocks and hotels are another church-based group of volunteers: the Red Frogs, so named because in their early days they became known for handing out jelly frogs to break the ice. They still do, tonnes of them. Brett informs me that it is the Red Frogs who organise the massive beach party. As if on cue, a group of four youngsters, barely older than the revellers themselves, walk past wearing matching black T-shirts and are cheered on by a group of schoolies yelling their approval: 'Red Frogs! Yeah! Red Frogs! Go Red Frogs!'

The Red Frogs have utterly infiltrated schoolies: not just on the street and in hotel lobbies, but in the apartments and hotel rooms themselves: cooking breakfast pancakes to provide ballast for grog-blasted stomachs, taking out the trash and cleaning rooms, endearing themselves to the students. Above all, they offer emotional support: everything from love gone wrong to suicide prevention. Every schoolie knows about the Red Frogs; they've been issued with a card with an emergency number, connecting into a 24-hour call centre. It is a highly organised and discreet safety net, helping young Australians through their rites of passage: drinking, drug experimentation and sexual coming of age. Churches were different when I was a kid.

I talk to a couple of girls, Emelia and Ash. They are down from Toowoomba for the week. Seven girls are sharing a one-bedroom apartment, paying $700 each. Emelia is tipsy and very chatty. She says her dad gave her $300 spending money, a carton of premixed alcoholic drinks and a bottle of vodka. Fours day in, the grog is gone and she's had to ring home for more money. I ask what she wants to get out of schoolies.

'Just to have fun. You know, to party. Not to worry about exams or uni or working or anything. I'm going to uni in Brisbane. It might be the last time with all my friends.'

We watch as three police pass by, manhandling a young man; it's difficult to tell whether they are restraining him or holding him upright.

'He's a toolie', judges Emelia. She explains that there are three groups here: the schoolies, the foolies—younger students who want to be part of the action—and toolies—older youths who come to party and, conventional wisdom has it, prey on the schoolies.

'What about boys? Do you have a boyfriend here?' I ask.

'No. Some girls come here just to have sex. They're mad. I was told there are something like five-hundred unwanted pregnancies every year.'

'Well, I guess these things can happen.'

'Rubbish. Look.' And she fishes around in her shoulder bag before retrieving a small plastic box. She flips the lid, revealing three or four condoms, proud of her new badge of adulthood.

'So you came prepared?'

'No. No way. They were handing them out at McDonald's. God, I'm not going to have sex. My parents would flip!'

I walk back towards the beach, invisible in my cloak of middle age as young Australia whirls around me. Suddenly, I've been here long enough. This is no place for adults. I straddle a pool of vomit and start walking back towards Broadbeach, away from the *Doctor Who* set and towards my own generation. I pass a girl, head in her hands, crying uncontrollably: 'I just wanna go home! I just wanna go home!' Two Red Frogs are with her, one has her arms around the girl's shoulder, talking softly and reassuringly. No place for adults, but would I let my own kids come here when they're older? Sure. Better here with the police and the paramedics and the Red Frogs than off experimenting without a safety net.

It's an extraordinary event: thousands of teenagers coming together to celebrate their common metamorphosis, emerging from their high-rise chrysalis to spread their wings each night under the lights of the beach. They come here from all over, from private schools and state schools, from country towns and from the suburbs, and they congregate for this coming of age. Where else in Australia, but at the beach? The beach that, from this week on, these young Australians will remember as pivotal in their lives, even if they struggle to remember all of it. The beach that helps makes us, the beach that helps define us.

⌐⌐

I pay my $19 and take the express lift up Q1, 'the world's tallest residential tower', up to the seventy-seventh storey. From the observation floor the view is uninterrupted: south into New South

Wales, north to Brisbane, west to the mountains of Lamington National Park and east out across the curving horizon of the Pacific Ocean. Q1 is among the twenty-five tallest building in the world, and from its eyrie the Gold Coast is laid bare, like a scale model. Running north–south is the white swathe of the beach, uninterrupted by headlands, a continuous ribbon of sand stretching 30 kilometres from Main Beach in the north to Coolangatta in the south. The high-rise apartments and hotels are concentrated in Surfers, but erupt here and there along the entire length of the beach. Cranes can be seen hovering, harbingers of more apartments, more hotel rooms. A few blocks inland from the beach, the Gold Coast Highway demarcates where the high-rises end and the canal estates begin. These stretch for kilometres, sun glinting off waterways, from the old centre of Southport across the Nerang River. There's the Isle of Capri and Mermaid Waters, Clear Water Lake, Lake Wonderland and Paradise Island. These are the preserves of the wealthy: local developers and businesspeople made good, mixed in with retirees escaping colder southern climes. Further west, beyond the canals, are the suburbs, as bland and as flat as any in Sydney and Melbourne. Here are the bungalows of the hospitality and construction workers, heavily mortgaged or expensively rented, with the air conditioner cranked up, a SUV in the drive and a pool in the backyard. And everywhere, like patches in a quilt, the green splotches of golf courses and the grey squares of shopping-centre car parks. Hovering on the fringe, the theme parks: Dreamworld, Sea World, Movie World and Wet'n'Wild.

The Gold Coast is no longer a stretch of beach, it's a city, with a population of about 600 000, swelling by around half a million more at the peak of the summer-holiday season. In the past fifty years, it's surpassed in size not just Canberra and all other inland cities, but also Hobart and Darwin, as well as all those old industrial ports like Newcastle, Wollongong and Geelong, the places that used to make things. The Gold Coast doesn't actually make very much at all, except money. There's plenty of that sloshing about the place. If the projections are to be believed, it will eventually grow larger than Adelaide, a city of more than one million people. Adelaide, with its agricultural base and manufacturing industry, was once Australia's third city. In the 1950s it had more than half a million residents and a symphony orchestra; back then, the entire Gold Coast had a population of 12000—the fibro village of Southport surrounded by dairy farms and swamp. Nowhere else in Australia has the growth been as spectacular; nowhere else in Australia has a city been so dependent on the beach.

All of Australia's capitals, except artificial Canberra, were established as port cities. The English settlers looked for a good harbour, with a reliable supply of fresh water. Arable land was much prized, but the proximity of a reasonable beach was neither here nor there. That Sydney and Perth have better beaches than Melbourne is due to luck; that Adelaide can still feel superior to Brisbane in at least this one regard is happenstance. But the Gold Coast is different; it is a city built on leisure and tourism, on sand and hedonism. This is no state capital with taxpayers providing economic ballast. It's a boom–bust place, where prices rise and prices fall, where fortunes are made and fortunes are lost, where real estate bubbles and froths and bursts.

Even looking out from the observation deck of Q1, with the reality laid out before me, it's hard to believe that the Gold Coast is so very large and so very successful. The nearest comparison I can make is Miami Beach in Florida, which shares the same gaudy aesthetic. But the high-rise skyline of Miami makes sense, sitting at the end of a peninsular thrust into the warming waters of the Caribbean, a few kilometres of beach to satisfy the demands of 300 million Americans living through the chill of a northern winter. But here in Australia, with 25000 kilometres of coastline, much of it warm and blessed with white-sand beaches, it is harder to explain the magnetism of the Gold Coast. Further south in New South Wales, there are beaches with barely a soul on them, beaches that rival any in the world for beauty. I can see them, or at least where they lie, from my vantage point on Q1's observation deck. I wonder why the Gold Coast is so successful, why it appeals to us so much, what it says about modern Australia. A city built on sand.

Surfers Paradise is an unlikely place to find a history museum. The city doesn't seem old enough to have any history, or old enough to care about it. Like a teenager having a growth spurt, it's self-obsessed, having too much fun today to worry about what has gone before or what lies ahead. Everything here is brand new, a ready-mix city rushing skywards towards the future. Nevertheless, there is a museum, and I set out to find it. It takes some time. The address I have locates it in Bundall, but I find it's been moved to Surfers Paradise. Not physically, mind you—the buildings and land are in the same place, but it seems some real estate developers didn't quite like the sound of Bundall, so they had the area surrounding the museum rezoned to Surfers. Overnight, property values put on a spurt. When I finally find the museum, Bob Nancarrow, a spry 71-year-old and President of the Gold Coast Historical Society, informs me that there's nothing new in a bit of creative rebranding. Surfers Paradise itself was known as Elston for almost half a century before Brisbane hotelier and entrepreneur Jim Cavill—the man the main street and mall are named after—successfully lobbied to have the name changed to Surfers Paradise in 1933. This was good for Jim's business: he had opened the Surfers Paradise Hotel in Elston eight years earlier. Lucky he didn't call it the Fox and Hounds. Then, in 1958, the 30-kilometre swathe of beach was officially branded 'the Gold Coast'. Ever since, tourist-hungry councils around Australia have been branding their own stretches of sandy seduction: 'the Sapphire Coast', 'the Diamond Coast', 'the Copper Coast'. What's next: 'the Bling Coast'?

Bob is a good person to talk to about the history of Surfers Paradise and the Gold Coast, because he's lived it. The city is so new that he can remember back when it wasn't a city, when the area was known simply as the South Coast. When he was a school kid in the mid-1950s there were still only about 7000 people living in Southport, with another 5000 scattered along the rest of the coast.

'It was very casual. The only place you'd wear shoes was to church on Sundays. You'd have a pair of Sunday school shoes and that was all you'd have. You used to go to school barefoot,' Bob reminisces. 'Southport was a community and everybody knew everybody. You'd go down the street and you knew everybody. If there was a bushfire coming in, you wouldn't ring up SES or any of them, because they weren't there. The men would get together and go and do something about it.'

What Bob doesn't know firsthand has been passed down through his family. His great-grandfather came to the coast in 1880, bought 88 acres and became a subsistence farmer, scratching a bit of income from a few beehives and some mango trees. The railway line from Brisbane reached Southport in 1889. (It wasn't ripped up until 1964.) Even in the very early days, there was some low-level tourism. Graziers with kids at boarding school in Southport, and well-off Brisbane families, would catch a ferry across the shallow Nerang River to the sandy spit of Elston.

'What changed the Gold Coast mainly was World War II', says Bob. 'The troops used to come north, because that was where the Japanese threat was. A lot of them got to know the Gold Coast then and decided to come back after the war. The 1950s were the start of the boom.' According to Bob, what helped set the Gold Coast apart was a new breed of entrepreneur who saw the potential to make money on the coast from tourism and property, and who understood the value of publicity. Entrepreneurs like Bernie Elsie, whom Bob remembers fondly.

'Bernie Elsie was a bit of a character. He was a plumber up in Toowoomba. He come down here and he was the first to do a lot of things. He was a bit of a wild sort of a bugger. You'd get along well with him as long as you didn't have any authority. He built motels and used to run a tourist boat up to Stradbroke Island. When he moved over to Surfers Paradise he set up Beachcomber. And then he used to have these pyjama parties. I think there might have been a bit of sly grog and whatever floating around. He used to get raided by the cops regularly because it wasn't a licensed venue. The next day the headlines of newspapers right round Australia would be full of pyjama parties at Surfers Paradise, and he got millions of dollars of free publicity. Set him up for life.'

Taking a leaf out of Bernie Elsie's book, a swimsuit designer from Victoria named Paula Stafford started making bikinis on the Gold Coast in the late 1940s. When a beach inspector asked a model wearing one of her creations to leave the beach in 1952, it also made the national papers. As did a story about visiting US entertainer Sammy Davis Junior buying bags of her designs. In staid 1950s Australia, the Gold Coast, with low-cut swimmers and risqué pyjama parties, was radiating some of its own rat-pack allure. The plumber from Toowoomba, the bikini designer from Victoria and the real estate hustlers from Brisbane had somehow managed to imbue the sleepy tourist village with a touch of stardust and glamour.

Bob left school and, like most of his mates, went into the building trades, becoming an apprentice plasterer. He was still an apprentice when he got a job working on Kinkabool, the first high-rise building on the coast. 'It was 1959–60. Ten storeys high. It was a monster thing!' he says with a laugh. 'It's still there on Hamlin Street. It's heritage listed.' And he laughs again.

I ask whether he realised what was coming and he shakes his head. 'I was only nineteen; it was a job, so who gave two hoots. Nobody imagined what that was going to be a start of. The next thing you knew high-rises were going up left, right and centre. Then people started to have second thoughts, but by then it was too late.'

If the Gold Coast boomed in the 1950s and 1960s, more was to follow. Bob has no doubt about the single biggest factor taking it from sleepy holiday hamlet to international tourist destination: the decision by premier Joh Bjelke-Petersen to abolish all death duties in Queensland in 1977. Instead of flying up for an annual holiday, southerners started retiring to the Gold Coast in the thousands, bringing the accumulated wealth of a lifetime with them. Retirement, old age and healthcare have been major industries ever since. In the era of the white-shoe brigade, wetlands were denounced as swamps and filled in to form canal developments, and the once hot-button issue of shadows on the beach was forgotten as the towers of Surfers Paradise grew higher and higher. Soon it wasn't just southerners, but Japanese and other foreign tourists sweeping into the Gold Coast. Everybody was making money: the developers, the real estate agents, the hotel and apartment operators, the tourism entrepreneurs. And everybody was happy. Everybody except locals like Bob.

'I don't particularly like the high-rise lifestyle, but I'm a minority. I live out at Tallebudgera Valley. It's rural. I go into Southport now and I'm the foreigner. The town outgrew me. The land value got too high for what was on it. So, all the houses got knocked down and became three-storey walk-ups, because you had to get more people into a smaller area.'

I ask if he ever sees any of his old mates. 'Occasionally we've had a class reunion, the 1953 scholarship class reunion, and it's surprising how many are still around the coast, but you never see them. They've all moved out. Not many locals made money here because they could not see the potential. They should have made millions.

'It does make me sad, to think of the lifestyle that once was here, and what is here now.'

But if Bob feels sad, he doesn't feel sorry for himself. He's still laughing with incredulity about it all as he gives me a quick tour of the gardens surrounding the museum's modest single-storey building. Out the back, he shows me three graves, dating back to the nineteenth century, when this was the site of a sugar mill. The inscription of one is still legible, despite the passing of more than a century: 'In Memory of George William Haly Hutton, Eldest Son of the Late Major General Hutton of H.M. Indian Army. Born October 1848—Died 26 January 1873.' I feel sorry for George. Sorry for his short life, sorry that in death, as he must have been in life, he was overshadowed by his more illustrious father. But in death, he may well have bestowed his most lasting legacy: it's the graves that protect the tenancy of the Historical Society and the continued existence of the museum. Without them, the land would long ago have been devoured by developers and covered in concrete.

The graves are on a ridge above the flat land that stretches out to the Nerang River and beyond that to Surfers Paradise's Main Beach. The rise isn't an anomaly; it's a remnant of a dune formed tens of thousands of years ago when this was the coastline. When Bob was young, the old dune, and others like it, stretched the length of the coast. Now they've all been flattened, bulldozed in the name of progress. That might be the source of some regret in a future where the sea is higher, the waves more aggressive and the weather less predictable. The flattening of the dunes and the transformation of wetlands into canal developments might not seem such a great idea.

Driving back to Broadbeach, the Gold Coast Highway is more like a car park than a road. The traffic inches forward, treacle slow, windows wound up and air conditioners cranking in the heat. The afternoon peak hour. Wedged between the beachside high-rises to the east and the canal developments to the west, the road is a series of bottlenecks. The cars have nowhere to go and the traffic lights struggle to prevent gridlock. The buildings beside the road are smeared with the red and yellow livery of fast-food outlets, and an erratic burst of wind blows matching packaging across the road.

As a 13-year-old I went to Sydney as part of a sporting team, and our coach guided us through the CBD navigating by the pubs, back in the days when there was still one on every street corner. He was a lousy coach, but his knowledge of pubs was legendary. You could do something similar nowadays in Surfers: navigating by junk food. 'Turn right at the second MacDonalds, then left at KFC, and we're there next to Red Rooster.'

An intimidating four-wheel drive, indicator insistent, pushes its way in front of me, as if this lane has a chance of moving any more quickly than the one it is coming from. On the back of the vehicle is a bumper sticker: a white Australia surrounded by black seas and nasty black letters written across the continent: 'FUCK OFF, WE'RE FULL'. I consider getting out and asking the driver what he's full of, but I suspect I know.

⌒

I drop round to have an after-dinner drink with some old friends, Jan and Peter, at their house in Burleigh Waters. It's a lovely house, in a quiet cul-de-sac; 'Canberra with palm trees', Jan calls it. There's a swimming pool in the yard surrounded by a sort of mini rainforest that Peter has established, an oasis. Jan and Peter moved up here from Canberra several years ago. They love it. They love the warmth and the laid-back lifestyle. Until recently, they had a boat, and used to putter up the Broadwater towards Brisbane and back again. Both Jan and Peter's parents have also made the move north, so there's not much the two schoolteachers miss about their former life in Canberra, except their friends and the capital's egalitarian social order. 'You notice it here. Canberra is such a middle-class city. Everyone is a public servant or a schoolteacher or something like that. Here there are people who are so rich you wouldn't believe it, then there are all these poor buggers working casual jobs in hospitality. There's hardly any middle class.'

Outside, as we say our goodbyes, Jan spots a blemish in the otherwise perfect streetscape: a large cane toad has parked itself on the front lawn. She nips back inside, returns with a spray bottle and gives the toad a quick blast. 'Dettol', she says with a wicked grin. 'That'll teach the sod.'

⌒⟶

The mid-morning traffic on the Gold Coast Highway has eased after its early morning peak, and I arrive at Bond University fifteen minutes before my interview. I've been here before, yet I'm still taken by the grandiloquent tableau of its main axis: two colonnaded buildings leading the eye through a giant arch to the decorative lakes in the distance. Like some giant *trompe l'oeil*, the architect has skilfully manipulated the perspective to make it all look much grander and more impressive than it really is.

The illusion appears to be working fine. Students loll on the grass, drink coffee in takeaway cups, exchange flirtations. The accents are Asian, American and European, with a booming Queenslander drawl thrown in for good measure. Australia's first and most prominent private university, with its appropriately Gold Coast motto, in English not Latin, *Bringing Ambition to Life*, appears to be prospering. Half the students are from overseas; the fees rank with some of the most expensive in the world. It's possibly the most tangible legacy of property developer Alan Bond. His business empire collapsed; Kerry Packer skinned him alive, and the yanks won back the cup. He stomped on Paul Barry's business card, faked mental retardation and ended up in prison for four years for fraud and bad acting. And yet not only does the university survive; it hasn't renounced its founder's name. It's an impressive display of loyalty in the notoriously fickle worlds of property development and academia. I find a plaque attached to a wall beneath a clock tower, gilt lettering shining against dark stone: 'To Brian Orr and staff with thanks for developing a magnificent campus. Alan Bond A.O. Bond University, May 1990.' The AO has gone, of course, repossessed by the government after Bond's conviction, but here on the Gold Coast no one is about to chisel out the two burnished letters of a self-made property developer.

There is no illusion about the Mirvac School of Sustainable Development building at Bond University and its six-star energy efficiency rating. The Professor of Real Estate and head of the Mirvac School, George Earl, gives me a guided tour of the 2-year-old building. It's a marvel of green engineering and design. Rain is collected from its roof, and its grey and black water treated, so 90 per cent of the building's water needs are generated on site. The roof itself is designed like an upside-down wing, sucking air into and through the building, cutting the costs of air conditioning in the sub-tropical summer. The building uses 70 per cent less electricity than a traditional building, with motion-sensor lights that turn themselves on and off to complement natural sunlight. It has windows that shut themselves when it rains and air conditioning that will operate only when they are sealed. Even the lift generates electricity when descending. It's exactly the sort of technology that will be needed if booming cities like the Gold Coast are ever going to become halfway sustainable.

George Earl bounces through the building, exuding optimism and enthusiasm with every step. He's just wrapping up a study of thirty-two energy- and water-efficient office buildings nationwide. It concludes that, on average, they only cost 6 per cent more to build than conventional office blocks. This building, he believes, is the future. That, and a bit of rebranding.

'You could say climate change is a threat to the Gold Coast because you have rising tidal water. According to the doomsayers, the place is a swamp and will go back to being a swamp. That threat is real—climate change is happening. But the opportunity is there to rebrand the coast as a place of excellence in sustainability and use what could be a problem to our advantage.'

As an expert on sustainability and real estate, George Earl doesn't subscribe to the 'fuck off, we're full' view of either Australia or his home city. Just the opposite. He believes the Gold Coast could easily accommodate one million permanent residents, if developed properly. For that to occur on a sustainable basis, there will need to be a move towards more medium-density housing. He says that the housing density on the coast, disregarding the high-rise strip along the beach, is about fifteen lots per hectare, compared to about thirty in major European cities. He says by moving towards twenty lots per hectare, with apartment buildings of 5–10 storeys, the Gold Coast could accommodate a lot more people without any loss of amenity.

'People say that small-lot housing is the slums of the future. I disagree. Not if it's done well,' he says, telling me he lives in medium-density housing himself. 'I live on the lake, so it's very pleasant. There's walking, rowing, cycling. There's more interaction and social amenity in that area than there is in the urban deserts of the outer suburbs of Brisbane or Sydney.'

George sees the Gold Coast developing into a much more sustainable city in other ways as well. He says the economic base is expanding. Where twenty years ago the coast was totally reliant on tourism and property development, the advent of Bond University and the much larger campus of Griffith University, combined with the development of a teaching hospital and numerous private colleges, is building a larger middle class and smoothing out the boom–bust cycle that has plagued it in the past. Other industry is following.

George represents, I realise, a view of the world that has faded from fashion in recent times. It's the mentality of the 1950s and 1960s, of agriculture's green revolution, of the elimination of small pox, of the moon landings—a belief that technology and humankind's ingenuity could overcome any obstacle. That unbridled optimism has eroded in recent decades; as the world has grown smaller, its resources have appeared more and more finite. In this regard I am probably, for once, at one with the fashion of the day. I can't help thinking that we are exhausting our planet and that our politicians are lacking the will, the intellect and the courage to do anything about it. Kevin Rudd identified climate change as the great moral challenge of our generation, and then failed his own challenge.

Rudd also unwittingly revealed a rift in society when he embraced a federal Treasury report predicting the Australian population would increase from about 21 million to 35 million within forty years. The then Prime Minister thought this was splendid, declaring he believed in a big Australia. Rudd was replaced by Julia Gillard, who declares herself supportive of a 'sustainable Australia', whatever that means, while skilfully avoiding putting a number on an ideal population size. I suspect, in this poll-driven polity, her line is designed to appeal both to the environmentally concerned and the 'fuck off, we're full' crowd. It suggests that George Earl and Kevin Rudd are in the minority, and the community as a whole is growing more pessimistic about our ability to expand our population, protect our environment, address climate change and maintain our standard of living.

And yet George Earl, Pangloss incarnate, reckons that a big Australia and a sustainable Australia aren't mutually exclusive.

'I think we can support 30 or 40 million people in Australia. It's a fertile country—the sniff of rain and things bloom. We could utilise our land much better than we do. With green energy you can decentralise more easily than with conventional energy. There are ideal places to grow biodiesel and ideal places for solar and wind farms.'

Stuck back in the baking traffic of the Gold Coast Highway, I wonder if George Earl could be both right and wrong. The new technologies will make decentralised living more affordable, feasible and attractive, but that doesn't mean people will move. Menzies built Canberra and Whitlam built Albury-Wodonga to entice Australians away from the coast, and governments of both persuasions built the Snowy Mountains Scheme to supply sustainable water and renewable electricity to the hinterland. But Australians prefer to live on the coast. And most choose to live in large cities like the Gold Coast. I suspect George's vision of a low-impact, decentralised Australia will take some achieving, and that his other vision, of a medium-density Gold Coast of a million people living in apartment blocks may be the more likely future. Unless, of course, the climate remains unconvinced by the rebranding, and the Gold Coast finds itself rebranded 'the once and future swamp'.

Petrina Maisey is worried about the koalas. She lives in Logan Shire, in the rapidly diminishing gap between the northern Gold Coast and southern Brisbane. The area has branded itself as 'the Koala Coast'. She and other activists want to protect Bahr's Scrub, 800 hectares of bushland rapidly being eaten up by the great Australian suburban sprawl. Petrina is a diminutive woman, but unwavering in her beliefs, the sort of person who finds it difficult to take a backward step. You know the type. Not always the easiest to get on with, not the sort to accept an easy compromise so we can all get on with whatever it is we think is important at the time: picking up the kids, going to the mall, watching the latest must-see television. The sort of person who makes the rest of us feel insipid.

Petrina is driving me round Bahr's Scrub, extolling its unique environmental credentials. It's been a long day and I'm feeling tired. So perhaps it's just me, but the remnant forest doesn't look so impressive as we motor through the evening dusk. No Tarkine wilderness this; it's crisscrossed with roads and dotted with water tanks and communications towers. Suburban man is never far away. I'm not sure which is sadder: that it's not larger and more impressive, or that this is all that's left. But Petrina insists that it's definitely worth saving. 'There are rare and threatened plants here, some of which don't exist anywhere else, and dry lowland rainforest. There's a campaign to get that declared as an endangered ecosystem,' she says as she drives. 'It's a biodiversity hotspot. There are more species here than in Lamington National Park.' I look into the gloom, trying to see it through her eyes.

Bahr's Scrub is earmarked for development. We pass a site where the bulldozers have already breached the periphery, laying the groundwork for a new shopping centre. Petrina looks grim, saying she doesn't come this way often because it makes her too sad. She says that Bahr's Scrub is an important koala habitat, but successive councils have refused to recognise the fact, even though neighbouring Redlands Council, with a more activist constituency, has had its shire declared prime koala habitat. Logan City Council has now recognised the existence of the koalas, but, according to Petrina, only with reluctance. She says the policies to protect the animal are inadequate.

'But isn't it true that they are planning wildlife corridors?' I ask.

That elicits a derisive snort from Petrina. 'Come on, I'll show you one of the wildlife corridors.' We drive just a few hundred metres before she pulls the car up on the side of the road. 'There you are. Down beside the road. Where those house are.'

'They have houses in wildlife corridors?'

'Sure. What did you expect? Bushland?'

'Strangely enough, yes.'

Petrina explains that the wildlife corridors consist of large established housing blocks of about ten hectares, some with native bushland and others that are cleared for horses or other activities. She says no one is happy: environmentalists believe the corridors are patently inadequate, while the property owners are up in arms because they are prohibited from subdividing while all around them their neighbours are making a motza selling land off to developers. She says that in places, some of the wildlife corridors are only 10 metres wide. 'These areas are not environmental reserves. They are residential blocks, big residential blocks. These people can have cats, they can have dogs, they can have fences. Some of it is bushy, and some of it is not—but it's not bush. There are people who have cleared acreage, with an odd tree here and there. You are talking about rural residential basically.'

I ask what this means for the koalas.

'Each koala needs 50 hectares of land to survive. You can't squash them all into one area. You are trying to train them to move down corridors, expecting them to know somehow that there is more bush at the end. Also, of course, if they do get to another piece of bushland, there are likely to be koalas there already.

'Koalas are in very serious trouble. There's research going on that may prove the southeast Queensland koala is a distinct species, and if that gets recognised, then they're definitely facing extinction. It's even been said within twelve months, which is pretty heavy.'

'What? That they could be extinct within twelve months?'

'Yeah. We haven't provided habitat. We're lowering their genetic mass. We're putting them at risk.'

It's thought the koala population between Brisbane and the Gold Coast has halved in just the last three years, and if that rate of decline continues, the koalas will be gone in less than a decade. At the eleventh hour, local councils and the state government have begun to act, setting up reserve areas. But koalas living in isolated pockets of bushland will be prone to inbreeding and stress, as well as vulnerable to disease, feral animals and traffic. In the next twenty years, 21 000 new homes are planned for Redlands Shire and 90 000 for Logan Shire, as the last gaps between the twin sprawls of the Gold Coast and Brisbane are erased. It's expected 750 000 new dwellings will be built in southeast Queensland's growing conurbation. If I were a koala, I reckon I might put a 'FUCK OFF, WE'RE FULL' sticker on my gum tree.

Jupiters Casino glows in the night. I can spy it from the window of the automated monorail that carries me over the Gold Coast Highway from Broadbeach. Inside the casino, the gaming hall is awash with light. The red and brown carpet is harsh on the eyes and lush on the feet. Young Asians gather laughing around roulette tables, serious amateurs are concentrating hard at the $5 blackjack tables, and Chinese grannies are playing poker machines, clutching styrofoam cups full of coins. A sign points the way to the high rollers' room, but no one is ever going to mistake me for one of them. Instead, I descend some winding, carpeted stairs to the poker room. It looks like fun. A couple of dozen men are seated round three tables playing Texas hold 'em. These are not tourists, but regulars. Dress is casual, bordering on sloppy. Jeans, T-shirts, sandshoes, hoodies. Some wear sunglasses to disguise their emotions and hide their 'tells'. Most are in their twenties or thirties, with a smattering of middle-aged and elderly. Almost no one is drinking; the barmaid at the well-stocked bar is staring into space. I break her reverie and order a beer. A pretty young blond girl sits nearby watching her boyfriend in despair. She's dressed for a night out: short black dress, stilettos, black stockings. Hair coiffed, make-up perfect, jewellery just right. He sits oblivious at a nearby table, wolfing down a hamburger, eyes still glued to the game unfolding before him. On one table, a Slavic-looking body builder in a white T-shirt is doing well, on another a middle-aged Indian, a snappy dresser in a white suit, holds temporary possession of the largest pile of chips. Play on two of the tables is minimalist, the players making their calls and little else, emotions carefully packed out of sight. On the other, players are engaging in friendly banter, egging each other on and chiacking each other over tactics. I miss the cause, but from nowhere a dispute erupts. A young guy starts complaining vehemently, believing he has been short-changed in some way. A casino floorwalker moves in quickly and politely, suspending the game. He gives me a wry smile as he heads into a back room, finger pointing to the ceiling. I look up. Every few metres are black plastic orbs covering closed-circuit television cameras. All is seen, all is recorded. The dispute will soon be settled, but in the meantime the players take the opportunity to take toilet breaks, order food, or simply stand up and stretch. The eager young man, burger finished, spell broken, suddenly remembers his girlfriend, turns, places a greasy hand on her elegant thigh and asks if everything is okay. Her expression is one more of sadness than of anger. The floorwalker returns, overruling the complaint. The aggrieved party gathers his chips and what's left of his dignity and leaves. The game recommences, like a pool that has swallowed a stone.

Upstairs again, I take one last stroll round the gaming floor. Unlike the serious concentration of the poker room, most people are here for a night out, for a bit of fun. On one $5 blackjack table the long-haired teller is dealing slowly, explaining the rules of the game as he goes, while on the next table the game is flowing more smoothly. Most people are drinking, having fun, with only the occasional face set in concentration or contorted by obsession.

Past the card tables, beyond the 1-cent pokies, I happen upon an isolated island of silent drama. A single punter is playing craps, attended by three casino employees. I stop and watch. The man is in his fifties, dressed in an unbuttoned blue cotton shirt over a pristine white T-shirt, tan cargo shorts, brand new brown-and-white sneakers and Reebok socks. There is a Cartier watch on his wrist. He has a huge quiff of greying hair, brushed up and back in the style of the former Bosnian Serb leader Radovan Karadzic. Lying before him in a purpose-made groove in the table is a multicoloured sausage of casino chips half a metre long. I look at the colours, trying to determine their denomination. There are plenty of black chips, worth $100 each, but I can't be sure if the other colours are worth more or less. The game is being played at a furious pace, Radovan throwing the pink plastic dice as soon as they are returned to him. His face is expressionless, spellbound. He leans on the table, gathering the dice, and, unhurried yet urgent, flings them against the far end of the table with a dismissive, backhand gesture. Every now and then he looks over at the spread of chips he has placed upon the felt grid, adjusting their position, perhaps following some intricate and sophisticated system. There is little or no eye contact between player and tellers; all communication is via the movement of dice, chips and tokens. One young teller wields a long, hooked stick, pulling in the thrown dice, returning them to Radovan untouched by human hand. Another teller is overseeing the numbered grid where the bets are laid, and flips the silver disc indicating whether a throw is on or off. A third casino operative, an Asian man in his fifties, looks on, supervising. The game is moving too fast for me to follow; win or lose, there is no movement of a chip for a dozen or more throws: it is understood between player and tellers that a bet lost is a bet automatically renewed, that wins are being tallied to offset losses. Radovan throws, the teller flips the silver disc, the long, thin stick pulls in the dice, Radovan throws again. How long for each cycle? Maybe fifteen seconds. How much is being bet? I can't keep up. The teller with the stick is quiet, efficient, deferential; the teller overseeing the bets is motionless with concentration, small beads of sweat on his brow; the supervisor is silent and unmoving.

A couple of other punters wander over, and we whisper among ourselves, trying to determine the rules of the game, the size of the bets, the flow of wins and losses. Two well-dressed young Asian men approach, one carrying a plastic container of chips, including plenty of black ones. He asks to join in. The teller overseeing the bets shakes his head, not taking his eyes from the felt. 'Sorry, not now.' The two gamblers look more surprised than offended, and leave with a shrug. Even I know that this is unusual. Craps is a social game, sometimes with the two ends of the table in play at the same time, players and spectators often cheering each other on. Think Sean Connery in *Diamonds Are Forever*. Not here. This is a silent, almost solitary pursuit, a private compact between the player and the house. Radovan doesn't even look up to see who is watching. He just keeps rolling. There's a brief pause: the supervising teller relieves the man administering the betting, and a new supervisor appears. The game goes on, Radavan implacable, the tellers near motionless with concentration. And then the break. A last roll and Radovan's sphinx-like demeanour gives way, his eyes tighten with annoyance and he turns from the table, looks to the floor and lets out one short, impassioned 'Fuck!' He gathers his few remaining chips and strides towards the exit. The tellers watch him go and then, as one, let out a long sigh of relief. Most of Radovan's long, multicoloured sausage remains in its groove on the table.

'Excuse me', I say to the supervising teller. 'I couldn't keep up. How much was he betting?'

'About $3000 a throw.'

'Cripes. So how much did he lose?'

'Don't know. A lot.'

With the pressure off, the teller is happy to explain the rules, give me a better understanding of what has transpired. He explains that there is no craps table in the high rollers' room.

'So why didn't you let those other guys play?' I ask.

'He doesn't like it. He plays very, very fast.'

'So he's a regular?'

'Yeah. Might come in once or twice a week. The table is usually only open on Friday and Saturday nights. Not many people play craps. But if he calls, we open it up for him.'

'One last question. There's no skill or strategy involved, is there?'

'No. None whatsoever. You want to have a go?'

'No thanks.'

Out in the sultry midnight air, I give the monorail a miss and start walking back towards my Broadbeach apartment. An elevated walkway snakes out from the casino, across an ornamental creek and a road to the Gold Coast Convention Centre. About halfway along the walkway I start encountering groups of well-dressed people, men in dinner suits, women in evening gowns, heading towards Jupiters, either to their hotel rooms or for a nightcap and a flutter. Soon the walkway is dense with them; they're pouring out of the convention centre. Some sort of annual dinner or convention or awards night: dentists or developers or car salesmen. Whatever it is, there has been an open bar. As I reach the convention centre and walk over to the traffic lights on the Gold Coast Highway, I can smell the lingering fug of Bundy rum. Some of the penguin-suited men, aged in their fifties and sixties, are near legless, exchanging stream-of-consciousness idiocies in over-loud voices, swaying erratically as they walk, held erect by irritated wives. One grey-haired gent displays the signs of an impending vomit attack, while another lurches out onto the highway and is hauled, laughing inanely, back to safety by his partner, unaware how close a speeding black SUV came to killing him. A couple of kilometres further north, schoolies will be heading towards the climax of another night of revelry. Maybe I should call, see if they can spare a few Red Frogs.

⌒

Forget Dreamworld, forget Sea World, forget Movie World. The best theme park on the Gold Coast is Sovereign Islands. There are plenty of gated communities dotted around the coast, small enclaves of privilege hidden from sight, retirees secure behind 24-hour surveillance. Sovereign Island is no such place. Here the gates are flung wide during daylight hours, the great unwashed invited inside to marvel at the wealth, the success, the extravagance of its denizens. Peter has picked me up from Broadbeach and driven me up here to see the great Gold Coast divide for myself.

We drive in across the bridge from Paradise Point, past the Champs Elysees Hair Salon and along the Sovereign Mile. The islands are low-lying, made from reclaimed land and shaped liked the fronds of some cartoon plant so that every house has both water frontage and road access. The street names are comically regal: Excalibur Court, Sir Galahad Close and Queen Guineveres Place, as well as Hampton Court, King James Court, and King Arthurs Court. But if there was ever any intention for the islands to have some sort of quaint medieval ambience, it was long ago overtaken by the competition to build the biggest, most opulent, most ostentatious edifice in whatever architectural style appeals to the owner. There is only one castle. Down the end of Knightsbridge Parade, it's a $20 million pile that looks like a teenager has designed it on his computer. There are turrets, topped with faux ramparts, but the scale is askew. It's not made of rough-hewn stone, but uniform sandstone bricks, and attached to the front, as if by blue-tack, is a sort of rendered concrete McMansion portico. Perched on either side are a couple of huge bronze-effect eagles, wings outstretched. The 2427-square-metre castle was built by a man named Ron Litherland. He spent twelve years designing it, then four weeks living in it before putting it on the market. Apparently the former Brisbane truck driver turned internet entrepreneur decided a mega-yacht would be more to his style. I hope, for his safety's sake, that he doesn't design it himself.

We pass the home of Michael Issakadis. An article in the *Gold Coast Bulletin* has alerted me to the fact that the retired lawyer has three Rolls Royce limousines in his garage, and is planning to acquire a fourth. The article says Mr Issakadis doesn't play favourites, he drives a different car every day. Surely then, he won't be content with just four; he must want seven.

It would appear that status on Sovereign Island is measured in many ways. Square metres of floor space are important, so is the size of the indoor swimming pool and the screen in the media room. Internal elevators are a must, and the capacity of the underground car park tells neighbours all they need to know about the owner's success in life. More than ten car spaces and more than ten bathrooms, and you're definitely on the up.

All the houses on Sovereign Island are big, and many have motor yachts gleaming at the end of private jetties. But there the uniformity evaporates, as different owners build different visions of perfection. Some are merely McMansions on steroids, but others are strange and fanciful, borrowing features hotchpotch from different periods and styles. Here, a widow's walk, there, a columned façade from *Gone with the Wind*. Peter slows as we pass a blend of mausoleum and masonic hall, sitting squat and heavy at the corner of King Arthurs Court and Queen Guineveres Place. We idle outside a square, modern mansion, two-storeyed but dwarfed by its own three-storey portico, supported by two columns plated in scarlet steel—two enormous phalluses standing before the subdued tones of the house itself. We stop outside Madison, a kind of Tuscan palace spreading across several blocks on palm-lined Britannic Crescent. With well-proportioned wings, Juliet balconies already attracting climbing vines and shutters painted a pleasing shade of blue, it almost passes, but attached to the front, as high as the house itself, is another enormous drive-through portico, the sort you might find outside a five-star hotel or an up-market resort. Perhaps that's the template for luxury and wealth: a Singapore Hilton or a Bangkok Shangri La. We drive on, and I admire the names: Rivage Royal, the Villa Amalfi and the grammatically challenged Chateau de Rêves. My personal favourite is Palazzo di Venezia, a massive edifice built across three urban blocks. Peter stops the car to give me time to take it all in. A low, cream-coloured wall separates the house from the road, and set in the wall is a portico supported by Doric columns of faux marble. On either side of the portico, set on plinths to welcome visitors, are two life-sized statues of black-skinned Moors, dressed in the flowing white robes of North Africa and holding sheathed swords. The Moors stand guard over a green wrought-iron gate, which supports a golden lion in heraldic relief, wearing a crown and rampant, one paw raised to its mouth as if yawning. Past the gate, across the drive where black limousines wait, two life-sized horses of burnished silver stand for no apparent reason other than to impress. One can only guess what sumptuousness awaits the visitor should he or she pass yet more columns, this time Ionic, and enter the house proper. But, for all his luxury, the Doge must be feeling a little put out. Next door, an even more grandiose mansion is under construction, covering four housing blocks with a grander portico and, no doubt, an underground garage the size of a football field. There's an arms race underway on Sovereign Island, and it isn't pretty. Maybe climate change and rising sea levels have an upside after all. Who knows, perhaps Palazzo di Venezia is more appropriately named than the owner imagines. And next door, the new place could be called Atlantis, with a helipad atop the portico.

⌒

It's easy to laugh at the rich; it's trickier with the poor. The shelter for homeless youth in Southport is a deliberately anonymous affair, with bars on the windows and locks on the door. It's the Gold Coast without the gold. Explaining it to me is Jason, a youth worker who has spent the last year running the refuge. He leads me through the lounge, where a young man with bleached blond hair and a collection of tattoos on his arm is reclining on an old couch watching daytime television. The youth acknowledges our passing with nothing more than a curling of his lip. Jason leads me into the office and locks the door behind him. It's no reflection on the youth watching television; it's a rule turned to a habit—unlocked doors can lead to temptation. We sit, and Jason explains that the shelter has been operating for thirty years, yet its seven beds are still the only emergency accommodation for homeless youth in a city now numbering more than 600000 people. It's temporary shelter: the kids can stay a maximum of twelve weeks, then it's back on the streets if nothing better has been arranged in the meantime. It's rolling crisis management that leaves Jason frustrated.

'It will take at least six weeks before they can tell me what their real shit is. And just as we're starting to rock and roll, to get something going for them in their life, it's time for them to go,' Jason explains. 'They say to me: "Well, what is the fucking point?" and I'm like, "Well, what is the point? Because I know you have to leave." It's bandaid bullshit, that's what it is.'

Jason, originally from New Zealand, does not share the glass-half-full optimism of George Earl. For Jason, the glass is half empty and someone has pissed in the wine. He says life on the Gold Coast is tough for minimum-wage families, and the margin between doing all right and life falling apart is perilously thin. Many come, attracted by the tourist-brochure lifestyle, only to find housing expensive and good jobs hard to find.

'The workforce is largely transient, doing casual jobs in the hospitality industry. If you're casual, you can have your shift cancelled with an hour's notice. And those jobs don't finish at five, more likely to start at five. Weekends and nights and that sort of thing. Kids come home from school, there's no one home.' He says some families simply can't cope. There's alcoholism and domestic violence and worse. Kids leave home, not because they want to, but because they are forced out by circumstance.

Jason tells me the story of Susan, a 17-year-old drug addict who has been through the refuge three times this year. There's frustration in his eyes and despair in his words as he tells me there are no refuges or rehabilitation centres that can give her the help she needs. He believes she will be dead before she is twenty-five.

'On many levels she already is dead. She's just like a leaf blowing in the wind, she rolls from place to place. In a job like mine, you have these people come through, and they haunt you. I'm always going to wonder what happened to her.'

The sun is setting, and the skyscrapers are casting their long shadows across the sands and out over the tumbling breakers. I wonder at this glittering new city built on sand and reclaimed lagoons and drained swamps. It still doesn't appear quite real to me, as if it's constructed of façades, like some monumental film set. Maybe it's the newness of everything, the impermanence. A place where a 50-year-old high-rise is heritage listed, seen as quaint for being only ten storeys tall as it's dwarfed by gleaming new towers the same way it once towered over beach bungalows. The economic foundations seem tenuous, reliant on the continued influx of tourists, retirees and money. The urban environment seems unsustainable, with an ever-increasing population, chronic water shortages and rapidly disappearing rainforest. Yet it exists, it flourishes, arguably the most dynamic and successful Australian city of the past half a century.

My thoughts are interrupted by the sight of a retired couple, taking turns photographing each other on the wide expanse of the beach. I do the right thing, offering to snap them standing together. Photographs taken, we talk as we stroll together towards Surfers Paradise. His name is Artie, her name is Gabrielle; he is English, she is Italian—they live in Italy.

Artie tells me they are a bit disappointed by the Gold Coast. The weather has been cool and raining during their visit, not the golden warmth they'd been expecting. I explain that the travel brochures haven't been deliberately misleading, that it's La Niña causing the unseasonably cool spring, the first in more than a decade.

'Not to worry. You've still got this,' he says, extending his arms in a gesture straight from his adopted home. 'It's worth coming all the way just to walk on this beach. You can't do this in Italy. All the beaches are private, chopped into segments, and the public ones are full of rubbish. Here you can walk for miles. You Australians, you don't know how lucky you are.' And then with a slight frown he asks, 'But what is this schoolies thing? I don't get it.'

5

TOWARDS SYDNEY

Main Beach at Byron Bay—a mixture of schoolies and backpackers.

The old Hyundai has seen better days. There's a hairline crack snaking across the windscreen and the squirter thing on the bonnet is suffering from the automotive equivalent of a prostate problem. I press the button, but the stuttering ejaculation of foaming water dribbles out onto the hood; none reaches the windscreen. At the next set of lights, I jump out and pour water on the windshield from my drink bottle and turn on the wipers to clear the smeared insect that has been nagging at me for the last few kilometres. In my imagination, the hairline crack extends another centimetre at the touch of cold water. I'll need to sell the car soon, maybe when I get back to Canberra, before its more vital organs start collapsing. It's been a workhorse, all right. We bought it new and stuck it on the mortgage, back when we bought the house, before we were married, before we had kids. There's an idiosyncratic dent in the back bumper, where I reversed into a pole at the hospital the day my son was born. He's twelve now, his sister eight. The car is fourteen.

The sense of time passing shifts focus as I proceed down the Gold Coast Highway, reaching Coolangatta and the New South Wales border. Back when I was eight we came here as a family, driving all the way from Canberra in Dad's brand-spanking Toyota Crown, the vinyl seats alive with their aroma of newness. We stayed in a holiday flat near Greenmount Beach. It was on the second floor of a two-storey fibro place, reached by exterior stairs of greying wood. I remember my mum making fruit salad—a revelation. There was real fruit: pineapple and mango and banana and passionfruit. Until then, I thought fruit salad was peaches and pears out of a tin. What else can I remember? Not much. Going to the 'world famous' Currumbin bird sanctuary and being shat upon by myriad lorikeets, going to Sea World and feeding smelly pilchards to a seal. And getting sunburnt as all hell.

I rein in the Hyundai at Greenmount, and recognise almost nothing. The old holiday flats are gone, of course, replaced by a twenty-storey apartment tower, all mirror glass and white concrete balconies. Reflection on the Sea, it's called, the largest and most conspicuous of the seaside high-rises, at least for now. In fifty years it will either be demolished or heritage listed. Inside its beige apartments a new generation of children are laying down their own memories of coastal holidays. I wonder what may greet them in their middle age. Some things, however, don't change. Across the road, the beach is much the same, as is the pine-topped headland of Greenmount itself. I walk down onto the sand and another memory comes back:

the waves full of bottle-blue jellyfish the size of grapefruit, and my 10-year-old brother Brendon, a Huck Finn kid with brown skin and hunter-gatherer tendencies, plucking them out of the water and holding them upside down, before slaughtering them on the rocks below the headland, their jelly blobbing this way and that.

There are no jellyfish today, and the weather has turned fine and clear, the sun already warm, the greyness of the previous days evaporating away in a harbinger of summer. There are plenty in, swimming and surfing, making the most of the fine weather. I go for a quick swim myself, between the flags in the lee of the headland. The water feels clear and good. I like the fact that the beach here, at the tail of the 30-kilometre stretch from Surfers Paradise, has a curve to it. It feels less exposed, and the waves are more regular and well defined, the water translucent and less choppy than the churning breakers on the exposed beaches of Surfers and Broadbeach. I climb the headland, up the footpath beside the road, wet feet slipping in thongs. From the lookout, New South Wales is a stone's throw away, the Tweed River guided out to sea by twin breakwaters.

Back in the car, I cross the river and the urban environment changes. Suddenly, there is almost no high-rise. It's a different world. Back in 1997, the recently elected government of Bob Carr reformed coastal planning regulation. Before then, local councils made development decisions. Carr didn't ban high-rise outright, but he went close. The height of buildings outside cities, towns and designated growth areas is now restricted to less than 14 metres (or four storeys) and buildings in built-up areas can only exceed this height after an environmental impact assessment, public consultation and, most importantly, the approval of the state government. Brown paper bags to councillors would no longer be enough. Buildings would not cast shadows on beaches or waterfront open space before 7 p.m. in summer. Carr introduced other reforms as well: he banned building on undeveloped headlands, and on already developed headlands new buildings would be restricted to existing scales and heights; no new developments could impede public access to beaches and foreshores; building on beaches and their dunes was prohibited, with special exemptions for surf lifesaving clubs; and canal developments were banned outright for their impact on water quality, flooding and wetland ecosystems. This, of course, offers another explanation for the boom on the Gold Coast. It's the southern-most point on the east coast where canal developments and high-rise can sprout unimpeded.

Yet as I drive through Tweed Heads, I have to doubt how well all this has worked. The coastal strip is predictably pleasant, but in the hinterland the suburbs sprawl, flattened by the approaching heat of summer and the planning restrictions of the state government. High-rise would be permitted here, more than one kilometre from the coastline and the river, but there's no premium without water views. If the Gold Coast has its problems, so too does Tweed Heads. There are reports of teenage gangs and indiscriminate violence. I recall what George Earl had to say, contrasting the cosmopolitan ambience and ecological sustainability of well-planned medium-rise with the urban deserts of suburbia. I wonder, with more and more people pouring into coastal communities, what is the optimum town-planning solution. I don't much like high-rise, but kilometre after kilometre of soul-sapping suburbia baking in the subtropical sun doesn't hold much appeal either.

⌣⟶

South of Tweed Heads, on an impulse, I turn right off the Pacific Highway and head into the hinterland towards Murwillumbah. Something like 85 per cent of Australians live within 50 kilometres of the coast, but most of them aren't sitting on water views. I find myself interested in what is happening here, back from the beach. The road is flat and straight and the traffic sparse and fast, the constraints of Highway 1 left behind. I wind down the windows and crank up the Hyundai's tinny old stereo. There are cane fields on either side of the road, glowing green after recent rain. The breeze carries a hint of sweetness, of molasses and treacle and golden syrup, smells from childhood, growing stronger as I pass a sugar mill. The road shadows the southern bank of the Tweed River, shards of sunlight flashing from the water through the riverside foliage. Ahead are the coastal ranges, and the jagged, olive profile of Mount Warning, gathering clouds about it in an otherwise clear sky.

I stop in Murwillumbah for lunch, hungry after my Coolangatta swim. I eat a kebab upstairs at the Sunnyside Mall. I came to the mall last time I was in Murwillumbah, in late September 2004. I was on the road, covering the federal election, and between the campaign launches of John Howard and Mark Latham in Brisbane, I ventured down to Murwillumbah for a much smaller launch: the opening of the campaign office of the sitting member for Richmond, National Party MP Larry Anthony. Richmond was on a knife-edge: one of the seats Labor needed if it were to win power. Anthony was a popular local member, an effective junior minister and a National Party Brahmin. Yet there was an inescapable impression that he was going through the motions as he declared open the office in the Sunnyside Mall. Larry's dad, former deputy prime minister and party leader Doug Anthony, was there, old and bald, with eyes so puffy they were almost closed, but cagey and astute as ever. 'It'll be tough', was all he could offer me by way of comment. Richmond was an Anthony-family fiefdom. Doug's father, Larry Senior, had held it for twenty years from 1937, until Doug held it for another twenty-seven years until 1984. A couple of interlopers, the Nationals' Charles Blunt and Labor's Nev Newell, kept it warm until Larry Junior was old enough, at thirty-four, to take up his legacy in John Howard's 1996 landslide. But by 2004 he was in serious trouble. As he frankly conceded as I interviewed him, his enemy wasn't Labor's Justine Elliot or her leader Mark Latham; his enemy was demographics. The old National Party loyalties were breaking down. The primacy of sugar and bananas and the industries of the hinterland was diminishing as sea changers and retirees flooded into the beachside enclaves of the coast. The world was changing, and there wasn't a great deal Larry Anthony could do about it. Latham lost the election, outmanoeuvred by John Howard and defeated by his own poor discipline, but this wasn't enough to save Larry and the family dynasty. Justine Elliot won and still holds the seat. It will doubtless return to the conservative side of politics sooner or later, but it's more likely to go to the Liberals than to the Nats. The rural communities of the coast are no longer what they used to be. Larry Anthony's old campaign office is now a hairdresser—The New U.

Outside Murwillumbah I pick up a hitchhiker, a young bloke called Joel. He tells me he's unemployed and lives with his mum up the road near Uki. He reckons there's not much work about, so he hitches into Murwillumbah most days just to hang out. We pass a huge house, perched up on the side of the hill, where it commands spectacular views out across the Tweed Valley. 'See that house', says Joel. 'The bloke who owns it won the lottery. Twice. First time he won, he built the house. Second time, he moved it up the hill. It's too big for one slab, so it's built on two, but the slabs are drifting apart. The house is splitting down the middle. He needs to win a third time.'

Past the house the land begins to rise, and Mount Warning dominates the skyline. It stands 20 kilometres inland, yet Joel tells me it's high enough to be the first part of mainland Australia to catch the rays of the rising sun. I ask him if he's climbed it. 'Oh yeah', he says. 'It's great. Not easy, but the view is unreal. Lots of people climb it, most during the day, but some at night, so they can be there when the sun comes up. The blackfellas don't like it, but what the heck.'

'So, like Uluru?'

'What's Uluru?'

'Ayers Rock.'

'Yeah. Same deal. The blackfellas don't like people climbing and people climb anyway. National Parks don't have no problem.'

I drop Joel at a farm gate, and keep on my way. It's occurred to me to venture a little further inland, up through the rainforest and hobby farms and communes to Nimbin, hippy capital of Australia. The Gold Coast, with its explosive growth, has rattled me a little, got me thinking, as has George Earl's vision of high-density housing. It is not just population growth that's driving change, it's economic growth. Every year the national economy grows by on average 3.5 per cent. Economist Ross Garnaut, in his reports on climate change, estimated that by 2050 Australians would be twice as wealthy as they are now and the economy two and a half times as large. Treasury reckons the population will grow from about 22 million to 35 million during the same period. Other economists have calculated that economic growth of at least 3 per cent per annum is required to prevent an increase in unemployment. Like some giant shark, the economy cannot simply stand still: it must keep moving forward, devouring more and more resources, creating more and more wealth, to keep joblessness at bay. Larger houses, more cars, bigger air conditioners. Is there no other way? Maybe the hippies of Nimbin have found it.

The hippies first came to Nimbin in May 1973 for the Aquarius Festival, Australia's answer to Woodstock. Before then, Nimbin was unheard of, a timber and dairy town in slow decline. Then the hippies and the freaks, the down-to-earthers and the alternative lifestylers, the new agers and the old radicals rolled into town for a ten-day party disguised as a serious exploration of getting back to nature, rejecting capitalism and living communally. Many words were spoken, much weed was inhaled, manifestos were drawn up, guitars were strummed, and people got their gear off and went skinny-dipping in the river. It was a brave new world, sponsored by Peter Stuyvesant. The cigarette brand, which had hitherto been promoted as the preferred toxin of the jet set, had identified the hippies as a profitable new market, in a classic 'get 'em while they're young' campaign. The smokes were manufactured by German multinational Reemtsma Cigarettenfabriken, a company that had prospered under the patronage of the Nazis, and was now displaying a certain agility in product placement. You can understand their logic: hippies were rumoured to smoke just about anything, from banana skin scrapings to buffalo poo, so why not tobacco? As for the festival's name, it derived from the belief that the world was entering a new utopian age, the Age of Aquarius, after spending the past 2000 years or more wallowing through the war-ravaged Age of Pisces. Trouble was, no one was exactly sure when the new age was due to kick off, as astrology would have to be one of the most imprecise of the imprecise sciences. If it were a science at all, estimates for the beginning of the new age ranged from halfway through the fifteenth century to the start of the thirty-seventh century. But May 1973 was as good a time as any, and Nimbin could justly claim to be as well connected to the earth's ley lines as anywhere else. Who could argue otherwise?

I was too young to make the Aquarius Festival, and didn't hear of it until a few years later—1976—when the whole thing was repeated on an even larger scale at the Cotter Reserve outside Canberra. This time 10000 people turned up, including my friends, Ben and Margaret Ann, and me. We hitched out from the suburbs to see what all the fuss was about. The sight of lots of people walking around naked had instant appeal to a 16-year-old boy, and later in the week Ben and I returned and camped out there. No doubt, in among the wigwams and geodesic domes, there was a lot of serious talk going on about alternative economic models, getting back to nature, and subverting the dominant paradigm, but I was more interested in hanging out and picking up on the vibe. For a suburban boy it was a strange new world: 10000 people gathered together, many of them convinced humankind was on the cusp of this new, utopian age. There was talk of revolution, but I never really got the revolution thing, because whenever you asked someone when it would come or what it would be like, they'd simply take another toke on their joint and say, 'It's coming man, I tell you, it's coming'. What I especially didn't get was the nexus between smoking dope and revolution. As far as I could see, smoking dope was to get high. Yet here were all these people who believed it was some revolutionary act, and that simply by smoking pot and collapsing into a torpor, you were bringing the great day closer.

At the Cotter, surrounded by the campsites of the gathering tribes, a stage had been set up in a natural amphitheatre. Bands played through the afternoon and into the night, music being another essential ingredient in changing the world, whether strummed acoustically round a camp fire or feedback blasted Hendrix-like through a mountain of Marshall stacks. One group, with massive white speaker bins, performed a note-perfect rendition of Led Zeppelin's 'Stairway to Heaven'—staggering in both its virtuosity and its complete lack of originality. Later I lay on my back watching the stars next to a girl whose name I forget. The night was warm, the air was clear. Away from the city lights, with only candles and camp fires to dim the starlight, the Milky Way was a clearly defined spray across the sky, with the Horsehead Nebula a black patch against the luminescence. Gradually at first, then more and more intensely, a swathe of shooting stars began flashing through the atmosphere, and hippiedom held its collective breath. It was mid-December and the earth was passing through the annual Geminids meteorite shower, but none of us lying there in the dark knew that. For a moment it seemed as if a new age might in fact be dawning.

'What are the stars?' whispered the girl beside me.

And so, stupidly, I told her. Massive thermonuclear reactions, every star another sun, the universe unbelievably big, billions of stars, billions of suns.

She listened for a while, then got up. 'What sort of fucking idiot do you take me for? There's only one sun—Ra.' She stalked off into the darkness and I never saw her again. More fool me. Perhaps I should have been more poetic. Angels, I should have said, or souls awaiting reincarnation. Or perhaps I just made a lousy hippy.

I'm thinking of this as I turn off the Kyogle Road and head up the hills towards Nimbin. The landscape is green, the road winding, carving through patches of old dairy farms and residual rainforest. I negotiate a tight bend and have to brake hard; there's a peacock strutting about in the middle of the road, lapis lazuli breast iridescent, tail feathers trailing. It saunters off to one side, and I motor on. A peacock in the middle of the road. After an absence of decades, I'm being welcomed back into the kingdom of the hippies.

I cross a bridge and I've arrived, not just in Nimbin, but magically back into the 1970s, like a new-age Brigadoon. I walk along the main road, under the shop awnings, among people of all ages dressed like they've been beamed in from the Haight-Ashbury or Carnaby Street or the Cotter. There's cheesecloth and tie-dye, dreadlocks and shoulder bags, beads and beards and scarves and sandals and headbands, and long, long hair. The Sex Pistols have not yet made it to Nimbin; disco and new wave and grunge and rap and hip-hop and house and electro still lie somewhere in its future. Blazoned on the T-shirts hanging for sale are the faces of Jimi Hendrix, Bob Marley and Che Guevara. From a shop comes the sound of Janis Joplin singing … *Oh Lord won't you buy me a Mercedes Benz*. For just a moment, the illusion holds and I wonder if the hippies have indeed created an alternative reality. No sooner do I consider the possibility than my thoughts are interrupted by a decidedly modern looking youth: short hair, baseball cap, wrap-around mirror glasses, acrylic basketball shirt.

'Want to buy some weed?' he hisses.

Squatting in a doorway next to us, another young man sucks through a plastic-bottle bong with a steady, intense intake of breath, holding the smoke in with concentrated effort. Only lungs inured by long practice can pull a bong like that, and only the most habitual smoker wouldn't bother seeking some privacy. Eyes open, I keep walking, past shops called Bringabong and Happy High Herbs and the Gorgeous Joint. More T-shirts hang for sale: Fight Terrorism, Smoke Homegrown, and Legalize It. Across the road, the Nimbin Hotel sports a sign declaring its sponsorship of the local soccer team, the Nimbin Headers. I walk across to the Hemp Embassy, with its Hemp Bar. A sign on the exterior wall reads: 'How absurd is a law that seeks to classify a plant as a crime, as if there were something feloniously wrong with nature'. Tacked to the wall is another banner, multicoloured letters on a blue background:

> Nimbin Street Code. Respect Bundjalung Law. Don't fight, steal or be greedy. Have integrity—be kind, honest and fair. Respect all people. Children are watching and model themselves on your behaviour. Help keep Nimbin funky, friendly and free. Don't force your addiction on others. Work it out. Be responsible—leave your dog at home. We care about our children, please be mindful of their safety. Life is sacred, including yours. Karma is for real, love is for real. Nimbin tolerates most things but violence is not ok.'

Nice sentiments, but Nimbin would be lucky to boast half a dozen streets; a written street code suggests not all is well in the magic kingdom.

A couple of Japanese girls, decked out for the day in psychedelic headscarves, Janis Joplin glasses, flares and newly bought beads, giggle as they pass, followed by a couple of towering blokes speaking Dutch. Nimbin is a well-established stop on the backpacker trail.

Buses bring them up for the day from Byron Bay to smoke a bit of dope and snicker at the quaint idealism of their elders. It's like a Gold Coast theme park without the entry fee. I follow the Japanese girls into the Nimbin Museum, a converted shopfront promising '8 rooms of magic'. Inside are the multicoloured flotsam and jetsam of four decades of alternative living, with cut-up Kombi vans and old magazine covers and clothes from the local op shop and a defaced Kevin '07 poster. The rooms follow a rough chronological order. The first is dedicated to the local indigenous people, with a few amateurish paintings of dinosaurs thrown in for good measure. The next room pays half-hearted tribute to the pioneers, the dairy farmers and the cedar getters: 'The first settlement and house was started in 1882. In fifty years the forests were decimated and farming was in full swing.' A sign above the next doorway ushers the visitor into the real heart of the museum, 'And then came the hippies'. There are posters from the original Aquarius Festival, more cut-up Kombis and a poster of the Mona Lisa sucking on a joint. There's an old ad spruiking Dr Poppy's Wonder Elixir, With Cannabis Extract, 2/6 a bottle, and the bust of a policeman with porcine features and blood-soaked tusks. 'Paranoia or Reality?' asks the sign on the bust. There is little coherence to the museum; like the 1970s, it's a colourful mess.

I have lunch in the Nimbin Café. On the wall are flyers advertising houses made of hemp. I wonder what the big bad wolf would make of that. There's another poster, a photograph of a single seven-pointed marijuana leaf. 'Perfection', says the title. There are some old-timers here, sitting around smoking rollies and playing Bob Marley songs on the guitar. 'Bad boys, bad boys, watcha gonna do? Whatcha gonna do when they come for you?' sings a dark-skinned guy in full hippy regalia and a large skull tattooed on his back. It's a little bit of the 1970s, preserved in aspic, or perhaps hash oil. The beards are streaked with grey, teeth yellowing, rheumy eyes sheltering behind prescription lenses in John Lennon frames. I watch as one old bloke assiduously rolls a joint, taking his time to get it just so. He holds it up to the light, revolves his wrist slowly as he admires its form from all sides, then lights it with an old Zippo. He gently draws in the smoke and gently lets it out again. A little sigh of contentment and he passes it to his neighbour. I consider conversation, but I fear I might get the same old response: 'It's coming man. I tell you. The revolution. It's coming.' Let sleeping dogs lie. If there's an economic model here to challenge the Gold Coast, I can't see it through the smoke haze. Time to go.

But I'm not done yet. On the community noticeboard, near the Bob Marley T-shirts, I find something more promising: among the notices advertising guitar lessons, naturopathic massage, tribal-style belly dancing lessons and traditional wisdom treatments is a flier: 'Phil Emmanuel plays Nimbin'. I check the date. Tonight. Phil Emmanuel in a local hall sounds pretty good. So I book into Granny's Farm, down by the river, a short walk from the Bush Theatre, where the guitar hero will be playing.

⌒

I wander over to the venue in the early evening with the sun setting behind me. Nowadays it's called the Bush Theatre, but once upon a time it was a butter factory. It's a beautiful old place, maybe three storeys tall, with rendered brick walls and leadlight windows. It sits in the bush beside the river. I pay my entrance, buy a beer and sit on a log overlooking the river, watching the fruit bats sweep through the crimson sunset and something swimming in the shallows: a platypus perhaps, or a water dragon. A couple of itinerants, an American named Douglas and his English girlfriend Tanya, who are also staying over at Granny's Farm, join me and we discuss the merits of Nimbin. They love it. Not so much the hippy ethos as the landscape. On an evening like this I can appreciate it; there is little in Europe that could match it.

A few power chords ring out from inside, followed by a cascade of reverberating arpeggios. Phil is powering up, and I follow the crowd inside to marvel at the maestro. But Phil, like Nimbin, is a bit of a disappointment: too flashy by half. In quick succession he plays a Bach fugue, the William Tell Overture and the theme from *The Benny Hill Show*. His unintended best comes after his set is finished, when he gets up and jams with local outfit Express, a trio channelling Cream and the Jimi Hendrix Experience. Express gets the crowd pumping, up on its feet, and in the thick air of marijuana smoke, I'm transported back to my youth. When Express cranks it up another notch, turning the Marshalls up to eleven, and it's too loud for those of us who retain most of our hearing, I retreat outside, buy a beer and sit at a trestle table by the glowing coals of a fire. Much better. The music pours out of the open doors, out across the river, up the hill into the town.

I'm joined by a couple of ageing hippies. The woman has auburn hair and is wearing glasses with thick lenses. She's nursing a bandaged hand; she suspects she has been bitten by a red-back spider and is on heavy-duty antibiotics. The man has sparkling blue eyes, a piping laugh and an explosion of hair and beard, all of it so grey as to be bordering on white. We get to talking. The woman is Kali, the man is James. Neither of them is looking too happy, despite the party mood, the music and the ready supply of beer and dope. They exchange shakes of the head and disappointed looks. I ask what's wrong.

'Oh, we've just been to our AGM. It was a bit disappointing.'

'AGM? AGM of what?'

'Our power company.'

'You own a power company?'

'We don't own it. We have shares. We helped found it,' Kali says, using her good arm to point out a poster over on one wall of the old butter factory. 'Solar installation by Rainbow Power Company', says the sign. 'Appropriate Energy Systems.'

'Tough times?' I inquire.

'No. Just the opposite. We're raking it in. It's the government's feed-in tariff. Suddenly, everyone wants solar.'

'And that's a problem?'

'Yeah. We're making too much money.' She sees the quizzical look on my face and explains, 'That's not why we established Rainbow. We went through lots of tough times, people volunteering their services just to keep it going. Now it's all about professionalism and expanding and business plans. They're investing in real estate, of all things. People are thinking too much about the money.'

'Real estate is a Ponzi scheme', interjects James in a quiet voice. 'People say there's a bubble. Well, a bubble is a polite word for a Ponzi scheme. It's the last ones who buy in who are always burnt.'

James and Kali, I discover, are Nimbin originals, present at the Aquarius Festival and founding members of what is arguably Australia's most famous commune: Tuntable Falls. We exchange memories of the Cotter in 1976. I recall music and dope smoking and skinny-dipping. They remember the manifestos and debates and the spirit of change. For me it is the distant past, inhabited by another person bearing my name, a prototypical me; for them it's part of a continuum, of debates and issues that are still very much alive. I ask how the Tuntable Falls commune is faring. Kali says it's faring well, more like a private village than a commune, with 250 inhabitants. She says different authorities treat it in different ways. The school has been operating well for thirty years, but issues surrounding land use and housing persist. She recounts how building inspectors condemned a house, a small, wooden A-frame, because it was sited too close to a neighbouring house. When contractors arrived to demolish it, they found it already gone, with nothing left but the stumps. The communards told them they had pulled down the house and recycled the materials, preferring that to outsiders destroying their creation. But it hadn't been destroyed. Instead, about fifty of them had picked the house up off its stumps and carried it a short distance to a new set of stumps.

I ask how communal the place is, whether it operates as a subsistence cooperative. It doesn't. A few people grow vegies or have chooks, and there are some cows, but most people work outside Tuntable.

'Do you work?' I ask.

'Yes', says James. 'We do some electrical jobs. Kali has just been down to Griffith installing a micro hydro plant, and I've just got back from New York. I was helping with some generators.' It seems that James and Kali are in demand. The skills they developed pioneering alternative energy so they could escape mainstream society and its electricity grid just happen to be the same skills that the electricity grid and mainstream society now desire. They tell me they don't seek out work; they get it through word of mouth. That and the internet. Tuntable Falls is not the isolated place it may once have aspired to be.

Kali says the ideals of the 1970s are under threat, not because ageing hippies are feeling impoverished, just the opposite. 'Property values are going up and there's the temptation to subdivide. It's multiple-occupancy title, but people have their own agreed areas. Now some are making applications for development. Some are getting them, others aren't. People are starting to think about property values.'

'Really?'

'Yes. We're thinking of inviting a few of the town junkies in, just to lower the property values,' says James with a smile.

Kali adds, 'We have a sister commune down near Byron Bay. Right on the coast, beautiful spot. Now it's worth millions, and there are tensions over the way ahead. We came up here to escape the bourgeois lifestyle, and we're ending up middle-class regardless.'

I consider this later as I sit writing my notes in the late-night calm of the verandah at the back of Granny's Farm, my ears still ringing from Phil Emmanuel and Express. I'm glad I met Kali and James—glad the hippy dream endures. In many ways, the hippies were the first greens, back before there were Greens. They rejected capitalism and consumerism and private ownership and championed communalism, sustainability and equality. Somewhere, it all got mixed up with Eastern mysticism, bad hair and worse drugs. In the wide sweep of history, there have been worse movements and uglier ideals. But there's no getting away from globalisation. Back in the 1970s you could band together, buy a bush block for next to nothing and drop off the side of civilisation. It's harder nowadays. Real estate prices, and rates, keep climbing. Now the sea changers and tree changers can move in next door, power up using solar or wind or micro hydro and plug into the world wide web through the new NBN. There's no more running, no more hiding. A revolution is coming, all right, but not the sort that comes from smoking dope, no matter how many bales of the stuff you inhale.

Byron Bay is swamped with people. Another, more low-key schoolies week is underway. It feels different from Surfers Paradise. For a start, the adult population hasn't been sent scurrying for cover—it's still here, shopping in the main street, swimming at the beach, sitting in the cafés drinking lattes and reading the capital-city broadsheets. The morning is clear and warm, and the main beach is crowded with listless youth, the density highest where the sands abut the town centre. I drive a short way south and park the car at the southern tip of the main beach where it curls into the beginning of Cape Byron. There are plenty of young people hanging about, but judging by the accents, they're backpackers, not schoolies. I wander down a short track to the end of the beach and across the sand to a large outcrop of rock on the point: Fisherman's Lookout. The council has built a wooden platform here, and I climb the stairs to take in the view. It's summer-hot, effacing the greyness of Surfers, and waves are rolling in, blue crystal tubes cresting alongside the point. Below the platform, dozens of surfers, from young kids on boogie boards to retirees on malibus, patiently queue for waves. A sign tells me this is a favoured place to view dolphins and migrating whales, but there are no cetaceans disporting themselves today. The view is exhilarating all the same. Looking north along kilometres of beach, beyond the surfers, the town is largely hidden from view. There is the blue of the water, the white of the sand, the green of the dunes and the darker blue of the coastal ranges. On the sand, children play with buckets and spades and splash in the shallows.

It's hard to imagine it now, but Byron Bay was once an industrial town, built on a foundation of killing things and extracting wealth from nature. Timber, dairy, meatworks, sand mining and whaling. It was said that the town stank: stank of the abattoirs, stank of the dairy, stank of the whale works. Whaling here was not some nineteenth-century relic. The Byron Whaling Company operated from 1954 to 1962, harpooning humpbacks as they passed the cape in their annual winter migration north. At first, there were so many whales that the rendering works couldn't cope. Less than a decade later, numbers

141

had declined to such a degree as to make the industry unviable. The 'extractive' industries are gone now. The cedar getters ran out of cedar, the whalers ran out whales and the sand miners ran out of support. The butter factory moved to Lismore, while the meatworks closed in 1983. Byron Bay was left to live off the richest resource remaining: stunning natural beauty. The surfers were the first of the new breed to discover it, revelling in the break below me, with a sea breeze to quarantine them from the death smells of the abattoirs. Soon after, the hippies and the new agers, travelling north for the Aquarius Festival, thought they'd found their own piece of nirvana, and Byron Bay began to morph into an alternative-lifestyle mecca. By the 1980s a plummeting Australian dollar, the rise of backpacker tourism and the town's laid-back ethos put it firmly on the backpacker route heading north up the coast from Sydney to Cairns.

I keep walking south, along a rainforest path, across a small headland and down onto Wategos Beach. It's a beautiful beach, modest in length, north-facing and cradled by headlands at both ends. The sand is broad and white, the waves clear and cylindrical. I'm not the first to appreciate it. Dotting the rise above the beach sit the multimillion dollar houses of the wealthy. Byron is different from the Gold Coast, but the pressures are the same: too many people, too much money, too little space. Here, though, the alternative residents have not packed up their teepees and surfboards. Their numbers are large enough to guarantee a solid bloc on the local council, and so the worst excesses of development have been stemmed. Famously, locals overturned a development application for a Club Med resort back in the 1990s. There is no high-rise and, to this day, McDonald's and KFC have been prevented from opening franchises. Yet the pressure is constant.

The federal government is busily laying the National Broadband Network, fibre-optic cables to carry the information revolution into the homes and businesses of 93 per cent of the population. The political argument revolves around cost and need and the benefit to the economy as a whole. The most significant impact is likely to be felt in places like Byron Bay and other attractive non-metropolitan regions of Australia. Services, including education, tourism and finance, which make up some 70 per cent of our economy, will be delivered remotely. I continue along Wanegos Beach, past three young girls sprawled on beach towels. The three girls aren't talking to each other, each engrossed in her smart phone. Connected.

I head up the path as it continues away from the beach towards the Cape Byron lighthouse, on the most easterly promontory of the Australian mainland. Paved with concrete bricks to prevent erosion, it's a well-maintained path. And it needs to be. I pass families and couples and groups of young people, speaking Japanese, Spanish and German. It's not at all overcrowded, but I wonder what it must be like in summer when the holiday crowds arrive. I come to a path leading to a lookout. I wonder if this is it: the most easterly point. I turn to follow the track, but I'm distracted by a pretty girl in a bikini, miss my step and go over on my ankle. The pain is sharp and immediate, and I collapse onto the ground.

'Are you okay?' asks the girl, her accent from the English Midlands.

'Sure', I lie, rubbing the ankle, already rueing my decision to wear thongs. The girl moves on, and I stand, rearrange my camera, water and backpack, and hobble on. The pain isn't diminishing, but I push on to the lookout, figuring it a better place to rest than on the path. It is not the most easterly point, and there are no seats. So I stand on one leg, stork-like, trying to enjoy the view and wishing the pain away. A couple from Dubai—an Australian guy and his Russian girlfriend, both in their twenties—walk down and join me. They either don't notice my strange stance or are too polite to inquire. They tell me Dubai is over, and they're on the lookout for the next big thing, somewhere where they can make serious money. They ask my advice.

'China', I suggest, but the guy demurs. He wants the boom, but wants something more laid-back. 'Byron Bay?' I ask.

'No. Dubai is going to shit, but it's still tax-free. There are too many regulations here, too much tax.'

I think of the hippies, suddenly wealthy without trying to be. The couple leave me and head off on their quest for easy wealth. I don't like their chances, not if they're asking advice from the likes of me, hobbling along with a twisted ankle, wondering how to get back to my 14-year-old Hyundai and whether I'll be able to drive it when I do. I take a breather beside a sign that congratulates me on my efforts. It says walking is a cheaper, healthier and environmentally responsible way to go, that driving releases between 200 and 450 grams of greenhouse gas per kilometre, while walking generates none. Which is probably right, provided you don't breathe. But I'm breathing heavily, and sweating, and by the time I get up to the lighthouse, my ankle has given up on me and is abusing me for my pig-headedness and general stupidity. One reason I wanted to come here is because it is another place we stopped off on our family holiday back in the 1960s. I don't remember details, just that it was the most easterly point, and the unassailable whiteness of the lighthouse. The view up and down the coast is something: Cape Byron's natural elevation its response to Q1. Another sign informs me the Pacific bottlenose dolphin is commonly seen from this point. I scan the waves, but I see no dolphins, just a couple of bulk coal carriers heading north from Newcastle.

Next day, my ankle is still voicing its complaints, but I push on. There is something I want to see. This time I drive north, parallel with the main beach. I take the car as far as I can, then get out and hobble down between the dunes. It's called Belongil Beach, although it's really an extension of the main beach. I've come at a good time. It's early afternoon and the tide is almost at its height. The waves are gentle today, but they still wash across the beach and up against the dark boulders and white sandbags protecting the land above. In no time, the sand is completely submerged and I'm wading. The water feels good, cool on my glowering ankle. It would be a very different story if the tide were any higher, or the waves any stronger. And if there were a king tide and a storm, then the sandbags and the boulders would struggle to restrain the power of the Pacific. The waves would carve into the land behind the beach, undercutting dunes laid down decades ago, and undermining the millionaires' houses that sit above the sea. It's already happened several times, most recently in 2009, when many metres of land were lost to the ocean, sending residents scrambling to shore up their properties. I realise I'm wading through a battlefield, out in no man's land, between the advancing army of waves and the defensive line of sandbags, rock walls and concrete fortifications.

Painfully, I scramble out of the water and up some stairs to a guesthouse, Beaumont's Beach House. The views are stunning, the edge of the property precipitous. Inside, I catch the owner, Margaret, just as she's about to go out. I ask her about the erosion of her property. She says she can live with the sea, its comings and goings; it's the council she finds outrageous. She says it wants residents to take down their protective walls. 'Outrageous', she repeats. She tells me she has to go, but that I should call her neighbour, John Vaughan, who can explain the ongoing drama.

When I eventually get onto John by phone, he's just walked in the door from New York. Nevertheless, he's more than happy to give me his version of the battle of Belongil Beach. John reckons that beach erosion first became a major issue back in the early 1970s, when a series of La Niña years swept sand out to sea and threatened houses. Residents responded by building ad hoc protective works, including rock walls. He says of the 150 residents along the beach, thirty-three have beach frontage; of those, thirty-two are protected by rock works, his own place the sole exception. In the ensuing decades, more benign weather saw the beach rebuild itself and efforts to protect it lost their urgency. In 2001, the council filled in some of the gaps with interim measures while they prepared a coastline management plan. Two-tonne, sand-filled geo-textile bags were put in place to protect John's property, as well as council land.

When in 2009 severe storms again carved away the beach, threatened properties and inflicted considerable damage on the protective structures, residents asked the council to repair the damage, but the council refused. It had moved to a policy of letting nature take its course, developing a coastal plan that stipulated that the 2001 measures should not be repaired. John says council was moving towards a position that all protective structures, including the rock walls built as long ago as the 1970s, should be removed. He says that when residents started repairs themselves, the council took them to court. A protracted case followed, costing millions. The residents' legal costs were met in part by their insurance companies.

'Well, the court case ran its course and finally ruled that the residents—namely myself and a couple of others—did have the right to rebuild [the 2001 works] because they were approved works', says John. 'Those works have been repaired and council has subsequently repaired, to a certain standard, their own to try and bring them up to the standard of 2001 consent.'

The residents may have won the battle, but the war is ongoing. John believes the council still wants to remove the protective works and abandon the houses to their fate. 'Their coastal management plan had *retreat* in it and all of these structures were meant to be pulled down', he says. 'While the case was being heard, the council abandoned its coastal management plan. There is now no plan, so they've got to start the process again.'

John accuses the council of hypocrisy, because while its plan called for retreat along Belongil Beach, it also called for the maintenance of existing protective structures that prevent erosion on the main beach opposite the town centre. 'It's not a natural process here at Belongil Beach. There's a big structure by the swimming pool, 1.2 hectares of man-made retained headland. There's a series of groynes and a rock wall that wasn't there in 1880 or 1890. It completely stabilises the main beach, which in turn deprives us at critical times of sand nourishment.'

John explains that the localised effects at Byron Bay can be explained by a much larger regional phenomenon: strong north-flowing currents that carry sand from northern New South Wales and deposit it on Moreton, Stradbroke and Fraser islands, the largest sand-island system in the world. He says every grain of sand on those islands has been carried past Byron Bay and that this massive transport system affects practically every beach over a 300-kilometre stretch of coastline. Beach stabilisation in one area can deprive a beach further north of sand. He points to the Gold Coast, where sand dredging and pumping, so-called 'beach nourishment', is actively pursued, as it is north of Brisbane at Noosa. He tells me that the rock walls protecting the mouth of the Tweed River, the ones I saw from

Greenmount headland, deprive the beach at Coolangatta of sand, and so it is pumped north instead under an inter-state agreement that costs millions a year.

There's another case, one John doesn't mention. In the 1970s there was a small village called Sheltering Palms near Brunswick Heads, about twelve kilometres north of Byron Bay. Cyclone Pam ripped away a large section of the shoreline in 1974, breaching the dune system and allowing seawater to penetrate into the low-lying land behind the houses. Within three years the settlement had been lost to the sea, with the government buying out residents. Suddenly I appreciate why the insurance companies backed the residents of Belongil Beach. Imagine the tangle of liability and litigation should councils start endorsing private property being dragged out to sea.

⌒

King Canute, legend has it, attempted to hold back the sea, commanding the incoming tide to desist. The tide paid no attention and the royal feet got wet. Canute was the King of Denmark, Norway, England and of bits of Sweden. His name is more accurately transcribed as Cnut, son of Sweyn Forkbeard. They had good solid names in those days. There are two versions of the story; both are almost certainly apocryphal. In the first version, an arrogant Cnut commands the sea to withdraw. When it does not, he realises the error of his ways and, falling to his knees, acknowledges that only Jesus, the King of Kings, has the power to command nature. The second version has a pious Cnut commanding the sea to desist, knowing full well that it will not, as a demonstration to his sycophantic courtiers that his powers should not be compared to the Almighty's. In both versions, attempting to hold back the sea is shown as folly. The Cnut story, which emerged in the twelfth century, may have drawn on older tales and legends. There's a nice one concerning the sixth-century Welsh Saint Illtyd. He was supposedly the son of Bican Farchog, which can't have been much fun. According to legend, Illtyd lived in a bounteous valley by the sea, but the tides kept invading the land. Three times he built a dyke to keep back the waves, and three times the waves broke through the dyke. Illtyd was about to quit the land when he was visited by an angel in a dream; the angel instructed him to drive the sea back with his staff, invoking the power of God. The next day, Illtyd did as he'd been instructed, and the sea dutifully retreated. Illtyd then struck the ground with his staff, and a spring of fresh water emerged on the shore where the sea had withdrawn. The sea never again invaded the land and Illtyd and his followers remained, living happily ever after in the valley. Saint Illtyd: patron saint of property developers.

⌒

Byron Shire Council is located in Mullumbimby, 20 kilometres from Byron Bay. I drive up to hear the council's side of the story. Mullumbimby is a pretty river town, sitting a winding 10 kilometres upstream from Brunswick Heads. There is little traffic as I drive in, pass a large construction site, and turn into the council. I find Ray Darney, not a councillor, but the Executive Manager for the Environment and Planning. The man in the hot seat. Except he doesn't seem to be suffering too much heat. He invites me into his office, happy to discuss the battle for Belongil Beach.

I get straight to the point, asking whether the council believes the protective rock walls on Belongil Beach should be removed altogether. 'We haven't said that outright, but what we are trying to do is to keep the beach in a natural environment rather than a protected environment. As sea levels rise and storms increase, quite often, at high tide, you can't use the beach at all. Whereas in a natural environment, the sand and dunes recede and you still have a beach. That's the problem at Belongil—you are protecting private assets to the loss of the beach environment.'

Ray believes the situation at Belongil can only get worse. The council accepts rising sea levels are a fact of life, a fact that needs to be incorporated in its planning and its building codes. It bases these on federal government projections that the sea level will rise 0.5 metres by 2050 and 0.9 metres by 2100. So any new developments must be above the 2100 line. This affects a larger area than might be imagined—not just areas directly adjacent to the sea, but any land that adjoins tidal estuaries. The land on Byron's coastal strip is flat, so there is the potential for rising sea levels, high tides, floods and storm surges to combine and cause widespread inundation. Even Mullumbimby, 10 kilometres up the river from Brunswick Heads, is potentially affected. And Ray says Belongil is certain to be affected.

He shows me a map of the beach and points out a road called The Esplanade, which used to run between the houses and the beach before it was washed away by the sea in the mid-1970s. He also shows me how the beach backs onto Belongil Creek, and that a combination of sea-level rise and floodwater would see the houses attacked from all sides. 'When you add sea-level rise and flood modelling from the Belongil Creek, there is practically nothing there in fifty years. There's a double jeopardy with the pressure from the ocean and sea-level rise up the mouth of the creek. Probably the only way you could really protect it would be to rock line the whole creek and its frontage. Make it like one of those American islands,' he says.

Rock walls and beach nourishment are a fact of life up and down the east coast. I ask why Byron should be any different. Ray says the council reflects the beliefs of the local community, which is overall more pro-environment and more anti-development than in many other shires. 'We emphasise environmental issues, the retention of our green areas and landscapes. If you compare us to the Gold Coast, that southeastern corner of Queensland is projected to have an extra two million people during the next twenty years. This area is more reluctant to develop in that style,' he says. 'The population of the shire is about 34 000 now. We see that growing by about one per cent a year.'

The council has blocked Club Med, KFC and McDonald's opening franchises in Byron Bay. Ray asks if I noticed the construction site across the road from the council offices. He tells me it's a new Woolworths, being erected against the wishes of many locals and without the approval of the council. 'Woolworths was approved by state government, not by Byron Council. Since it started building there, there's been a fair bit of local angst. There are letters in the paper saying Woolworths shouldn't be here, it's not what they want to see in Mullumbimby.'

And if Woolworths is coming to Mullumbimby, then McDonald's may soon be erecting its golden arches over Byron Bay. The council's planning powers are being emasculated by the state government. Large-scale developments, like the Mullumbimby supermarket, can be approved by regional planning panels appointed by the state government. At the same time, Sydney has 'streamlined' planning provisions, removing the distinction between takeaway food outlets and restaurants, and removing references to drive-through takeaway. It's these provisions the council has used in the past to block McDonald's and KFC.

'I expect if we were to continue down the path of trying to protect what is near and dear to us, it will cost us a lot of money in court', Ray says. 'The government, in my opinion, haven't allowed for enough diversity in the new planning documents. I believe the planning provisions are going to be more strictly dominated by the state government, and the difference between Byron Bay and other towns won't be as easily discerned in the future.'

Labor has come full circle. It started its sixteen years in government using its powers to overrule local councils to prevent overdevelopment, and to protect the coastline. Now it's imposing development even where local people don't want it. It's the same old story: a tired government, weakened by flagging popularity, falling prey to the lobbyists, cutting desperate deals to shore up waning support. Labor's time in government is coming to an end, but a new Liberal government is hardly going to be anti-development. As Bill Clinton put it: 'It's the economy, stupid.'

⁓

I find the beach by mistake. Driving south from Byron Bay, a false memory lures me from the highway. I turn off towards Iluka, mistakenly thinking it's a place I hitchhiked to as a teenager. The town is not what I was thinking, sitting quietly across the river from Yamba. I eat an early lunch, some forgettable fish and chips, and head back towards the highway. Leaving town, I realise I must be close to the ocean. Sure enough, when I pull over and cut the engine, I can hear the surf pounding its persistent rhythm from behind a wall of sand-dune scrub. A short path leads me to the beach, and what a beach it is: long and broad, with fine white sand squeaking underfoot. My ankle states its muted complaint, but I'm not listening. I'm captivated. It's called Ten Mile Beach and seems even longer, stretching hazily into the distance, not straight, but a long, perfectly curved crescent, a 16-kilometre parabola, backed the entire distance by the low, green scrub of Bundjalung National Park. And on this day, I have it all to myself. It's just gone noon, but there is no other human being in sight. There are tyre marks, perhaps left by a fisherman too lazy to walk, and a volleyball court painstakingly marked out by clumps of kelp. But these indications of humanity only emphasise my solitude. I love it. The waves here are consistent, not squabbling and crossing each other as they do on the straight-line beaches of Surfers Paradise. Here, accommodated by the mathematical curvature of the beach, they approach with well-ordered regularity, building and curling over into cylinders many hundreds of metres long, crashing in synchronised thunder. I change into my swimmers, half run, half hop, ankle indignant, into the sea and plunge into the waves, diving under the storming foam, then under the curling lips, until I'm far enough out to turn to face the sand, attentive to the waves and their regular beat. I time my swim to a wave's advance, gather pace, launch myself forward just as the wave peaks, stretch out my arms, hold my breath and feel the power of the swell lift me. The tip of the wave comes over my head as it takes all of my weight, carries me hurtling towards the beach, before depositing me gently in the shallows, energy spent. I do it again. And again, and again. It's too good to stop. I'm not sure of all the mechanics of bodysurfing, but the variables must be many and unpredictable. Waves can look impressive, but lack power; they can look gentle, but pitch you forward into the bottom. These waves look as if they might dump you, the way they curl into tubes before breaking, but they're perfect, simultaneously smooth and powerful, every one a winner. I bodysurf until I need a rest, then swim out the back and float until I'm ready for another bout. It's at least an hour before I emerge and lie exhausted on the sand. Still I have the place to myself. Where is everyone? Are they really all at the Gold Coast and Byron Bay? Above me, there are a few wisps of white cloud, high and thin, way up in the stratosphere as if spray-painted on heaven's dome.

I consider this beach, and the currents that sweep past it, transporting a gazillion tonnes of sand north each year to deposit on Stradbroke, Fraser and Moreton islands. Does this beach, Ten Mile Beach, advance and retreat? Do its well-vegetated dunes surrender themselves in the face of storms, then creep back seawards during more clement weather? I guess they do, I guess it must. But with no human boundaries, no residential blocks, there is little to measure the movement. There are no groynes here, no breakwaters, no seawalls. Instead, the beach seems timeless. Yet all up and down the east coast of Australia, harbours have been carved, waterfronts developed, mangroves removed. I wonder what will happen if and when the sea levels rise, if and when the storms become more frequent and more violent, if and when more and more people move to coastal strips. Who will decide what is protected and what is surrendered? And does protecting one section of beach necessarily come at the detriment of some other, less-populated section of beach? Will this beach, so perfect in its curve, fall victim to some rearguard action being fought over the horizon to the south? Is that what Belongil really represents, an intertidal zone where the land is not so universally prized as to be automatically protected, but not so universally disregarded as to be automatically surrendered?

But the sun is warm. I begin to doze. In my stupor, an image of the Gold Coast comes to me, a massive engine, its furnace fed by shovel loads of money, with huge dredging machines pumping sand out onto the beaches, and huge marketing machines pumping out tourists to lie on them. I hope the dredges don't get the sand from Ten Mile Beach, and I hope the marketers don't suck me in either. I like it here, lying with my eyes closed, listening to the waves crashing with studied regularity.

⌒

I sit beside the Overseas Passenger Terminal at Circular Quay and contemplate the Sydney Opera House, this country's most famous building. It sits serene, white sails floating above the water, aloof from the bustle of the city, oblivious to the thrumming traffic of the Harbour Bridge. A flower, I decide, with the ferries buzzing around it like bees. Australians may not care much for opera, but they revere this building. It's such an original and striking piece of architecture that it would be special anywhere; sit it at the top of Martin Place, in among the city skyscrapers, and it would still be a standout. And yet its location is special: historically, as it sits upon Bennelong Point, overlooking the site of European settlement; symbolically too, as it sits directly on the waterline, where the land meets the sea. For Australians, this juncture between the elements seems to hold a special attraction. There are some 22 million of us; almost 19 million live on or near the coast. Eleven of the twelve largest cities are on the coast, with Canberra the only exception. Governments have tried to populate the interior, pouring money into the capital, into Albury-Wodonga, into Bathurst-Orange, but most of us prefer the coast. Mining companies, flush with money to tempt workers from the seashore, still need to fly in and fly out workers from the coast. The bush may loom large in national sentiment and our sense of identity, but the beach rivals it on both counts and trumps it on lifestyle and amenity.

I walk around Circular Quay, threading my way through milling tourists and buskers, acrobats and mime artists, past the ferry terminal and beneath the railway station, up into the city. Here I find the Museum of Sydney, a new building constructed upon the bones of Sydney's original government house. The museum displays various artefacts from the early days of settlement and explains how the soldiers, convicts and free settlers struggled to survive and prosper. But there's nothing here explaining a special affinity for water, a love for the beach or a national obsession with water views. I'm about to leave the museum when I notice a prominently displayed reproduction of a famous poster, an image so familiar that I almost overlook it. It is from the opening in 1932 of that other iconic Australian construction, the Sydney Harbour Bridge. It's a poster many Sydneysiders would be familiar with, reproduced regularly in newspapers to mark anniversaries of the opening. The bridge itself is in the background, a pastel silhouette against a summer sky. The foreground is dominated by a surf lifesaver wearing a red neck-to-knee bathing suit; he's bronzed, muscular, glowing with health. He stands proud and confident. In one hand he holds the staff of a billowing Australian flag, while his other arm is spread in a welcoming gesture, inviting the viewer to join a seated couple, also wearing swimming costumes, who have apparently come to witness the great event. It's an intriguing image, given the bridge is located nowhere near a surf beach. Yet it is a surf lifesaver that has been chosen to represent a young and vital nation, who holds erect the national flag. Not a bushman, nor an Anzac, nor an idealised construction worker. A lifesaver. But why? How did this come to pass?

In the years before Federation in 1901, the quintessential Australian was depicted as a bushman: independent, loyal to his mates, a pioneer carving a new country from the wilderness. It was a stereotype incorporated into the Anzac legend, where the light horsemen were the elite, soldiers from the bush, somehow superior to the men of the coast and the suburbs. *The Bulletin*, fiercely republican, idealised the bush and the bushman, seeing in him the foundations of a national character different and better than his English forebears. Writing in the magazine in 1889, Banjo Paterson was dismissive of the ocean, looking instead to the bush as the shaper of a new nation in his 'Song of the Future':

> We cannot love the restless sea,
> That rolls and tosses to and fro
> Like some fierce creature in its glee;
> For human weal or human woe
> It has no touch of sympathy.
>
> For us the bush is never sad:
> Its myriad voices whisper low,
> In tones the bushmen only know
> Its sympathy and welcome glad.

I leave the Museum of Sydney and head up the hill to the State Library, looking for answers. How is it that in 1901, the beach and the surf were absent from our national identity, yet by 1932 the lifesaver trumps the bushman and the Anzac? I already know part of the answer. Council by-laws prohibited bathing at city beaches throughout the colonies between the hours of six in the morning and eight at night. At Federation, the beach lifesaver did not yet exist. Then in 1902, the publisher of a Manly newspaper, WH Grocher, took on the authorities, wading into the sea (apparently he had never learnt to swim) on three successive Sundays, challenging the police to arrest him. On the third occasion, watched by thousands, the constabulary obliged and detained him. But according to Grocher, the Inspector-General of Police met him the next day with 'merriment', informing the publisher that no magistrate would convict him, and that police would not be making any more arrests, provided men wore neck-to-knee costumes and that women 'did not expose their breasts'. Next year, Manly Council repealed its ineffective by-law. Sea bathing, as it was known, quickly experienced a boom in popularity, as Australians increasingly headed to the beach to escape the heat and fetid air of the cities.

That still doesn't explain why a lifesaver should become such a symbol of nationhood. The bridge opened in early 1932; Don Bradman was at the very height of his powers, so why not a cricketer? Phar Lap was in America, set to conquer the world, so why not a jockey? Charles Kingsford Smith was breaking aviation records, so why not a pilot? At the library, I can find no trace of Grocher's editorials. Instead, I read Manning Clark's 1979 lecture 'The Quest for an Australian Identity', but the celebrated historian barely mentions the beach. I plumb his six-volume *A History of Australia*; the beach is described as the scene of struggle between swimmers and sunbakers on one side and those railing against the morals of mixed bathing on the other, but there is nothing about national identity. Bradman rates numerous mentions, Boy Charlton none. I search Geoffrey Blainey's *A Shorter History of Australia*, and Start Macintyre's *A Concise History of Australia*, and still I am none the wiser.

It's left to a thinner, less celebrated work, *Sand in our Souls: The Beach in Australian History*, published in 1991, to go some way to explain the importance of the beach to our national identity and the elevation of the surf lifesaver to hero status. Its author, Leone Huntsman, explains that swimming was popular from the earliest days of settlement, that the local Aboriginal people were great swimmers and divers, and that the soldiers, convicts and free settlers were quick to follow their example. But by the late nineteenth century, Victorian prudery was at its height and swimming in public was outlawed. Manly was developed as a resort, but only for the properly attired. Swimming was confined to pools hidden from view behind fences and walls, either in the harbour or at rock pools like those found at Bondi and Coogee. Inside the pools, bathing was segregated: men only, with certain times set aside for women. Those who dared swim at beaches risked arrest, with the police becoming increasingly zealous.

After Grocher challenged the prohibition at Manly, bathing became popular, but beachgoers were still not at liberty in the first decade of the new country. Men and women were not meant to mix in the surf, a practice euphemistically referred to as 'continental bathing', while sunbaking was still prohibited outside fenced-off, segregated enclosures. Bathers were required to proceed directly from changing sheds to water and back again, or to wear a gown or mackintosh. This is much the same scenario that Manning Clark refers to: swimmers pushing for greater liberty, moralists pushing back. Huntsman observes that lifesavers, required to dash into the surf at a moment's notice to rescue the drowning, were exempt from the mackintosh rule. I imagine they became the envy of many a harassed, raincoat-wearing swimmer. At the same time, suntans were becoming popular, a sign of health and vigour and, just possibly, a symbol of rebellious youth. Perhaps by 1932, the lifesaver was seen not only as a hero for rescuing the drowning, but as a symbol of progress, of a new country that had thrown off the dead weight of Victorian prudery and English colonialism, a sign that there was something modern and progressive about swimming at the beach.

As the popularity of the beaches grew and grew through the 1920s, the pleasure of swimming and sunbaking coincided with a new ideal: that of physical perfection and, Huntsman suggests, racial purity. Perhaps this is the key I've been looking for; I start joining the dots. Australia was a new country and Australians were to be a new race, albeit a white one. It was a sign of our youth, our vigour and our independence: the English were notoriously either poor swimmers or not swimmers at all. Australia was not alone in this pursuit of physical fitness. Darwin's theory of evolution had seized the imagination of political leaders, with many subscribing to the pseudo-science of eugenics; physical health was seen as reflecting mental and moral superiority, just as it had once done in ancient Greece. The martial callisthenics of Aryan youth captured in Nazi propaganda films were not so very different from the militaristic marching of Australian surf carnivals of the day. The differences are many and obvious, but the admiration and desire for physical perfection and regimentation are strikingly similar. Australians began to believe in our physical superiority: our soldiers on the Western Front had been fitter, stronger, a better calibre of men; our sportsmen and women were stronger and more successful; our society healthier than that of the pallid, damp cities of England. And on the beach, everyone could share in this national myth making. For it combined with another emerging myth, also developed in contrast with the old country, that Australia was a classless society. If this was never actually the case, then at the beach it came closest to reality, where the accoutrements and posturing of quotidian life were stripped bare, and the well-chiselled body of a young factory worker could put that of a middle-class lawyer to shame. Beach gymnastics, body building and the high dive became the vogue, Australian swimmers began winning Olympic medals and swimmer Annette Kellerman became not only a Hollywood star but, according to a Harvard professor, the embodiment of a perfect woman. The photographs of Max Dupain and the art of Charles Meere celebrated the physicality of the beach.

I think that is why the Sydney Harbour Bridge poster features a lifesaver and not a bushman: by 1932 the lifesaver represented the future, the bushman the past. The lifesaver on the poster inviting the citizenry to join in the opening celebration for the bridge is also inviting them to join in the future. The mythology of the beach had been established as an integral part of the national identity.

The walls of the Manly Life Saving Club are thick with memories, coated with photographs, plaques and honour boards, every available centimetre plastered with history. Here are framed photos of the club's greats: Harold Hardwick, Olympic swimmer and winner of gold medals, on successive days, for swimming and heavy-weight boxing at the 1911 Empire Games; Andrew 'Boy' Charlton, triple Olympian and winner of the 1500-metres gold medal at the 1924 Paris Olympics; and Noel 'Tiger' Ryan, acknowledged by the Americans in 1931 as the most outstanding athlete in all of Australasia. Here also are the modern-day ironmen like Guy Leech and Craig Riddington. There is a huge wooden surfboard encased in protective glass, with many dozens of names in gilt, acknowledging club members who served in World War II, discreet asterisks noting those who died. There are other honour rolls: the club's twenty-two Olympians, the winners of the club championship races stretching back into the 1920s. Three brass plaques, tarnished by verdigris in the sea air, commemorate three lifesavers who died while on patrol, attempting rescues or competing for the club. It's a strange mix: the clubrooms are modest and functional, but their walls are like a shrine.

Behind closed doors, the back rooms of the club are packed to the roof with even more memorabilia: display cases are strewn with medals; surfboards and surf skis of wood and fibreglass are stacked to the ceiling. There are photographs, blazers, surfing magazines, swimming costumes, lifesaving equipment and a trophy case cram-packed with silverware going back more than a century. It's a well-ordered mess of memories. Showing me through the jumble of history is club member and unofficial historian Ray Moran. He says the club wants to build a proper museum open to the public, but for the moment the priorities are storage, preservation and cataloguing.

Ray explains Manly figured large at the beginning of both surf lifesaving and surfboard riding in Australia, back in the first decade of the twentieth century. Ray says board riding came to Manly within years of legalised bathing; a local named Tommy Walker bought a wooden surfboard for $2 in Waikiki in 1909 and brought it back home. But it was a series of surfing exhibitions by Hawaiian Duke Kahanamoku in 1914 and 1915 that planted surfing firmly in the Australian imagination. At first, the boards were used as lifesaving tools and for inter-club races, but increasingly there were those who simply liked riding them, standing upright for the thrill. Ray explains the distinction between the Life Saving Club, established in 1911, and the club it grew out of: the Manly Surf Club. Ray says the surf club is more of a swimmers' club, a 'gentlemen's club', rather than being involved in beach patrols and lifesaving. From the early days, it seems there was a division between the well-drilled and disciplined lifesavers and those who were more interested in simply enjoying the surf.

Ray's own story is instructive. He grew up at Yamba on the Clarence River in the 1940s and 50s. His father tied a rope round his waist, threw him off the wharf and dragged him along until he could swim. He joined the Yamba Surf Club and began surfing.

'I got my first board in 1957 or 1958. I found one under the club in Yamba. It was a barber-pole board, black and white striped. No one knew who owned it, so I started surfing on that, on a toothpick, as they were called. They were narrow and long, built for racing and competition, for speed, not for steering. We didn't have cars, so we didn't carry boards from beach to beach. They were too heavy. We just left them at the surf club. About twelve months later, we got some money together and some of the boys got balsa boards. They weighed 30 pounds and they cost 30 pounds.

'Then we got cars, and then the music started, and we all started on the move. A lot of guys left the surf clubs and we went up and down the coast looking for waves. I was amongst the first group of guys to start doing that sort of thing. It was fun times. We lived on hamburgers and god knows what. We lived in the back of cars and the front of cars, from beach to beach. It really started to kick along from about '58.

'It was an alternative lifestyle. It was the start of long hair. We spent hours trying to bleach our hair. It was blond to start with and we used to get in the first-aid room and use the peroxide. We had Ajax cleaner in the kitchen of the surf club, so we used to wash our hair in Ajax just to get bleached hair. The lemon-drop kids. We had lemon juice in it. All the things that you try when you're sixteen years old.

'We had our own bands, Johnny O'Keefe and the Deltones and Little Patty, we had our own sort of style. When we went up the coast, we could stay at the surf clubs. All the clubs still had beds in them, so we had free accommodation, which was pretty handy, and a kitchen to cook your food. So we'd go to Queensland, we'd go to Currumbin and they'd come down to New South Wales. If someone passed you with boards on the car, you'd know them, where they were from. You'd have been drinking with them or surfed with them somewhere along the coastline.'

As the 1960s unfolded, boards got smaller and riders started leaving the surf clubs, forming new board-riding clubs, or simply striking out on their own. Ray moved to Sydney in 1964 and joined the Manly Pacific Board Riders. Similar clubs were opening all along Sydney's beaches, with skills tested in inter-club competitions. Surf magazines started appearing. The first world surfing championship was held at Manly in 1964. An estimated 60 000 people turned up to watch Midget Farrelly from nearby Dee Why win the crown ahead of the more-favoured Americans. Board riding was no longer the preserve of the beachside cognoscenti; it had entered the consciousness of the wider public. Boards grew lighter, cheaper, more manoeuvrable. Competitive surfers remained club members, but surfing increasingly became an individual pursuit. As the 1960s folded into the 1970s, surfing became associated with hippiedom, drug-taking and the counterculture. The contrast with the well-drilled pre-war lifesaver, marching behind the flag, couldn't have been starker.

Ray was never a member of the counterculture, remaining a member of both the lifesaving club and the board-riding club. Membership of lifesaving clubs was onerous: new members were required to patrol the beaches for the first ten years of membership. Ray was lucky; he'd already done five years of patrols before moving to Sydney. After his ten years he was on 'active reserve', and free to surf where and when he could. Nevertheless, the lifesaving clubs remain popular even today. Manly has plenty of members, and parents like to join their kids up to the 'nippers'.

I ask Ray if the clubs reflect the multicultural nature of modern Australia, or whether the stereotype of the blond-haired, blue-eyed, bronzed Aussie endures. He reckons the latter. 'You go to a surf carnival and it's fairly Australian. It's probably the only sport event that I know of like that, when you go to a surf carnival and they're all original Aussies, maybe with a few Poms thrown in. The white Anglo-Saxon sort of thing. There are few exceptions. Board riding is a bit different, [with a] more international feel to it, whereas surf clubs are still mainly [white] Australians.'

As we talk surrounded by a century of surfing paraphenelia, an old mate of Ray's drops in: Ian 'Wally' Wallace. Wally is seventy now, looking a bit woolly round the edges, thanks to a perfunctory and haphazard approach to shaving. In his day, Wally was a big-wave pioneer, surfing Hawaii in the early 1960s and travelling to Peru. His eyes sparkle water-blue as he recalls his glory days, when he'd buy surf magazines to see if he was in them. As often as not, he was. Wally doesn't surf anymore, but swims every day; says he hasn't missed a day in twenty-three years. Ray still surfs everyday; he's heading up to the Central Coast tomorrow. I ask them what appeal the sea holds for them, these two ageing men who appear strangely young when they speak of it. Wally smiles fondly. It must have been a cheeky grin in his youth. 'Oh, the girls on the beach, the sun, the sand between your toes. You go out and crack a few waves, come up and lie on the sand, talk about the wave you caught. Stuff like that,' he says.

'I don't know', says Ray. 'I think once it's in your blood, it's there for good. I have that attraction to water. I'll never give up swimming or surfing. Even when I'm on my knees, I'll be doing it. I've lived by the water, by the river and the sea. I bought my house in Manly to be by the sea before everybody wanted to live here. It's my way of life. There's been no sea change for me: it's been my life since the 1950s.

⌣⌐

I venture by train to Cronulla, 35 kilometres south of the Sydney CBD, the city's only beach accessible by train. I once met a German in Berlin, a huge man, easily two metres tall, who told me he had learnt to surf at Cronulla. He'd rented a flat in Kings Cross, but his malibu longboard was too large to fit into a taxi, so instead of nearby Bondi he had taken the train every day to far-off Cronulla. It had been an embarrassing experience. At his first day of surf lessons, he'd been put in a class of seven- and eight-year-olds, with a sixteen-year-old as an instructor. To make matters worse, most of the kids were better than him. He persisted, but by the end of his first day, his chest had been rubbed raw by the sand embedded in his waxed board. Returning to Kings Cross, he had followed his youthful instructor's advice and gone to a pharmacy and asked for some Vaseline, not even sure what he was asking for. When the young man behind the counter presented him with a small jar, the German responded, 'No, I need a big one. It is for my nipples.' The assistant promptly propositioned him. 'It is an interesting place, Kings Cross', the German told me.

It's not only foreign tourists who have made their way to Cronulla over the years. On summer weekends, the trains bring people from the western suburbs to the sand and the sea. Many are from ethnic backgrounds; successive generations of migrants and refugees have had their first experience of an Australian beach at Cronulla. But Cronulla and the surrounding Sutherland Shire are by reputation predominantly Anglo-Saxon, and resentment of the interlopers has waxed and waned over the years without ever vanishing completely. In December 2005, Cronulla was the scene of a race riot, exposing a simmering fault line in Australian society. The police had seen the problem coming, but were unable to defuse mounting racial tension. An internal police memo written two months before the riot had warned: 'Many local beach users have the opinion that Cronulla beach's [sic] are for locals only and show an obvious racial prejudice against middle eastern males. This area will have to be addressed to prevent … this escalating into more serious incidents.' Yet as spring turned to summer, the heat on the beach increased. Scuffles erupted sporadically between locals and Lebanese, even as police tried to keep a lid on tensions. According to police, on Sunday 4 December three

'Caucasian' surf lifesavers were passing a group of 'middle-eastern' youths when both groups accused each other of staring. 'I'm allowed to, now fuck off and leave our beach', said one Middle Eastern youth. 'I come down here out of my own spare time to save you dumb cunts from drowning, now piss off you scum', retorted a lifesaver. A fight ensued, police were called, offending comments were noted down. The constabulary, keen to showcase their diligence, issued a curt media release. The media latched on with glee. The next day pyro-mouthed talkback-radio announcer Alan Jones ignited with indignation, branding the beach visitors as 'middle-eastern grubs' and calling for a rally to be held at the beach the following Sunday. The scene was set, and over the next week an estimated 270 000 text messages, many inciting racial violence, bounced around between the young men of the beaches and the young men of the hinterland. An official investigation into the riots and the police response, called Strike Force Neil, later quoted some of the most inflammatory messages. 'Every fucking aussie. Go to Cronulla Beach Sunday for some Leb and wog bashing Aussie Pride ok', and 'Just a reminder that Cronulla's 1st wog bashing day is still on this Sunday. Chinks bashing day is on the 27th and the Jews are booked for early January,' texted the skippies to their mates. 'All leb/wog brothers. Sunday midday. Must be at North Cronulla Park. These skippy aussies want war. Bring ur guns and knives and lets show them how we do it,' and 'Lets get hectic and turn gods country into wogs country. Habib will be cookin victory kebabs after. Tell all your cousins,' texted the Lebs to their mates.

Both sides agreed on one thing: if there was to be a battle between old white Australia and new multi-hued Australia, then the beach was the place to have it out. Not in churches or mosques, but in this country's spiritual heartland.

On Sunday, 11 December, 5000 'Aussies' converged on Cronulla to 'win back the beach'. Some merely wanted to show solidarity with lifesavers; others were draped in the national flag; some were wearing T-shirts sporting slogans like 'no lebs' and 'aussie pride'. As the day wore on, and the beer worked its sinister magic, various splinter groups set upon a number of hapless beachgoers arriving by train, including a couple of Sri Lankan boys. Twenty-six were treated for injuries despite the massive police presence. As evening fell, a convoy of about forty cars from the suburbs arrived at the southern beaches carrying up to two hundred Middle Eastern youths intent on revenge. Cars were trashed, windows broken and two pedestrians seriously wounded in separate knife attacks. The next evening some 2800 people gathered at Lakemba mosque, with the Imam calling for calm. Police surrounded the mosque, preventing a small group, some reportedly armed with guns, from again forming a convoy and heading towards the beaches. In the weeks, months and years that followed, tensions gradually eased, but the violence and prejudice remain a nasty reminder that Australia is not always the tolerant and multicultural place we like to believe it is.

The train pulls in to Cronulla, close to an hour after it left Central. I alight, walk out through the station and past a block of shops full of ice-cream freezers and deep-fryers, to the beach. It's a great beach, long and curved, with a broad sweep of fine, white sand. Cronulla Surf Life Saving Club stands proudly down at the edge of the sand, a three-storey art deco building, old enough to warrant a coat of pastel yellow heritage paint. The Australian flag flutters patriotically on a pole above it. Half-a-dozen teenage lifesavers, including a couple of girls, loiter on the steps, wearing their trademark red swimming shorts and gold rash shirts. The girls are wearing broad-brimmed hats, but a couple of the boys sport the iconic red-and-yellow skullcaps of the lifesaving movement. All fit the police description 'Caucasian'. Down on the beach there is a red tent fly sheltering those on patrol, the obligatory flags marking the safe swimming zone, and an inflatable dingy parked ready to go by the waterline. It's a cool day, a working day, but there are still about thirty people in the water, another twenty lolling on the sand. Most are white, but there are also some East Asians, a few Pacific Islanders, a couple from the Subcontinent and others who may or may not be Southern Europeans or from the Middle East. Pretty much a typical Australian beach. If there is any tension here, I can't sense it.

Before I leave Sydney, I go for a swim at Bondi Icebergs. The sea baths sit at the southern end of the beach, the pools set into the rocks, the clubhouse climbing up the cliff behind them. Officially, summer has already begun, but the water is unbelievably cold. It's a Friday. The seawater pool is emptied, cleaned and refilled on Thursdays, so on Friday it has the coldest water of the week. It comes as a shock, a breath-stealing chill, as I plunge in and start stroking. No wonder some of the other swimmers are in wetsuits. It's too cold to idle at the end of the pool, too cold to adjust goggles, too cold to luxuriate. I swim hard, trying to generate a little warmth. No long, slow strokes this morning; instead I put in a few quick laps, arms flapping, rushing the swim so I can get out again before the tight band gripping my skull solidifies into a permanent headache. Yet despite the chill, it's good to be back in the pool, moving up and down with the sunlight glancing off the surface. When I lived at South Bondi in the 1990s, I used to swim here most mornings, at least in the warmer months, unlike club members who pride themselves on swimming all year round. The best days are when the sea is up, and the waves surge over the edge of the concrete wall, foaming into the pool, pushing swimmers from the direct line of their laps. I used to love that, being shoved back and forth, tracing a haphazard route compared with the straight black line on the bottom of the pool. This morning I do my laps, not even a dozen before I'm driven out by the cold. But by the end I've acclimatised a little and start to enjoy the clean exhilaration of the water. I climb out. My head is tight; my nose is running, and I feel a little dizzy as I stand. But I feel good. I sit for a moment to gather myself on the white tiers, like giant steps, that lead down from the change rooms to the pool. The pool and club have been rebuilt since I was a regular: the old place was riddled with concrete cancer. I had feared what might have replaced it, but the pool and the white tiers feel very much the same as always, just a little cleaner and brighter. I lie in the sun, letting the warmth flow back into me. It is such a delicious feeling. The physicality of it, the shock of the water and the warmth of the sun. The feeling of muscles stretched and worked. I walk up to the café. The coffee tastes like it has been brewed in heaven.

It's a special place, Bondi. It's Australia's most famous beach, a glorious hotchpotch of humanity. It's special for my family, too. Our son was conceived in a house just up from the beach. Later, after his Canberra birth, we returned for a few months, living in a holiday apartment up at North Bondi. My wife still remembers the sleepless nights, kept awake by an insistent baby and the all-night partying of the British backpackers next door. She still shudders at the sound of Britpop band Oasis. But during the day, she could walk the stroller along the promenade, while the waves sang their lullaby to our boy. He wasn't so old, a few months, when he was introduced to the sea, baptised into his birthright, his toes dipped in and out of the paddling pool in the shadow of Ben Buckler. Who could not love it?

I shower and change, and take a walk down along the promenade running above the beach. It's still early on a working day and the beach is a serious place to be. Joggers run along the sand close by the waves or pound along the concrete walkway. An ambitious group of three are doing beach sprints where the sand is softest. Young men are bare-chested; svelte women are lycra clad. Older women power walk, huffing along, raising weights with their arms as they go, fighting gravity with steely determination. The thin white wires of iPod earphones are ubiquitous, the exercisers enclosed in their own worlds, thinking through the challenges of the day ahead. Off the point, black-clad surfers queue impatiently for lacklustre waves. Soon they will be at work, and the beach will relax. The holiday-makers and the shift workers, the students and the retirees, the dreamers and the layabouts will move down onto the sands and stretch out, reading books or dozing.

I wonder what the beach means to us now, how we might react if, like Belongil, the beaches we grew up with started getting sucked out to sea. There was a time when the lifesaver became a symbol of a young country, of who we were and who we wanted to be. That time has passed. He won't feature on the poster, or even the email, announcing the opening of the broadband network; no refugee kid will see him as a symbol of the future. Our identity is more complex, our aspirations more diverse and far-reaching. The idealised lifesaver of the collective imagination has been retired to the collective past, having played his part in guiding us here like the bushman and the Anzac, the convict and the larrikin.

For many of us, the beach is personal: not some sweeping metaphor for our country, but a treasured part of who we are as individuals. It's a place to relax, a place to exercise, a place to play. A place to fish, a place for contemplation, a place of beauty. A place for parties and picnics and evening drinks, for baptisms, marriages and the scattering of ashes. For prayers, religious and secular. In the vast and polluting city, here is the one place that remains as nature intended, below the high-tide mark as unspoilt as the day Grocher waded into the Manly surf. On the sand and in the water, there is a sort of innocence to be found here, where the artifice falls away, where we are children again, playing in nature. It's what still bewitches the likes of Ray Moran and his mate Ian Wallace. It's there for all of us. The beach.

6

BERMAGUI

Disaster Bay—south of Eden.

It's winter. The winds are carving in from the south, slicing through Canberra's leafless suburbs. In the alps, the resorts are reporting metres of snow and temperatures bottoming out at minus twenty. I should be going skiing; instead I drive towards the coast. It's a bleak July day, grey with high wind. Roadside paddocks have been bleached bone by frost, their grass still long after the summer's drought-breaking rains. Ten kilometres from Braidwood I pass a large rock beside the road, a rock that for decades has been painted with colourful birthday wishes, marriage proposals and the exultations of graduating high school students. Today it's monochrome. The black-and-white message reads, 'NEGATE EVERYTHING'. The poplars lining the road beyond Braidwood, green in summer, golden in autumn, are grey skeletons against a darkening sky.

I haven't been to the South Coast since Easter, when we went down as a family. Now I arrive to find my parents' beach house at Broulee looking forlorn. Grapefruit and lemons lie rotting on the ground, and a dead passionfruit vine has been blown away from its trellis against the garage wall. The winds have stacked leaves up against the front door, obscuring the doormat: 'Grandchildren Spoiled Here'. Inside, the house is clean and waiting, untouched since my mother returned to Canberra after our Easter visit. I pile my bags inside, turn on the power and fire up the totally inadequate heater. I brew a cup of coffee in a house unusually quiet, summer clamour replaced by winter solitude.

Reminders of my father are everywhere. Photos on the wall, a half-finished wine cask on the kitchen counter, his shaving gear still perched on the laundry shelf. I guess we lacked the emotional wherewithal to clear it up at Easter. Dad made it down here one last time just after Christmas, even as the last vestiges of his health began to collapse. It seems like yesterday. I'd driven down with the kids on Boxing Day, one of nature's great annual migrations: wildebeest across the Serengeti, lemmings off cliffs, Canberrans to the coast. We descended the coastal range from Clyde Mountain and reached Nelligen at the foot of the hills, 10 kilometres inland from Batemans Bay. Here the traffic on the Kings Highway stopped flowing, cars bumper to bumper. Gridlock 10 kilometres from anywhere. Perhaps a prang, more likely just congestion where the Kings Highway joins Highway 1, the Princes Highway, just outside Batemans Bay. We waited for a while at Nelligen and I told the kids of my early ventures to the coast, sitting between my parents on the bench seat of the pastel green FC Holden, my older brother and sister squabbling in the back. In those days, we'd stop at Nelligen to wait for the ferry to take us across the Clyde River, a few cars at a time, back when Canberra was a town and Batemans Bay a village. The bridge across the Clyde was put up in the early 1960s, yet sitting with the kids in the Boxing Day jam, the traffic was moving more slowly than in the days of the ferry. I finished my story, and still we hadn't moved. 'Tell us another one', said my son. Aged twelve, and yet to start high school, he was already refining the mocking attitude of a teenager. 'C'mon Dad. Another "back in my day".' With the kids getting restless, I'd decided on adventure instead, turning right onto the dirt of the Runnyford Road. I'd always known it was there, seen it on some of the more detailed maps, but had always been in too much of a hurry to explore it. I knew it was unmade and twisting, the slow way round, but compared with the sclerotic highway, on Boxing Day it offered the quicker route, bypassing Batemans Bay and delivering us onto Highway 1 well south of the congestion. So I took the turn and in moments we were free. Free from the traffic, from any traffic, winding through the towering trees and the man-high ferns of the rainforest. Windows down, there was nothing to hear except the sound of the engine, the tyres splashing through puddles on the clay road, and the birdsong of the bush. It had been raining and the downpour had released the smell of the eucalypts, a fragrance of freshness and invigoration. We wound our way up a ridge, and eased down the other side through the speckled light of the canopy. Past Runnyford, a hamlet struggling to justify its dot on the map, we crossed a tributary of the Clyde, more like a lake than a river, over a high wooden bridge, single lane, no passing, no overtaking. An old bridge, white-painted rails and hardwood planks clanking under us. A couple of blokes and their sons fishing from the bridge were the only people we saw on our detour. It was the last time I took the old Hyundai to the coast, and with its high clearance and manual gears, it handled the winding roads with workman-like aplomb, like an old dog chasing rabbits in spring. The kids were looking out either side of the car, intrigued by the bush, hoping to spot a wallaby. After forty minutes, we emerged onto the Princes Highway at Mogo, traffic moving smoothly. Ten minutes later we were at Broulee, opening up the house, settling into the rhythms of the annual beach holiday.

Mum and Dad arrived a couple of days later. Dad insisted on driving, my mother sitting beside him, as always. I wonder if he knew how ill he was, what force of will made him insist on driving. The doctors had taken him off chemotherapy just before Christmas, saying he was handling the treatment so well he deserved respite from nausea for the holiday. Instead of beginning to feel better, he was beginning to feel weaker and his appetite was disappearing altogether. They spent three days with us, happy as ever to be with their grandkids. But despite his brave face, Dad just got worse and worse. He still insisted on getting out of bed, having a shower and a shave, and getting dressed, but the effort left him so weak he couldn't do much more than doze in front of the cricket. At first we rationalised his condition as a reaction to the withdrawal of the chemotherapy, but it became more and more obvious that he needed attention. Mum decided she should drive him back; there was no longer any question of him driving.

Then Dad decided he wanted to go back via Runnyford, on the winding dirt track through the bush. He'd been intrigued by our venture and wanted to see it for himself. Perhaps, like me, he'd long been aware of the road's existence but had never taken the opportunity to explore it. Now he wanted to take the bush track, but I vetoed it. He was too ill, and I was concerned about what would happen if something went awry. His car was a low-slung automatic and my mother was unused to driving on bush tracks. Phone reception on the road would be patchy at best: if she had a flat tyre or slid off the side of the track, they'd be far from help. Mum was anxious to get him back to the doctors; she thought the highway made sense as well. Dad could see our logic. 'Never mind', he said. 'Next time.'

Now Dad is under the altar at the local church, his urn kept company by the ashes of a couple of other congregation members patiently awaiting final internment or dispersal. It sounds like a comfy enough place to be, in company with some old mates. Mum is trying to round up family members for a final ceremony. We're going to plant Dad in the churchyard, with a shrub to mark the grave. No headstone, no plaque. According to his wishes. Just like his funeral: family only, a single-column notice in the *Canberra Times*, a cardboard coffin.

My brother and his family are overseas; my sister's kids are grown up. One is in Taiwan teaching, her other son about to depart for Japan. The extended family is beginning to fragment. In its entirety, its final iteration, it only lasted for eight years, the age of my daughter Elena, the youngest of her generation. But during those years, my parents, my brother and his family, my sister and hers, and my wife and our two kids were about as close as a family could be. And the coast house was central to that. It was here that we gathered every year in summer and most years at Easter. We all lived in Canberra, so we'd see each other regularly, getting together for meals or barbecues or going out to a restaurant. Mum and Dad were the babysitters of first and last resort. But such occasions would only last a few hours. At the coast we were all together for days, sometimes weeks, up to a dozen of us packed into the two-bedroom Broulee house, with people sleeping upstairs in the loft and on the lounge-room sofa bed, and even out on the deck. During the day we would split up, with expeditions to the various beaches, my brother off cycling or fishing, my wife Tomoko venturing into Moruya markets, Dad pottering round the small garden or watching the cricket or writing his never-to-be-published book. Dinner was the time we all came back together, taking turns at cooking. For New Year's Day and Easter Sunday, Dad would fire up the barbecue and roast a turkey breast or a leg of pork. And then we would all sit together at the table and eat and drink wine and talk and laugh and argue.

It's a common enough story, unremarkable, typically Australian: families, large and small, from the bush or the suburbs, congregating at the coast at summer. For the fortunate few, at their own beach house, for others a favourite rental, booked faithfully every year, or a spot at the same camping ground or caravan park, with other families in adjacent spots year after year. A time when parents can leave work and pressures behind and spend time with their kids: swimming, fishing, surfing, boating, playing beach cricket, barbecuing, riding bikes, flying kites, reading books, listening to the cricket, watching the Sydney to Hobart sweep past. And as the kids grow into adolescents, the holidays at the coast becomes the backdrop for more memories: a first kiss, a summer romance, illicit drinks, the first toke of a joint, virginity lost. Here then is the summer of our collective past, a slice of our national identity not forged in war or moulded by hardship or purloined by politicians, but shaped by leisure and indolence, by the annual respite from daily life, when we have the time to reflect on a year gone by and the challenges ahead. We recuperate in the restorative surf; we read books bought long ago but hitherto unopened; we take long beach walks and formulate New Year's resolutions that survive until the end of the holidays and no further. It's a place that resonates among passing generations of Australians. No wonder sea changers or retirees dream of escaping to the beach; they want their futures to echo the idealised memories of the past. We may ponder the historical significance of the city beaches, with their strutting egalitarianism and lifesaver demigods, but perhaps the affection Australians hold for the beach derives not from a Sunday at Bondi but from these extended holidays: that long weekend, that week every year when we are allowed to relax, slough off the exoskeletons of profession and propriety for the briefest moment, become closer to our true selves, and the selves we would prefer to be.

Tomoko and I once rented a house at Broulee with some friends, back before we were married—a big posh house up on the headland. It was brand new, with raked ceilings and a gourmet kitchen, marble-clad ensuites and a lounge room of timber and stone and a wall of windows looking out into bush and blue sky towards the island. Throughout the house were photographs and paintings of the old house, a fibro shack, some with family members, some of just the house. The new house was impressive and functional, a good investment attracting premium rents. But there were no pictures of the new house, only those of the old beach shack where the family had grown and prospered.

In Europe, we holidayed with Australian friends based in Brussels, spending time in country houses in France, far from the sea. Our friends had been in Europe for several years, and had finally eschewed the Mediterranean coast, deciding it was impossible to replicate in Europe the timeless lassitude of an Australian beach holiday.

Our house at Broulee is not an old-style fibro shack, nor is it an ostentatious beach palace. It's just a modest brick semi, on a small block a couple of hundred metres back from the beach, entirely unremarkable. At first, I thought it rather plain, too suburban, not the weathered refuge of the imagination.

Not long after my parents bought it, my mother collected photos of all the family members and placed them in a large picture frame, the kind with postcard-sized windows cut in the matte, and hung it above the dining table. Every year or two she puts up a new one, so that the recent history of the family is recorded along the wall, stretching from the dining table to the end of the open-plan living area. Walk along the wall, and children grow to adulthood, babies appear and burgeon, adults grow thicker and greyer. There are larger photographs, group pictures taken every Christmas after lunch. It has become my responsibility: herding the family outside, taking the photo, then printing it and framing it for the house. I haven't printed and framed last year's yet. It's an incomplete photo, my brother and his family absent, but it's the last one including my father. Sooner or later, I will get around to it, but not just yet. Now, as I wait for the coffee to percolate, I examine the family history, individual and collective, arriving at the last photo on the wall, taken at our house two years ago, the last photograph with all fourteen members present.

The coffee pot signals its readiness with a throated gurgle. I pour the steaming liquid into a thermos cup and take it outside with me. There's still time before dark to pay my respects to the beach, a three-minute walk to the end of the street. But at the gate, I change my mind and head towards the bush instead, what's left of the rainforest. It's where my father liked walking.

My parents bought the house in the early 1990s, but memories of Broulee go back much further. I was eight when we spent a week there with some of neighbours in a fibro house raised on brick piles, kids squashed into bunk beds. In those days, Broulee stretched just two blocks back from the beach, with dirt streets, water tanks, bore water and septic tanks. I struck up a friendship with a boy I knew from school named Peter. We invented a game as we ran through the sand dunes by the beach. We'd collect empty drink cans, beer or soft drinks, it didn't matter which, and bury bundles of them in secret spots in the sand. Next day we'd search them out, digging them up like pirate treasure. The game ended abruptly. We'd just successfully exhumed a hoard when I felt something crawling on my arm. A huge red-back spider, scarlet stripe glistening against black. I looked up at Peter, his eyes wide, his mouth open. I held my arm as still as possible, held my breath, and brushed the spider off. We were up and running before it landed. We ran and ran and ran until we could run no more.

I'm in the bush now, walking along a sandy track. The eucalypts here tower above the undergrowth of ferns, a vestige of rainforest caught between the spreading suburbia of Broulee and the main coastal road. It's quiet here, the bush softening the Doppler hiss of a car rushing past in the distance. Above me a kookaburra begins to laugh. Other memories crowd in. Hitching to Broulee from Canberra aged sixteen with my best friend Ben, staying at the house of our friend Carole—a bunch of teenage kids with not a parent in sight. Ben and I riding old bikes down to Carter's store to buy grog, dropping our voices low and acting with studied nonchalance as we bought sweet alcoholic cider and Blackberry Nip. Rosie drinking too much Blackberry Nip and vomiting on the daisies.

The track abruptly comes to an end. There are bulldozers and a wide swathe of cleared land. Beyond are new houses, some under construction, some already showing the first signs of occupation. There is nothing coastal about them; they are the same brick boxes found on the fringe of any Australian city. I walk around them. There are signs: 'Land Sale! Broulee Beach Estate' and 'Banksia Village'.

We all remember our favourite beach from the first time we stayed there, from our childhoods or from when we finally bought a holiday place as an adult. After that, it becomes part of us, and we resent the newcomers, those who build in the bush and those who crowd the beach. We want it to stay as it was the first time we saw it. I'm like that. Broulee is already too suburban for my liking. I have a mate with a family house at Depot Beach, an idyllic spot surrounded by national park. Year after year he has railed against the council for incrementally sealing the road in to the beach from the highway, resenting the fact that a better road is sure to bring more people. But not my father. He was always intrigued by the new developments, by who was building what and where. He was of an older generation, who believed there was plenty of room for everyone, the more the merrier.

I remember him in the hospice, less than a week before his death. The cancer had taken over, his body wasted, but his mind clear. He'd already taken me through all the details I would need to know: share holdings, bank accounts, insurance. He'd told me about Broulee, the title deed held by a solicitor in Batemans Bay, how I would need to get the title changed over into Mum's name alone. He wanted me to install a reverse-cycle air conditioner to keep the house warmer in winter and cooler in summer, so Mum would be more comfortable. One of myriad minor things left undone. We'd discussed where it might best be placed, various local tradesmen who might be able to install it. 'Beautiful Broulee', he said with a sigh, 'beautiful Broulee'. He knew he would never see it again.

The water hits me like a shock. It's freezing. I must be mad. It's worse than Bondi Icebergs back in December. Now it's the middle of winter and I'm recovering from a cold. I can hardly breath, it's so icy. About 14°C, I'll learn later. But the sun is out, the wind is low and there is something I want to see, if I'm not driven from the water by the cold. My gonads throb and a headache emerges from the depths, wraps itself around my skull and begins to tighten like a vice. I'm wearing swimmers, a rash shirt and a snorkelling mask. I'm not sure why I'm wearing the rash shirt; I'm not about to get sunburnt in July. I searched for my brother's wetsuit, but he must have put it in storage. I haven't bothered with a snorkel or flippers; I won't be in the water long enough. I swim hard and fast, still struggling to get my breath working properly, getting my bearings from the rocky outcrops and the seagrass bed. I'm off the side of Broulee Island, now part of the Batemans Bay Marine Park. The whole island and an area extending a couple of kilometres out to sea have been declared a sanctuary zone: no commercial fishing, no recreational fishing, no collection of shells or seaweed, dead or live. Since 2007, only swimming, snorkelling and surfing have been allowed.

I'm here because I want to see the abalone. It was once one of my favourite spots to dive for them, and I want to see how they are faring since the sanctuary has been declared. I get far enough offshore to start a series of short dives, out among the pink rocks where the shellfish live. I scan a likely spot, tilt my body, pitching my legs into the air, using their weight to drive me quickly down, equalising my ears as I go. A rainbow wrasse, initially slow to react, decides discretion is the better part of valour and scurries off into a crevice between the rocks. Not only is the water cold here; it is deep. Normally, I would have come at low tide, but today I've come in the early afternoon when the sun is warmest, despite the tide being close to full. The rocks are a couple of metres down, and the headache intensifies with every centimetre of depth. At the bottom of my dive, I hover momentarily, using my hands to sweep aside the seaweed, searching among the crevices for the familiar grey lumps, before returning to the surface, lungs busting. Quickly, within a couple of minutes, I perform another half a dozen dives. Already the temperature is getting to me and I'm growing tired. I'll have to give it away any minute, or risk hypothermia. After all, what am I trying to prove? If there are no abalone, it doesn't mean the sanctuary isn't working. The whole South Coast is notorious for poaching, and the criminals aren't going to be any more hesitant breaking the law inside a marine sanctuary than outside it. When you see abalone, cut from the shell and sealed in plastic wrap, selling for more than $100 a piece at Sydney airport, you can understand why. And it's not just poachers. A virus has hit the shellfish along a huge stretch of coast reaching down into Victoria. I realise I am on a fool's errand. Time to give it away. But just as I'm preparing to head back to shore, I spot a circle of sand on the ocean floor among the rocks, a familiar underwater landmark, unbelievably intact in the constantly changing undersea environment. Once, I spotted a couple of shark eggs resting there, a discovery to exercise the mind and discourage loitering. I swim past the patch, further out to sea, pitch forward and dive. There, just inside a protective crevice, as if waiting for me, are not one but two good-sized abalone. I get right up close to make sure, give one a pat, and head back up, breaking the surface with a celebratory spurt of water.

⌒

The drive south from Broulee is redolent with memories. The coast road meets the highway across the bridge from Moruya, by the riverside pub where Dad, my brother Brendon and I went for a pre-dinner beer one New Year's Eve. I pass through Moruya itself, where Dad would look for hardware bargains at Crazy Clints. Further south, the turn-off to Tuross Heads, another favourite haunt of Canberrans, and earlier memories. We spent a week there when I was a kid, and my father transformed from a workaholic disciplinarian into a relaxed and doting dad, shouting us a chocolate-coated ice-cream each afternoon, a Streets Heart—unprecedented luxury in a Paddle Pop childhood. Further south again, I drive across the bridge into Narooma, and more memories emerge from the shimmering waters of the inlet: Dad and his great buddy John Delaney considering investing in oyster leases. There was money in oysters, Dad reckoned, plus the fringe benefit of all you could eat, an appealing pitch for the old boy. But the slimy grey meat wobbling in the shell looked in no way appealing to me; I couldn't understand its allure. Neither could my mother, and the oyster investment sank without trace. I continue south, alone with my memories. I detour into the heritage village of Tilba Tilba, now bypassed by the highway. It's a pretty village, but I recall my parents being decidedly unimpressed. Perhaps, having spent several years living in quaint rural villages in northern Tasmania, it had nothing very special to say to them. I wonder why, of all things, I should remember this. We must have called into the town once, forty years ago. Why do we remember the things that we do?

⌒

Any conventional ranking of the great American writers of the early twentieth century would put Ernest Hemingway and F Scott Fitzgerald at the top of the list. Not in Bermagui, New South Wales.

In Bermagui, Hemingway and Fitzgerald are joined, perhaps eclipsed, by a third American literary lion: Zane Grey. He was named Zane after his birthplace, Zanesville, Ohio. Lucky for him he wasn't born in Dorking.

Grey, like Hemingway, was a pioneering big-game fisherman, and even if he couldn't match the younger man with the pen, he could certainly give him a run for his money with the rod. Certainly Hemmingway read Grey's fishing books, and by some accounts, the two men were friends. Yet while Hemingway principally fished Florida and the Caribbean, Grey ventured further afield, to New Zealand, Tahiti, Nova Scotia and, of course, Bermagui. He spent a considerable amount of time in the town; in 1936 and 1937 he was patron of the Bermagui Sport Fishing Association. He even wrote a book about it, *An American Angler in Australia*, helping put the town on the world fishing map, even as it struggled to establish its place in more mundane atlases. Zane Grey wrote Westerns and remains one of the best-selling authors of all time. So forget *The Great Gatsby* and *For Whom the Bell Tolls*; pick up a copy of Grey's masterpiece instead: *Riders of the Purple Sage* (aka *Writers of the Purple Prose*). It's a western set in Utah, is explicitly anti-Mormon and possesses precious little in the way of literary merit. It was nevertheless a blockbuster, providing Grey with the wherewithal to indulge his passion for fishing. One of his sons reckoned Grey spent 300 days a year on the end of a line, which is a pretty good effort considering he also authored about ninety books, churning them out at a rate of two, three, even four a year during the 1930s. Unlike Hemmingway, who used his knowledge of game fishing to pen *The Old Man and the Sea*, Grey kept his fiction on dry land. However, he did write a number of non-fiction books, including eight about fishing, as well as other adventure-laden accounts, such as *Roping Lions in the Grand Canyon*. I can't help but think of Grey, with all his manly pursuits, as a kind of Hemingway Lite, even though *Riders of the Purple Sage* was a bestseller when Hemingway was still a schoolboy. Perhaps Zane was something of a role model for Ernest. Who knows?

In *An American Angler in Australia*, he describes Bermagui as he found it in 1936.

It seems, as the years go by, that every camp I pitch in places far from home grows more beautiful and romantic. The setting of the one at Bermagui bore this out in the extreme. From the village a gradual ascent up a green wooded slope led to a jutting promontory that opened out above the sea. The bluff was bold and precipitous. A ragged rock-bound shoreline was never quiet. At all times I seemed aware of the insatiate crawling sea. The waves broke with a thundering crash and roar, and the swells roared to seething ruin upon the rocks. Looking north across a wide blue bay, we could see a long white beach. And behind it dense green forest, "bush," leading to a bold mountain range, and the dim calling purple of interior Australia. This shoreline swung far to the north, ending in a cape that extended out, pointing to Montague Island, bare and bleak, with its lighthouse standing erect, like a gray sentinel.

I find Bermagui much the same as Zane left it, minus a few of the more overwrought adjectives. I walk up from the main street, past the Zane Grey caravan park, to find the slope he described still rising above the town to the headland, where it provides the same view out across the bay towards Montague Island. The long, white beach remains unspoilt, as is the bush, although the 'dim calling purple of interior Australia' seems to have been lost in translation. The Montague Island lighthouse is not so much a sentinel as a speck on the horizon. But Grey is right on the money about one thing: the beauty of the spot. It's a clear winter's day, the sky cloudless blue and the sea calm. I search for signs of Grey's camp. I find a rock with a plaque, but there is no reference to the American. Instead it simply states: 'In memory of Terry Hardy. Missing at Sea. 3-5-1993. Always remembered.'

Grey describes Bermagui with a fisherman's eye: his gaze from the headland is directed out to sea. So while he described the rugged cliff below his camp on the ocean side of the headland, he ignored the sheltered beach of Horseshoe Bay, which forms a perfect crescent and faces the more sheltered waters of the bay. It sits between the headland of Grey's camp and a second headland overlooking the entrance to Bermagui harbour, home to the town's fishing fleet. I walk down onto the beach. Even in winter, the north-facing beach is warm, and I remove my shoes and paddle in the water. A man emerges from the surf, and we exchange pleasantries. A retiree, he informs me he swims most days, all year round. He tells me Bermagui is the best-kept secret in Australia, and on a day like this, it's hard to disagree. I even contemplate a swim, but in my bones I still feel the chill of my abalone dive. I climb the western headland and look down upon the bay once more. There's another rock, a more elaborate plaque, quoting Tennyson:

In Memory of Kevin Walker Fenton. Died 8.5.1989. Collision at Sea.

Sunset and evening star
And one clear call for me
And may there be no moaning
of the bar, When I put out to sea.

Aged 58 years.

Floating in the rocks below the headland, a dead seal is bobbing in the swell, its two flippers erect, like twin dorsal fins.

Bermagui was a fishing town when Zane Grey staked his camp seventy-five years ago, and it remains a fishing town today. Commercial fishing, game fishing, recreational fishing. It's the one thing that keeps the place going, that and a trickle of retirees and sea changers. I continue down the other side of the headland, down to the boat harbour. There's a ramp for enthusiasts to reverse their boat trailers down into the water. Nearby, a couple of long concrete tables sit, each equipped with a series of small hoses. These are filleting tables, placed by the council to assist anglers. It's an offence to fillet fish at sea, because it could disguise the taking of undersized or protected species. No one is using the tables right now; it's too good a day. All the fishermen are at sea. A sign by the tables reads: 'The disposal of fish offal in adjacent waters is prohibited. Littering or polluting waterways is an offence.' A trailer sits by the tables bearing a sticker: 'Fish Offal Trailer'. I look inside. In among the malodorous guts, scales and bones of table fish lies the head of a tuna, at least twice the size of my own head. I try to estimate the size of the original fish. Longer than the trailer, no doubt.

Zane Grey's camp up on the headland was an elaborate thing, consisting of a dozen tents set on wooden floors, with a separate kitchen and dining tent. But he needn't have bothered. For then, as now, the Bermagui Hotel commanded stunning views across Horseshoe Bay and out to sea. Nowadays, the hotel is painted in heritage colours, russet and cream, but in Zane Grey's day it was painted white. It was still white when I stayed there for a couple of nights twenty-one years ago while filing stories on the 1990 federal election. It's one of the small mysteries of Australia: why old buildings are painted colours they never originally bore in an effort to make them look more authentic. We paint things to match our image of how the past should have looked, rather than how it actually did. On this trip I'd originally booked into the motel at the back of the hotel, disbelieving my own memory of its stunning location. But checking in, I can't resist swapping to one of the rooms on the first floor, with its own small balcony, looking out past palm trees to the beach and sea. The Zane Grey suite is already booked, so instead I'm in the Lady Elouisa suite next door. I ask the owners who Lady Elouisa was, but they don't know. 'A friend of the original owners' is the suggestion. It seems unlikely: not many members of the aristocracy were swanning around Bermagui in the nineteenth century. More like the name of a shipwreck, I reckon.

The bar downstairs is all but empty when I descend after night-fall. A solitary local sits nursing a beer, looking out towards where the sun set three hours ago. The barman is staring blankly into space and I feel almost rude interrupting his reverie. He tells me the kitchen is closed, but they can still put something in the deep-fryer for me. He says the veal chops are good. I give it a pass and order a beer instead. I take my schooner further into the bar. On the walls are mounted the plastic casts of huge fish: marlin, tuna and swordfish. There's a blue marlin, well over two metres long and, according to the plaque below it, 928 pounds. That's 421 kilograms, five times my weight. It took an angler called David Mercer three hours to land it in January 2000. It's almost twice as big as the largest fish Zane Grey caught in 1936.

For Zane, the ocean was vast and fish stocks were inexhaustible. In the 1930s, this was the conventional wisdom, decades before industrial trawling all but depleted the cod fisheries of Newfoundland and the North Sea. After catching a yellowfin tuna off the coast of Bermagui, he enthused about setting up a cannery.

> Yellow-fin tuna furnish California with one of its big commercial assets—a 50-million-dollar-a-year canned-tuna industry. There are floating canneries on the sea and canneries on shore. San Pedro, a thriving town, depends upon the tuna catch. For thirty years this business has been increasing. Large boats have been built, with refrigeration machinery and huge storage capacity, and these vessels ply far in pursuit of the schools of tuna. In 1927, when I found yellow-fin tuna at the Galapagos Islands, and showed motion pictures to verify it, the Japanese and American fleets were hot after these fresh schools. Five hundred tons of tuna, at a hundred dollars a ton, meant big profit.
>
> Australian commercial interests have something to think about. It can be depended upon—these yellow-fin tuna are more and more in demand. Japanese ships now come clear to the Californian and Mexican coasts, and down off South America. It will be a close run to Australian waters.
> The extent and abundance of this annual migration of yellow-fin tuna off the South Coast should be ascertained; and the result might well be a tremendous business for Australians, and what is more, a valuable and inexpensive food supply bound to take the place of the more expensive meats. In the United States the consumption of fish as food has increased forty per cent in the last ten years.

Poor old Zane. Apparently it never occurred to him that the reason the game fishing was so good in far-flung places like Bermagui was exactly because they didn't have fish canneries. But he wasn't alone. In those days, it was the common view: the oceans, like the planet itself, were inexhaustible.

Back in 1990, Bermagui was still a working port, a fishing port. I have vague memories of the wooden trawlers lined up along the dock, and of buying fish at the old co-op. But the trawlers have gone now and so has the co-op building. The harbour has had a makeover. A group of young children, five or six years old, are fishing from the wharf, sitting on the side and dangling their lines in the clear water. There are fish there alright, clearly visible, but none are biting.

'Can we fish somewhere else?' requests one small boy.

'No', says the man in charge.

'But we're not catching anything.'

'Well, that's the thing. You don't go fishing to catch fish. You fish as an excuse to sit and have a little think,' explains the man kindly. The kid looks at him like he's a complete idiot.

The fishermen's co-op still exists, only its buildings have been demolished and rebuilt. On my last extended stay it was a bustling hive of activity, taking in the catch from the town's trawlers and packing it off to the Sydney fish markets. In those days, there was also a shopfront where you could buy fish straight off the boats. Now the co-op has been split in two: a small building for processing fish and a retail outlet in a larger dockside development, a two-storey building with spotted-gum pillars and varnished stringy bark cladding. Both storeys have extensive decking overlooking the small harbour, with a couple of new jetties boasting an array of charter boats and rich men's runabouts. It's a smaller and more tasteful version of what you might find in Sydney's Darling Harbour or Melbourne's Docklands. There's a sign with a snappy logo featuring a laughing pelican and the words Bermagui Fishermen's Wharf. And there's the co-op's shopfront. The building contains a couple of restaurants, a café, a wine bar, a real estate agent, an art gallery, a clothes shop and a gift shop. Nowadays the members of the Bermagui co-op are as intent on reeling in tourists as they are on catching fish.

Upstairs, I find Rocky Lagana, lifelong fisherman and chairman of the fishermen's co-op. At forty-three, his hair and eyebrows are still thick and black; only his stubble is beginning to grey against his olive skin. We shake hands and he leads me from the offices along the decking and into a conference room. On the wall are photos of the harbour in its heyday, back when it was home port to sixteen trawlers.

Rocky tells me about himself. His real name is Rocco, a third-generation fisherman, his grandfather having migrated to Australia from Calabria before World War II. Back in Italy, the family were also fishermen. So there was no question that he too would go to sea and cast his own nets. At the age of fourteen years and seven months, at the end of year 8, his parents took him out of school and put him on the family boat, a 63-foot wooden trawler named *San Rocco*. Fishing was in Rocky's blood, so they told him. The reality was different.

'I struggled with seasickness when I was a young lad going to sea. I enjoyed the fishing, but couldn't really enjoy it because of my seasickness. I didn't want to go to sea for that reason when I was at school. It took a good twelve months to get completely over it. If I hadn't been fishing for two or three days due to bad weather, first day out I used to throw up. In them days my mum and dad had their own fishing boat and sort of said, "You've got to work", and "What are you going to do? You have to go fishing and keep the family business going."'

This was in Ulladulla, 200 kilometres south of Sydney. It was the early 1980s, a golden era according to Rocky. 'There were twelve to fourteen trawlers based there around that time, plus a handful of trapping line boats. It was one of the biggest fishing ports in Australia. It was a major supplier to Sydney in those days.' Seasickness aside, Rocky began to enjoy his new life. 'I think I liked it because I was a young kid and my friends were all at school and I was working and making money. I lived with my mum. She fed me, washed me clothes, and I felt like I was something bigger than I probably was. I was fifteen, and here I was working, and at the time, I was saving.

My mum took my pay and she gave me $50 per week to spend. She would bank my money.'

Not long after, Rocky's dad retired and sold the *San Rocco*. Rocky worked as a deckhand for another family for a couple of years before teaming up with his two brothers. The partners bought their own trawler for $620 000, assisted by their mother, who stumped up the deposit and went guarantor on their bank loan. And so, at the ripe old age of nineteen, Rocky had his own share in a boat and the future was looking bright. 'Yeah, it went well. We were young and wanted to catch the world. We thought the more fish we were going to catch, the more money we were going to make. So we worked the boat for gemfish along the east coast, but gemfish had already become a quota species at that stage, because there were already signs of overfishing. Still, we had enough gemfish quota in them days to fish in between Eden and Sydney. We went chasing them.'

Rocky explains that when they bought their boat, the brothers also received what were known as trawl units. The units weren't a quota or a method of limiting the catch; they were more a method of taxation. The operators of a boat were required to pay for units depending on its size and horsepower. Upgrade the engines, and the fishermen would be required to pay for more trawling units. There was no overall limit to what they could catch. It was a system that encouraged the fishermen to work their boats hard: they were paying for the units, so there was a strong incentive to catch as much as they could. What started to limit the catch wasn't regulation but the amount of fish left to be caught. There were already signs that the fishery along the southern New South Wales coast, as elsewhere, was becoming depleted. Towards the end of the 1980s the brothers moved their base to Eden, close by the Victorian border, where there were more species to catch and more areas to work. Then, in 1990, the world began to change. The government introduced quotas, with each fishing licence allocated a permissible catch based on their historic catch. The days of catching the world were over. For most fishermen, the quotas reinforced the status quo, but Rocky and his brothers were caught out. The quotas were based on their boat's historical catch, measured between 1982 and 1987. But during this period, the previous owners had operated it out of Bermagui, fishing for different species and at a lower intensity. Rocky and his brothers moved base again, to Ulladulla for four years, and then from 1995 to Bermagui itself.

The writing was on the wall, not just for the brothers but for the industry as a whole. 'There was too much effort in the industry', Rocky says. 'It had been overfished; quotas had to come down. In the government's wisdom they thought they would buy back fishing concessions, to ease the pain, to prevent half the industry going broke. [It] was in a lot of trouble. So, people had the opportunity to put in a tender of what they thought their business was worth and government accepted the majority of them. Not all—some were too high,' he recounts. 'I think they got it about 80 per cent right. They took out what they had to take out, but they didn't shut the doors on a few operators who came through the back door. Some people had two licences, sold one, then put the spare one back on the boat and continued fishing.'

That's not the only aspect of the system that rankles with Rocky. He's also opposed to the system that has separated fishing quotas from fishing boats, so that many of the quotas are owned by investors and money men, forcing fishermen to lease quotas. In his opinion, the government should own the quotas. But I can see the government's logic. Even if fish stocks appear to be recovering and the fishermen want to catch more, the owners of the quotas will want to keep them limited, increasing their value, just as the owners of taxi plates never want more taxis on the road, regardless of whether there are plenty of drivers and increasing passenger demand. This way, the government won't have to fight the battle to limit fishing quotas; it will always have allies inside the industry to do the fighting.

The quotas weren't the end of it; more change was on its way. In 2006, the New South Wales government proclaimed the Batemans Bay Marine Park, the nautical equivalent of a national park. It stretches some 100 kilometres down the coast from just south of Ulladulla in the north to Wallaga Lake, just north of Bermagui, in the south. It stretches from the high-tide mark to 3 nautical miles out to sea, the limit of state jurisdiction. The park is divided into a series of three zones. In sanctuary zones, like that covering my old abalone haunt near Broulee Island, no fishing at all is allowed, commercial or recreational. In habitat protection zones, nearly all commercial fishing is prohibited, with the exception of some low-impact techniques, such as trapping lobsters or harvesting abalone by hand. Even in the third, least-restricted general-use zone, trawling, dredging and long-line fishing are banned. So Rocky and his brothers, operating a trawler from Bermagui, found themselves locked out of a valuable fishing ground, a 100-kilometre stretch of ocean immediately north of their home port.

'We knew there was going to be a closure in state waters to ban trawling in the Batemans Marine Park. That was one of our main areas of summer fishing. We relied on it heavily to get through the summer months; with windy north-easters and the southerly current, we needed that area. We knew that once we lost it, life was going to be hard for us. To operate a boat out of Bermagui, we just weren't going to be viable. It came pretty much after the introduction of quotas, about three months later. It was a double bang.' Rocky and his brothers sold to the Commonwealth, and Bermagui lost another trawler.

'In the mid 1980s, they had sixteen trawlers working out of Bermagui, just trawlers alone. You're looking at anywhere to fifty to sixty people employed on the trawlers. Plus there were heaps of handline boats. Plus the co-op would have employed ten people permanent and casual,' Rocky recalls. The co-op had about forty members; now it's down to twelve. If a member doesn't put fish through the cooperative for two years, they automatically lose their membership. One member has recently retired, so soon it will be eleven members including Rocky, who doesn't fish but as manager has a special dispensation. Bermagui is down to one trawler, owned by an Ulladulla family that bases it here for nine or ten months a year.

The co-op didn't fold, however, and Bermagui didn't become a fishing museum. Rocky left the sea to manage the cooperative. They demolished the old co-op and built two new buildings: one for the fish and one for the tourists. 'We knew as a cooperative we couldn't sit back and do business the way we did twenty years ago. So, we got an architect, built the building. We slashed the running costs in half. And that meant a smaller cool room, a smaller ice machine, a skeleton staff.' A government restructuring grant of $1.2 million helped, but the fishermen stumped up the rest of the $4 million required and the co-op itself took out a loan of more than a million dollars. The new building, opened in December 2009, is impressive, designed by acclaimed architect and part-time resident Philip Cox. Rocky reckons it's doing okay.

'At the moment we're happy. We still need to cater for the very minimal operators we do have out on the water. The co-op works on commission basis from fishing sales. The fishing side is still the major income and the rentals are hopefully picking up the pieces. The co-op manages the docks. So the co-op gets an income out of the jetties and gets an income out of selling fuel and selling ice, and the co-op also runs a transport truck for their product. And we still cater for a lot of visiting boats from other ports, especially tuna long-line vessels. The majority of that is export. We send it off to an exporter and they export it. But we handle 'em and pack 'em.'

I ask Rocky what he thinks of the future of his town. 'It's a pretty town. My honest opinion on this town: it's expensive to buy real estate for what you do. I can't pinpoint why houses sell for what they do. I can't see what industry drives this town. There's sea changers. A lot of retired people from Canberra who don't want to go to Batemans Bay anymore, because they're over-populated. But there's nothing for me, and I've lived here for fifteen years and worked here for twenty. I don't believe the Bermagui public were aware how important professional fishing was and how much money it generated. I think people sat and said it's a shame what is happening with the fishing industry, but I don't think they realised the effects.'

Rocky has three kids. His eldest boy is now fifteen. At the same age he was already at sea, fighting seasickness and feeling pride in his pay cheques. I ask him if he would like to see his children become fishermen, a fourth generation in Australia, countless more if you count Calabria. 'No', says Rocky. 'Definitely not.'

In the evening, I return to Bermagui's Fishermen's Wharf. Strangely enough, there's no seafood restaurant, just Italian and Asian. I don't much fancy sitting in a restaurant by myself, so I order a takeaway pizza from the bustling Italian, figuring I can sit out on the balcony of the Lady Elouisa suite at the hotel and watch the moon float above Horseshoe Bay. But the waitress has a better idea. She suggests I wait in the wine bar next door. 'I'll bring it in. Eat it there. They charge two dollars eatage.' So I wait in the wine bar, sampling a smooth pinot while I wait. It's a cosy little place in winter, with folding glass doors shutting out the chill of the deck. There's a boisterous group, two middle-aged couples, full of laughter and banter. They each down a shot of grappa for good measure before they go. After they leave, the quiet descends. I'm the only customer, outnumbered two to one by the owners, Bruce and Janinka. My pizza arrives and I eat at the bar while we discuss wine, politics and Bermagui. Bruce and Janinka tell me their kids have grown up and left, so the wine bar is perfect. They have no staff, so even a solitary customer like me is enough to pay for the power. Best of all, they don't open until three in the afternoon. The couple are surfers. Most days they surf in the morning, year round. Then in the evening they run their wine bar, looking out over Bermagui's beautiful little harbour. It sounds like perfection.

⌣

I sit in the morning sun on Bermagui's main street, looking out over Horseshoe Bay and the ocean beyond, drinking my coffee and reading the papers. Even in the lee of the shopfront, the wind is funnelling in and nagging the edges of the paper, so that I find myself weighing it down with my coffee mug, my raisin-toast plate and my mobile phone. Even so, a story squirrels out through the obstacles and grabs my attention: 'BLUEFIN TUNA "CRITICALLY ENDANGERED"', states the headline. 'Australia's highly prized southern bluefin tuna is in dire trouble, according to a new global fisheries assessment by an international environment organisation', it reads. 'Of all the heavily fished tunas that face threats, southern bluefin stands out as a clear-cut case for "critically endangered" status, a scientific review by the International Union for the Conservation of Nature has found.'

The article goes on to quote research published in the journal *Science* that has concluded that the most efficient way to avoid further damage would be to shut down the southern bluefin and Atlantic bluefin fisheries altogether until stocks are rebuilt to healthy levels. It makes for sober reading. Another challenge to the Bermagui co-op, another challenge for the fishing villages of southern Australia.

I finish my coffee and meander across the road to the park and from there back towards the harbour and the co-op's tasteful new retail complex. The sun is shining and the water is calm and clear, but out at sea, the fierce wind has turned yesterday's blue glass into a wash of white caps. There won't be too many out fishing today, which gives me a good opportunity to gauge the boats that now call Bermagui home. I walk along the first of the three jetties. The moorings are full, but not with commercial fishing boats. These are private boats, some set up for fishing, others for cruising. There are boats from Melbourne and Brisbane, a sleek ocean-going catamaran and a small motor yacht called *Palao*, with its home port identified as London. Three people are eating breakfast in the shelter of its glassed-in cabin. At the end of the jetty, an old trawler floats. It's missing a name and much of its rigging, and its blue-and-white hull is badly in need of a new coat of paint or two. Some of the exposed woodwork is beyond repair and will need to be replaced. There's a bloke pottering about on board. At first I think he's working on it, but then he picks up a fishing rod and walks to the stern.

'What are you after?' I ask.

'Just some bait. It's too rough to go out today.'

'Your boat?'

'No fear. Belongs to a mate. He's meant to be fixing it up.' And he looks about, and shakes his head.

The next jetty along has three working boats tied up. There's *Melisa*, the last of the board trawlers; a smaller boat, *Consolato*, out of Eden; and a large, rather serious black boat, *Devocean*. And that's it. That's the entire commercial fleet sheltering in Bermagui harbour today. It's a different story across on the third jetty, a floating dock, where a dozen or so game-fishing boats are moored, gleaming in the sun. These are new-looking boats, snow-white confections made from fibreglass, some with three or four tiny decks held aloft by flimsy steel poles, crows nests for spotting fish. The boats look top-heavy and unseaworthy. These boats are purpose-built for reeling in blue, black and striped marlin, mako sharks, swordfish and yellowfin tuna. Bolted to the lower deck towards the stern of each boat is a solitary chair, large and solid looking, as if a dentist has decided to practise at sea. These are for the game fishermen, strapped in as they fight fish weighing several times their own weight. The game boats have names like *Mr Hooker*, *Slammer* and *Hardaraddit*. This, not a tuna cannery, is the industry that Zane Grey bequeathed to Bermagui. At the end of the row, in prime position nearest the shore, sits an old wooden trawler, *Binjarra*. With its wooden hull and cabin painted a simple white with blue trim, it makes something of a contrast with the flashy new game boats. A sign identifies its owner: 'BERMAGUI FISHING CHARTERS. KEITH APPLEBY.'

I find Keith living in a townhouse overlooking the harbour, a stone's throw from his boat. He's eating breakfast, eggs and baked beans on toast when I call in the next morning. He has a ruddy face, skin sandpapered by the weather. His receding hair is still ginger, but his beard is almost white. He tells me he came to Bermagui almost forty years ago at the age of twenty-one. His mother had died and his father had moved to the town to run the caravan park. Keith had already worked as an abalone diver and was at home with the sea. He had the idea that he could establish a full-time business taking people out fishing. They could come to Bermagui for a weekend or a week. He could supply the boat and the gear and the bait and, most important of all, the knowledge that would more or less guarantee they caught a fish.

'In 1983 I started up the charter boat. There were no charter boats on the southeast coast back then. The closest charter boat was at Batemans Bay,' he recalls. 'There was kind of a charter industry, but I was the first one to legalise it, to make it into a proper industry. Before that, tourists would come here and hire commercial fishermen to take them out on their boats. That was just the way it was. But I had a proper passenger-carrying boat and had to go away and get a licence to carry passengers, so I turned it into a proper business.

'It was the same boat I've got now, the *Binjarra*. The one down at the dock there. The first attempt didn't go so well. We set up the boat and it was wonderful. I had partners, and we got the boat set up and had it looking beautiful, and then sat back and waited. We had a total lack of knowledge about marketing. We sat back with this beautiful boat and all the knowledge about catching fish. And nobody knew we existed.'

Keith and his partners went bust. It was an inauspicious start to the professional charter industry, but he wasn't ready to call it quits.

'A bloke bought the boat off me, and I stayed on it. It didn't really look as if anything had changed, but he bought it. Actually, off the bank, not off me. The bank didn't like us not making payments. So they took it off us, he bought it from them, and I stayed on the boat. I rebuilt myself over a few years, bought another boat, which was the *Tarpin*, which I had up until about three years ago. Anyway, he went broke eventually and I bought the *Binjarra* back. That was about seventeen years ago, so I've still got it.'

Keith says there have been good times and bad times. Many of his clients are Victorians, and when the Geelong-based Pyramid Building Society collapsed in 1990 he felt the flow-on effects. More recently, the drought had a big impact. Keith reckons country people are more into boats and fishing than city people. 'They're more into greenies and whale watching. Yachties. We have more people from out west, farmers and the like.'

Nevertheless, the charter industry boomed. All through the 1990s and into the new century there were well over twenty charter boats in Bermagui, with at least five local residents running multiple boats. Keith himself ran the two boats, the *Binjarra* and the *Tarpin*, with skippers and deckhands and cleaners. He and his wife Anne would provide the fishermen with accommodation. Anne would get up at 3.30 a.m. and cook them all a full breakfast and at night they'd lay on a big barbecue and cook some of the day's catch over a few cold beers. Hard work, long hours.

'There were a lot of boats', says Keith. 'But now, I'm the only resident owner-operator in Bermagui. The rest of them down there are corporate boats that you see. Every charter boat. When I say a corporate boat, what I mean is they're all owned by companies or businessmen, and they charter the boats out to cover the costs. They wouldn't make a profit. It's just a way of covering their wharf costs, their fuel costs, their insurance fees, their survey costs and to keep a skipper.'

I ask what has changed, whether it's the fish or the people. Keith reckons it's the people. 'It used to be groups of people: eight to ten blokes would come and hire the boat for four or five days and we would go out every day. Nowadays, those groups have diminished. Some of them came for over twenty years. When I call them, they just say, "We can't get the numbers any more". Maybe it's that that generation, the outdoor types that went fishing and hunting, have gone through and passed on, and the new generation are more into the computer world or something like that. They're not as outgoing or outdoors as the last generation were. There are not so many young blokes any more. Not like there used to be.'

Keith is winding down his business now, looking for a less strenuous job as he heads towards retirement. One of the reasons he's still in business is that he's never gone chasing the big game fish, the marlin and the tuna. Instead he specialises in table fish: flathead, snapper, morwong and the like. And he reckons this has been one of the best years ever, that all the recreational anglers have been going out and getting their bag limit of flathead, day after day. And he reckons the good recreational fishing can in part be explained by the collapse of the trawler fleet.

'I used to work on a board trawler, and I would have to say it is one of the most effective ways of catching fish for market. If you are a commercial fisherman, it's wonderful. But when I jump over the fence and go on the other side and become a recreational angler, I'd say it's been one of the most detrimental forms of fishing ever introduced because of what it does to the bottom. The boards and the combination ropes and the wires, it drags along and takes all the seagrass off the bottom. You're not just taking fish; you're taking their ecology. There were areas out here where we used to trap crayfish. They don't exist any more, because of the rubber nets and boards. There were areas where I used to catch mowies, and those holes are gone, because they've been just dragged over and over. The area's been destroyed by board trawlers.'

If Keith doesn't think much of the trawlers, he doesn't think much of the fancy game-fishing boats that share the jetty with his *Binjarra* either. 'To the real fisherman a boat is just a platform to stand on. You can catch marlin off the rocks, which they do, and yellowfin. The general public thinks you need to be on a plastic boat with a fly bridge on it, otherwise you won't catch a marlin, but Zane Grey never had any plastic boats with fly bridges on 'em.'

I tell Keith about the article in the morning paper, about the decline in bluefin tuna. He has a little laugh at that, then tells me that I've arrived in town the week after a two-week run of bluefin that had anglers turning up in droves. He says there were seventy to eighty boats off the headland, reeling them in. Then the fish disappeared again overnight, and the people with them. Nevertheless, he concedes there has been a drop in the number of large pelagic fish being caught, fish like marlin, bluefin and swordfish, as well as yellowfin, the fish that follow the ocean currents.

'The yellowfin fishery used to be massive during April, May and June. Just hundreds and hundreds of boats here, maybe 200 a day, would be up off the headland during that period. And earlier, December to March, would be the marlin, and some of the charter boats were catching up to ten marlin a day. That decline in those fish stocks ... well I don't know if it is a decline in the fish stocks. It's the bait fish. If the bait comes here, then the fish come here. If they have something to feed on, then they will come here. I think the fish are still out there.'

I'm not sure. Maybe Keith is right, maybe not. He certainly knows more about fishing than I'll ever know. Perhaps the local fish, the ones that live on the reefs and the sandy bottom, are starting to rebound now the commercial industry has been wound back, whereas the larger ocean-going tuna are still falling victim to overfishing, much of it occurring in mid-ocean, outside Australian territorial waters. According to the government, yellowfin, albacore and broadbill swordfish are not overfished, while the status of marlin is uncertain. Only bluefin is officially overfished. Nevertheless, it's clear Bermagui's charter fishing industry, like its commercial cousin, is a shadow of its former self.

I thank Keith for his time, and ask him about the future, what it holds for fishing and for the town. 'Oh, there'll always be something there', he says. 'But Bermagui, because it's isolated and not on the highway, will always be very difficult. You're here for the lifestyle, not to make money. If you want to make money, you leave town.'

⌒

I wander around the Eden Fishermen's Recreation Club, the Fisho's as it's known locally, looking for a television set in among the poker machines and early starters. At noon today Julia Gillard is to announce details of the carbon tax and ensuing emissions-trading scheme. It's been a long time coming, from John Howard's promised scheme in the dying days of his government, to Kevin Rudd's 'greatest moral, economic and social challenge of our time', through to the final convoluted compromise negotiated with the Greens and independents. Today could be a red-letter day in politics: the day when the route ahead is finally outlined. The Prime Minister's announcement is only ten minutes away, but I'm having trouble finding a television. There's a big flat-screen in the foyer showing morning cartoons. *Wacky Races*. Camped on a sofa in front of the set are three elderly gentlemen drinking coffee. I politely inquire if they'd be interested in watching the prime ministerial announcement. 'Not much', says one old bloke, quite happy watching the adventures of Dick Dastardly and Muttley in reruns of the 40-year-old cartoon series.

I spy another set, somewhat smaller, over on the wall by the café counter. It's tuned to WIN, the regional affiliate of the Nine Network. The sound is turned down, but I soon work out how to crank it up. I order a coffee and settle in to watch live coverage of the Canberra press conference. I had thought the Fisho's might be an interesting place to gauge reaction to the carbon tax, but it's Sunday morning and, like most other people, fishermen have better things to do than hang around a pokie palace on a sunny morning. The only other people in the café area are a beefy bloke and his two kids, eating an early lunch of burgers and chips. The Prime Minister appears and

I turn up the sound a bit more. The beefy bloke looks at me as if I've just traipsed dog shit through the place. He steadfastly ignores the message from Canberra, engaging with his kids instead. 'We are seizing a clean energy future', says the Prime Minister, but at the Eden Fisho's no one is listening.

⌒

Down the road, at the counter of Eden Outdoors and Marine, Michael Mashado is too busy serving weekend anglers to have paid attention to the carbon tax announcement. But in between customers, he's happy to chat, and he's sure the tax will have a negative impact on the local fishing industry. 'They say they're not going to put the carbon tax on diesel, but they are going to take the fuel excise rebate off diesel. So if you look at a commercial fisherman paying an extra 30 or 40 cents on fuel, and burning 2000 litres of fuel a trip, price has to go up on something. They're getting 54 bucks a kilo retail for flathead tails now. It's not going to take much to put it up to 70 bucks a kilo. And you wonder why we're getting so much more fish imported.' It's not a bad point, even if Michael may be exaggerating the price. Australia possesses some of the largest fishing grounds in the world, yet we import two-thirds of the seafood we eat.

Michael is not impressed with government attempts to regulate fishing, especially the buy-back of commercial licences. 'Buying out the licences did bugger all because the blokes they bought out weren't operating anyway. And the ones they did buy out, they gave cash to go and start up other little fishing businesses anyway. They didn't get rid of half the licences they should have got rid of. Instead they bought out blokes who weren't making a go out of trawling, and now they've gone bottom lining. It's given the blokes who weren't making money out of fishing enough money to go fishing again.'

Nevertheless, he reckons if things stay the way they are at present, then the commercial fishery in Eden will remain viable. His main concern is a rumour that the state government intends to extend the Batemans Bay Marine Park all the way to the Victorian border. Much of the coastline south of Eden is already covered by land-based national parks, and Michael says conservationists like the idea of having an adjoining marine park. He says such an extension would not only damage commercial fishery, but could also injure the recreational industry, depending on which parts of the marine park are designated as no-fishing sanctuary zones.

Recreational fishers are Michael's customers. He sells equipment and bait to those who have their own boats or who fish off the rocks or the beach. He says the decline in the charter industry doesn't necessarily mean interest in fishing is waning. Instead, he thinks that many of the people who once would have gone out on charter boats now own their own runabout—that affluence has changed behaviour.

'Bermi's the same', he says. 'The boat ramp is chock-a-block. Not so much charters now days, it's Joe Blow towing his own boat. You look out here, you see blokes towing boats for two days, then turning around and going home. Just to have a shot at a bluefin tuna. It's been one of the best bluefin tuna seasons I've seen.'

I ask Michael about the story I read in the paper back at Bermagui, about the demise of the bluefin tuna and ask if he reckons they're endangered.

'Sure. Once upon a time, yeah, but not now. The last three years, you've gradually seen a tenfold increase. This year, I've never seen fish around a boat like I've seen bluefin. When you're fishing in an area on a dead flat day, and for a mile around you can see fish busting up, you look on the sounder and there's 40 fathom deep of fish. Poke your camera over the side and take a photo and you get a 50-kilo fish in your camera shot. The spotters for the fish farms in Melbourne, they have never seen so many fish.'

I ask why the fish are coming back. 'Because they've modified the commercial fishing. You've lost your purse seiners that used to net out here, that used to just take 100 tonne, but all this about them being endangered, I've never seen so many.'

⌒

From Eden, looking south across Twofold Bay, you can see the top of Ben Boyd's tower, rising above the bush on the distant headland. It looks like a lighthouse, except it's square, not round. Boyd was a Scottish entrepreneur and visionary who arrived in Sydney in 1842 aboard his own schooner, the *Wanderer*, the nineteenth-century equivalent of a corporate jet. He was set upon making a fortune in the new colony, and within months he was well on his way. As a London stockbroker in the 1830s, he'd become obsessed with the idea, even before he voyaged here. To help finance his grand scheme, he formed the Royal Bank of Australia, raising £200000 from debentures, money he packed in his bags and brought out to the colony with him. Within a year, he was rated as one of the wealthiest men in New South Wales. He owned fourteen sheep stations on the Monaro and a further four near Port Phillip, comprising more than 1500 square kilometres of land. Boyd and Company, borrowing heavily from the Royal Bank of Australia, also owned three steamers and three sailing vessels. Boyd's ambitions knew no bounds, and not content with Sydney, he decided his expanding empire required its own capital. He called it Boydtown, modesty not being one of his strong suits, and started building it on the shores of Twofold Bay, south of present-day Eden. He built a wharf stretching 90 metres out into the bay, so he could load the wool from his holdings in the Monaro directly onto his own ships. He built a fine Gothic church, various houses and stores, and a rather beautiful hotel, which is still operating today as the Seahorse Inn, snuggled in behind the dunes.

I drive from Eden along the highway, past the remnant township of Boydtown, and head towards Ben Boyd's tower. I turn off the highway and east towards the coast. It's a good road, sealed and well maintained. I've travelled it before, twenty years ago, when it led to controversy. It's the road that takes logging trucks to the huge woodchip mill on the southern edge of Twofold Bay. Nowadays, it's called South East Fibre Exports, but two decades ago it was called Harris Daishowa and was the centre of an environmental battle royale over the logging of old-growth forests. At regular intervals along the road are reminders of the controversy: signs in front of healthy stands of regrowth forest. 'Logged 1974', says one sign; 'Logged 1978', says another, the implicit message that regrowth is indistinguishable from old-growth forest. It was an argument I heard often in those days, that regrowth forest was superior to old growth: aesthetically, commercially and environmentally. South East Fibre Exports still processes a million tonnes of wood a year, exporting to Japan and Korea, but much of the heat left the debate with the signing of a Regional Forest Agreement in the late 1990s—although many environmentalists remain unhappy with the final outcome.

But I've come to see Ben Boyd's tower, not the woodchip mill. I turn off the road, park the car and take the short walk through the eucalypt forest to the tower. It's a beautiful building of honeyed sandstone, five stories high, its four walls tapering as they rise towards crumbling ramparts. There are four windows on each floor, one for each wall. It's a building of solidity, but the tapering walls and windows lend it lightness and elegance. Boyd wasn't just building a functional tower; he was making a statement. It was to be a lighthouse, a beacon to alert passing ships that they were approaching the glittering new capital of Ben Boyd's mercantile empire. Local stone wasn't good enough; he insisted Pyrmont sandstone be shipped from Sydney and master masons oversaw its construction. It would look completely at home among the colonial constructions of early Sydney; instead it stands alone, out of place in the bush. It remains an elegant overstatement—Ben Boyd's great folly. The colonial authorities didn't take kindly to this private-enterprise upstart and denied Boyd permission to operate the tower as a lighthouse. So it became a symbol of ambition thwarted, not of opportunity unlimited. Undeterred, Boyd put the tower to a more profitable use: whale spotting. Eden was already a prominent whaling port when Boyd arrived, and he soon muscled in on the action, operating nine harpoon boats. Whaling was a perfect fit for Boydtown, for its elongated jetty and for the trading ships of Boyd and Company. The tower, sitting on the southern headland of Twofold Bay, provided commanding views south down the coast as well as back across the bay. Lookouts at the tower would spot humpbacks coming up the coast on their annual migration and alert boat crews waiting in the sheltered waters of the bay, providing Boyd's whalers with a vital head start. But the same advantage could have been gained with a primitive wooden tower.

Boyd's ambitions, like his tower, proved too grandiose for Australia. Plans to import cheap labour from the Pacific foundered;

investors lost their faith, and Boyd lost their money. Just seven years after arriving in the colony, the empire collapsed and Boydtown was abandoned. Boyd was allowed his liberty and he departed the same way he had arrived, sailing away on the *Wanderer*, heading first to the Californian goldfields and, when that failed, back to the South Pacific equipped with another grandiloquent scheme: a plan to establish a 'Papuan Republic'. In 1851, he landed on Guadalcanal to go hunting and was never seen again. He was almost certainly killed, but that didn't stop endless speculation that the mercurial Scotsman was alive and well and off empire building in some far-flung El Dorado. Henry Lawson wrote:

> Ben Boyd's Tower is watching—
> Watching o'er the foam;
> Ben Boyd's Tower is waiting
> Till the "Wanderer" comes home.

The tower sits at the northern end of the Ben Boyd National Park and marks the beginning of the light-to-light walk, a three-day trek south along the coast to Green Cape. The day is clear and the winter sun is warm, so I put together a quick daypack and start out on the walk. The trail is clear and well maintained, and soon I'm engulfed in the forest, the silence accentuated by the distant sound of surf breaking on the rocks. The gums give way to tea-trees and banksias and the path becomes a tunnel through the overhanging foliage. Termite mounds line the path. Even high on the ridge above the hidden cliffs, the soil is sandy, grey on white. I pass through an open glade, ferns abounding. There is a sudden smell of herbs. It's like rosemary and oregano. Could this be a native plant, or is it a garden escape? I like the smell, hunt down the plant, rub the stubby leaves between my thumbs, put a sprig in my top pocket. Footprints on the sandy path inform me that others have walked this way since the last rains, but there is no sign of them. Twenty minutes into my walk I am feeling marvellously alone. The path winds back towards the cliff top, and looking north, I can see the apex of Ben Boyd's tower floating incongruously above the wilderness.

The path winds down the ridge, opening onto a small bay and a beach of dark-red gravel, so very different from the white sands of expectation. The russet gravel and boulders make for a sharp contrast with the deep blue of the sea and the cloudless sky. I sit on a boulder feeling the exhilaration of nature. The far headland reveals striations of red and tan sandstone. Off the point, shearwaters glide for a moment before plunging headlong down into the sea, hunting fish. A half-moon floats high and white in the early afternoon. As I contemplate the moon, a sea eagle floats into view, effortlessly riding the thermals. If it sees me, it takes no notice. I watch it for long minutes as it gradually circles towards the north. I should be getting back, starting the walk to the car, but the bay is sheltered, the sun is warm and the sound of the waves seductive. My reverie is broken by the sound of engines, and a powerful boat rounds the headland and enters the bay, followed by the white wash of its wake. The helmsman winds back the throttle and the white boat settles lower in the water. I wave, and the two men on board wave back. 'FISHERIES PATROL', says the writing on the hull. I pick up my bag and start heading back to the car.

I drive back towards Eden, but there is one more thing I want to do before returning to town. I turn off onto a dirt road and start heading back towards the sea. I bump along for 21 kilometres, stopping briefly to take in the panoramic views down across Disaster Bay. But I don't tarry, for now the sun is starting to get low in the western sky, its rays dazzling as they bump in and out of the rear-vision mirror. I reach my destination, the Cape Green lighthouse, high on the cape itself, where it juts out into the Tasman Sea. This is more your typical lighthouse: round, or at least octagonal, painted white, with small windows, solid in the landscape, with all trees cleared, and capped with the glassed-in turret housing the light and its Fresnel lens. But it's not the lighthouse I've come to see, and as I rush past it, I'm looking out to sea, already rewarded by the first flume. There they are: five or six humpback whales playing with the swell as they ease their way north. They are unhurried and unharried, coasting along the surface, sending plumes of spray skywards from their blowholes. They roll on their sides, hoisting first one flipper then another vertically into the air, a white flash, as if waving to the small group of us who stand at a lookout and ooh and aah at their slow progression past the cape. They roll through the waves, flukes occasionally rising above the water, the white of their flippers and the white of their flumes marking their passage.

Driving back to Eden, I feel a weight inside beginning to lift. All through my time in Queensland and northern New South Wales, I was weighed down with thoughts of what could go wrong: sea-level rise, coral bleaching, acidification, cyclonic destruction, beach erosion, the sprawling congestion of the Gold Coast. Deep inside it had combined with the grief over my father's death to embroil me in a pervasive pessimism, that climate change was coming to play havoc and we were not doing nearly enough to avert disaster. But now I consider what I might have thought visiting the far south coast of New South Wales twenty years ago—wholesale destruction of the native forests and unsustainable fishing. Yet, somehow, those disasters have been averted, at least in good measure. The state government has gazetted huge swathes of national park while retaining a smaller, more sustainable timber industry. It declared the Batemans Bay Marine Park, and fish stocks are rebounding, even while fishing remains an industry, albeit much diminished, in Ulladulla, Bermagui and Eden. Restrictions are in place to ease developments on headlands and beaches, and to keep high-rise to a minimum. Somehow, amid all the white noise of politics, things have got better.

And maybe no one was listening to Julia Gillard at the Eden Fisho's, but that doesn't mean the carbon tax won't be legislated. When it is, the price on carbon will most likely be here for good. Tony Abbott may say he will repeal it, cross his heart and hope to die, but even if he does win government, he won't necessarily control the Senate. He'll huff and he'll puff and he'll fulminate. He'll make all the noises the sceptics in his party want to hear, but that won't shift the Greens. And just quietly, Abbott may be happy with that. The world will move towards pricing carbon, and the heavy lifting will have been done for him. He's as likely to rescind the carbon tax as

Kim Beazley was to have rolled back the GST. It won't happen, no matter who governs. Somehow, through the posturing and politics, the babble and the blarney of the daily news, the governments of Australia are finally heading in the right direction. I hope it's not too little, too late. But I do have hope.

7

BASS STRAIT

Loch Ard Gorge—a place of death and beauty.

I drift south, across the border into Victoria. More weeks have passed. My travels down the east coast, originally envisaged as a summertime jaunt, relaxed and carefree, are coming to an end in August, hampered by grey skies and lingering grief. Yet the depths of winter are passing: the nights are at their coldest yet the days are growing longer. Today the sky is clear, and down along the sea, the promise of spring is emerging. There is wattle in bloom, flaring yellow in the speckled light of the eucalypt forests lining the Princes Highway. South I drive, further south, chasing memories. The highway cuts well inland here as it runs westward towards Melbourne, the coast itself largely left slumbering behind a protective blanket of national park.

We buried Dad's ashes in the garden by the church he and my mother helped build, just down the pathway from Mum's new apartment. It was 13 July, a cold and blustery day, the cloud-filtered light appropriately grey. We gathered those members of the family still in Australia, plus a gaggle of Mum and Dad's elderly friends. Dad's old mate Neville, the former bishop, led us through a couple of suitable prayers. Two holes had been dug, one for the ashes and one for a memorial shrub. Mum and my sister Gwyn had chosen it from the Yarralumla nursery, a nandina, a favourite of Dad's. It fell to me to empty the ashes into the hole. I was surprised by their weight, by their whiteness. I took some time, not wanting to simply dump them out unceremoniously. While I poured out my father's remains, elderly voices filled the silence.

'Where's Eric? He wanted to be close by Eric.'

'He's up on the bank a little, under that tree.'

'What about you, Molly, where are you going?'

'Oh, I've got my spot all picked out. Over there, under the azaleas.'

I finished my task, catching the eye of my twenty-something nephew Michael, his eyes watering from grief and suppressed laughter.

Now Neville has followed Dad's lead. A spry 89-year-old, with little sign of ill health, he fell down the stairs one night a few weeks later and never regained consciousness. For my mother, another small blow.

Such thoughts are exercising my mind as I pass through Cann River, a frequent ice-cream stop in my youth, when we would drive to Melbourne every summer to visit my grandparents. Not a lot has changed. The road runs a little straighter nowadays, with overtaking lanes and white lines marking the edges, but it's still the same highway.

Dad always drove at 50 miles per hour—80 kilometres per hour—in those early days of the FC Holden, before the advent of seatbelts, disc brakes and rack–and–pinion steering. It made for a long trip, plastered on the hot vinyl seats of the 1960s. Now I'm heading towards Orbost at 100 kilometres per hour, cruise control, air conditioning and iPod-fed stereo. It's a new car, modern and functional. The children threatened insurrection when I told them I was selling the old one, but it's gone now, and the new one is slowly gaining acceptance. A sign says I'm approaching Orbost. This was another staging post on our Melbourne trips; it was an undisputed fact in our family that Orbost pies were the best to be had anywhere, and I'm thinking maybe I should sample one, just for old time's sake. And then I see the sign to the turn-off. 'Tourist Drive', it says, depicting a loop off through Cape Conran, along the coast to Marlo, and then back to the highway at Orbost. 'Coastal and Snowy River scenic drive.' My mother was born near Marlo, within sight of the sea, an entirely logical location given her lifelong love of the beach and swimming. I take the turn-off.

The road leads through tall forest and then, as it approaches the coast, low-lying shrub. There's not much at Cape Conran: a car park, a boat ramp and a small jetty. I walk out on the jetty and look over Bass Strait, that wild and treacherous stretch of sea linking the Pacific with the Indian Ocean between Tasmania and Victoria. Like the Torres Strait, it's shallow, 50 metres deep on average, prone to passing storms and furious weather. When the current is running one way, and the wind the other, the waves can climb into cliffs of green garnet, threatening to smash or capsize any boat unlucky enough to be caught between their peaks. Bass Strait is just 240 kilometres wide, and not much longer from east to west, but in the days of sail and the early days of steam, it wrecked many hundreds of vessels, pounding them against the shorelines of Victoria or Tasmania or one of the fifty islands that dot the passage. Today, however, it's as calm as bathwater, the lowering sun polishing the surface to a peaceful sheen. Even so, the beaches here are wide and exposed, devoid of headlands and snug coves. These are not swimming beaches. Currents can sweep close to shore, pushing waves into erratic crisscrossed patterns; rips surge and recede, ready to sweep the unwary out into freezing waters. Ninety Mile Beach isn't far away—151 kilometres of unremitting sand and crashing surf. Had they been Australian, perhaps the Brontë sisters, lacking a good moor, might have located *Wuthering Heights* or *Jane Eyre* somewhere along this coast.

At Marlo, I call in at the pub, high on a rise overlooking the mouth of the Snowy River. The hotel is a long stretched-out affair of white weatherboard, almost nautical in appearance, as if a retreating flood has settled it atop the hill like some latter-day ark. From its verandahs and feature windows you can look out over the final bends of the river as it winds behind the sheltering dunes before entering the sea. I'd always thought Mum was born here, but she has told me her mother travelled into Orbost for the birth. Nevertheless, the pub was Mum's first home, where her parents worked as managers during the Great Depression. The family was forced to leave after the surrounding area was devastated by floods. Locals retreated to the pub, gaining shelter from the rising waters. But this was the Great Depression, and many couldn't pay. The owner went bust and had to sell. My grandparents returned to Melbourne. Mum was three. Nevertheless, seventy-five years later, hazy memories persist.

> I remember as a young girl being on the jetty, with lots of people and boats', she told me back at Easter, as we sat at the dining table in Broulee. 'Kids were jumping off the jetty. So I thought, I'd take a jump off the jetty. This must have been when I was under three. And I jumped in, and someone had to come and pull me out.
>
> It was a harsh sort of life, I suppose. Quite remote, es-pecially for my mother, who had come out from Wales. And they used to tease her about the tarantulas [huntsman spi-ders]. Said that they were Australian fleas. "Don't worry about them—they're Australian fleas", they'd say.

The view from the pub verandah is much as it must have been back in the 1930s, with little to interrupt the vista out over the mouth of the Snowy. Once again, the river is in flood, after a decade of drought and many more of dam-depleted flows. There's been enough rain up in the alps to leave it swollen and its banks broken, but it appears to be in no hurry. This is a slow-moving, dignified inundation, giving locals plenty of notice of the approaching peak. The land down by the sea is flat and the river winding, having lost the heady impetus of the mountains. It doesn't so much flood as expand out into low and lazy swamps, the water still, reflecting the setting sun, half-sunk trees cast as silhouettes in the glimmering mirror of watery sky.

Inside, the pub has changed since the days of my grandparents, but probably not an awful lot. There's a wide-screen television showing the AFL, and not a cigarette in sight, but there's a fire in the grate and the place has a comfortable, well-worn feel to it. The friendly barmaid, Nicole, tells me the place had a bit of a makeover in the 1970s, but that's about it. The walls are wood-lined, the lacquered pine already grown yellow with age. Here and there are photographs of fishing bonanzas, and some mounted fish. These are modest trophies, nothing remotely approaching the magnitude of Bermagui's game fish—table fish, plate-sized for the most part, platter-sized at best. The photographs above the bar have grown sepia with age: 219 fish caught with five rods, Easter 1911; 87 perch, date unknown; 54 bream with two rods, 29 October 1927. Fishing at Marlo, then and now, is estuary fishing, not game fishing in the open sea.

Nicole tells me the fishing is off at the moment. The favoured local theory is that a government campaign to clear the river of willows has left the banks vulnerable to flood waters and the main channel full of snags. She says so many trees and branches were being swept downstream at the height of the flood that the captain of the tourist steamboat the *Curlip* had to sleep on board to protect his vessel. But there is also a widespread belief that the floods are a good thing, breathing new life into a river that has been on life support ever since the Snowy Mountains Scheme stemmed its natural flows by 99 per cent. The locals believe the fishing will return better than ever. A more immediate problem is that the people who built on the river flats during the long dry years are now finding their homes surrounded by swamps. Come summer, the mosquitoes will play merry hell.

THE COAST

I leave the pub and wander down towards the mouth of the river. It must have been a tough, isolated place for my grandmother, recently arrived from her snug mining village in South Wales, looking after two small children. But I like it. Even in the peaceful sunset of a still winter's day, the coast here retains a sense of wildness, of understated power, of a sleeping giant.

⁓

An Air Canada plane is in trouble off the coast of Sydney. There has been smoke detected in the galley, and the pilot is dumping fuel out at sea in preparation for an emergency landing back at Kingsford Smith. The ABC is keen on the breaking story and keeps me well informed. The plane lands safely, and is soon in the air, bound once again for Vancouver. An oven has been replaced as a precaution. Utterly routine, assure the authorities—nothing to worry about, problem solved. Nice to have some good news for a change. Well, good news, if you weren't a sun fish basking off the coast, or a pod of dolphins, or my whales from Cape Green, minding your own business when, wallop, several dozen tonnes of avgas lands in your particular patch of ocean. I'm not sure how toxic avgas is, and no doubt it evaporates quickly, but I wonder about the mentality. Are pilots so quick to dump fuel over land? Probably, if the emergency warranted it. Yes, of course they would. I ponder the situation some more, realise my concerns are baseless. If the plane were high enough, the volatile fuel would vaporise before making landfall. In the long, long list of environmental concerns, dumping avgas must come pretty close to the bottom. After all, it's expensive stuff; airlines aren't going to be spraying it about willy-nilly. But I'm intrigued by my own sensibilities. Not long ago, I wouldn't have thought twice about the practice of dumping fuel at sea; now it sets off alarm bells. I discover I'm thinking about the ocean more. Not just the strip of land along the coast, or the waters where we swim and work and play, the bits that affect us directly, but the watery depths themselves.

⁓

My love of the sea comes from my mother. Dad was born in the bush near Bendigo, and his affection was always for the land. He liked nothing better than gardening, feeling the moist earth in his hands. Mum, born on the coast, loves the beach just as passionately. Even now, she'll bathe for hours in the gentle waters in the lee of Broulee Island. My daughter Elena is the same. Aged eight, she can stay in for hours. On New Year's Day, at Broulee, she went boogie boarding while I sat on the beach reading. While I read, the annual sandcastle competition got under way; fifty or so groups marked out their plots on the sand before the starting whistle. An hour later the sandcastles were finished, and the judges began walking through in careful consideration. There were chateaux, sharks, cars, aeroplanes, dogs digging tunnels, huge hands and mermaids. The winners were announced, and still my daughter was out in the surf, oblivious. Only when the tide started to encroach on the sand sculptures did I wade out and fetch her, so she could see them before their demise. And even then she was reluctant to come in. So like her grandmother. So I was surprised to learn when I spoke with Mum at Easter that she didn't really learn to swim until she was about twelve, down at Brighton Baths in Melbourne's Port Phillip Bay. It was rather late in the day, considering the beach had been a regular weekend destination for her throughout her primary school days. Her parents, having returned to Melbourne, ran a shop on Glenhuntly Road in Caulfield South, and the tram would take the family to the beach each Saturday afternoon.

'We went straight down to Point Ormond, where there was a big hill. Later on, a lot of people used to like going down there to see the troop ships off during the war. From the top of the hill you could see the ships out on Port Phillip Bay,' Mum recalled.

'We'd go down there to play in the water and pretend to swim. I would have been about five or six years old. They had a cement walk around the bottom of Point Ormond Hill, that's what it was called, and they had cement ramps going down from the walk down to the water. Sometimes, when the tide was in, the water would be a couple of feet deep at its highest. My brother found a little place that he liked, that he used to call his special place. You could see straight down into the water and you could see these coloured pebbles and shells and anemones. And it was quite a pretty little spot. And every time we went down to the beach we'd walk around the pathway and look for his special spot, which we enjoyed.

'Well it wasn't long, two or three years I would say, at the most, we went around to have a look at his special spot and you could hardly see in the water. The water was very cloudy. And I said to my mother, "What has happened? It used to be so nice and clear and you can't see it now." And she said, "Oh, it's the water that comes out of the Elwood Canal". She said there were a lot of businesses along there. I don't know what term she used, whether it was effluent or what, but she said there were drains that drained into the Elwood Canal and this would go directly into Port Phillip Bay.

'Then we noticed that where we used to swim, which was practically at the foot of this hill, we noticed the water was very cloudy. When we first went there, the waves were quite golden and sparkling in the sun, but it had changed so it was quite cloudy and you could no longer see the bottom. It didn't look very inviting at all. So we moved further south along Port Phillip Bay. There was a very popular beach, Elwood, that wasn't too far away, but it was a bit further to get to from the tram. We weren't so keen on Elwood. Then, because the train went straight down to Brighton Beach, I used to travel on the train with my father and mother. That was when I learnt to swim at Brighton Beach, so I was eleven or twelve.

'There were sea baths there, and the sea baths had a boardwalk on three sides of the square, and it went fairly deep into the water. I suppose it was [larger] than an Olympic pool. The water was very deep at the far end because there was a high-diving board. Well over thirty feet deep, so you could look right down through the big waves. They had these metal bars that went down almost to the sand at the bottom, supposedly to keep sharks and stingrays out. And that was beautifully clear. Although it was a distance away, we enjoyed going down there, because it was so pristine. You could see there were no rocks or anything on the bottom, and anything that was there, you could see.

'At sixteen I used to ride my bike down there. There were bike racks outside. You wouldn't need to lock it up; nobody would be taking it. You could have a good swim and then ride back. I used to take my bike on Saturday afternoon or Sunday. I'd be in about three hours, for as long as I could. I'd stay in until I'd start to shiver, then I'd come out and lie on the sand and warm up, then I'd go back in again. I was still swimming there when I was eighteen or nineteen. And then the water there—you could no longer see to the bottom. That was a fairly short period of time, really. People gradually moved further and further south along Port Phillip Bay until Sandringham became a more popular beach. And more people had cars, so they could drive down. But that was happening and people noticed and knew that the quality of the water was getting worse and was better further south.

'I didn't know about swimming pools until I went to high school, to MacRob. We always had our sports carnivals at the Olympic pool in Melbourne. And that was my introduction to chlorinated swimming pools. And of course to me it was nowhere near as good as swimming in the sea. I find it very relaxing in the sea. I like the smell; I like the sound of the waves. I like the look of it; I like walking along the beach, and how different it looks at different times of year. You have high tide; you have low tide; you have grey seas, and you have beautiful blues seas. The sea has so many moods. The beach is always different.'

⌒

I stop in Lakes Entrance for the night. In summer, it's a bustling tourist town, full of fishermen and families come to explore the Gippsland Lakes, but in winter it's a more peaceful place working to its own rhythms. I've brought my pushbike along for this part of the trip, and in the early morning I ride along the waterfront, next to the river. There's a pretty little harbour, made prettier yet by the sight of a working fishing fleet, small but still productive. I ride across the pedestrian bridge spanning the inlet, across to the dunes and the surf beach. There are suggestions of a storm and the breakers are already building, their surface brown with turbulence. It's a wild beach on a wild coast.

I eat fish and chips, and they are good. I have something of a weakness for an old-fashioned piece of battered fish. Chips are neither here nor there, but there is something comforting in a good piece of fish. I've been sampling the local offerings all the way down the coast, and Lakes Entrance is right up there with the best. The old-fashioned shop, with its deep-fryers and wire baskets, is selling a variety of local fish, none of them cheap but all of them fresh. I order flathead tails, taking them back to my motel room and eating them with a bargain bottle of white while watching the television news. The flathead is succulent, the batter crisp, the taste perfect. A little piece of heaven.

Next day I drive towards Melbourne. I'm still more than a hundred kilometres away when the rain hits, a front driving in from the west. The ABC radio informs me that the West Australian division of the Liberal Party has called for a royal commission into the science of climate change. Dr Mal Washer, a Liberal moderate retiring from federal parliament at the next election, calls the motion 'silly'. He's not wrong. Royal commissions are established to investigate corruption, serious wrongdoing or wide-ranging systemic failures. What are the West Australians suggesting? If they disagree with the science, they have every right to challenge it, preferably with science of their own. But the call for a royal commission is suggesting something far more sinister than the science being wrong; implicit in the motion is the suggestion the science has been deliberately manipulated, that some grand conspiracy is at play. 'Silly' is right. As I drive through the rain, I wonder where it was that we lost our respect for science and scientists. We live in an age of technological wonder, the beneficiaries of a rolling scientific revolution three hundred years and more in the making. Jet planes fill the skies; the internet spans the globe, and wonder drugs challenge the boundaries of mortality. We recognise the latest advances even as we take previous discoveries and inventions for granted. Our entire civilisation is built on science and technology. Each generation questions the benefits of such advances, ponders if we're removing ourselves too far from nature. There are those, like the hippies of Nimbin, who reject consumerism and attempt to return to a more natural life. But rejecting the products of science and technology, challenging the uses to which they have been put, is very different from challenging the veracity of science itself. I swear at the radio and turn it off. Silly indeed.

It's absolutely pouring as I enter Melbourne on the Monash Freeway. I've booked passage on the *Spirit of Tasmania*, but the ferry doesn't sail until evening. With time to spare, I drive down to Point Ormond, park the car and hope the rain will pass. There's no guarantee it will. This is no precocious spring storm, but the resolute soaking of a late winter front. The rain is constant in intensity and spread. The sky, the rain and the sea are grey—I have difficulty discerning one from the other. So I sit in my car, watching the sodden passing of the occasional obsessive jogger or cyclist. Who knows what is being flushed down through the Elwood Canal? Time flows on, and still the rain persists. Just as I'm thinking I will have to abandon my quest, the downfall eases enough for me to emerge. To the west, a schism of golden light has broken its way through the greyness. To my left lies a thin strip of caramel-coloured sand, to my right a concrete walkway winds beside the water round the base of Point Ormond. Point Ormond itself is little more than a gentle lawn-covered hillock, the height of a two- or three-storey house, topped by a white navigation marker. I walk along the promenade, wondering if it has changed much since my mother was a child. There's a low stone wall, and the water laps against the rocks below the path. I round the point and there, as if conjured for my purpose, is a gap in the wall and a shallow ramp dipping down into the water. In my mind, there can be no mistake. Surely this is my uncle Jim's special spot. Tentatively I edge down the ramp, careful not to slip on the slick concrete. A few drops of rain pockmark the water's surface, but the waves are gentle and the sea is clear. Really clear: clear like crystal, clear like gin. I look down through it at the rocks scattered on the sandy bottom and see a spray of small orange starfish. I take some snaps to show my mother and continue along to the Elwood Canal itself, pausing on the bridge as a surge of post-rain joggers passes me by. The water, even with the runoff from the rain, is transparent enough to reveal the bottom. Down where the canal meets the bay, I see another scattering of pale-orange starfish. Starfish are the nautical equivalent of coalmine canaries. They pump seawater directly into their bodies, with little or no ability to filter pollution or toxins—a living barometer of the environment. The starfish are another sign of hope. The people of Elwood wanted a cleaner beach and the authorities eventually responded. Maybe some businesses weren't happy with being obliged to dispose of their waste more thoughtfully. Yet no one, as far as I know, called for a royal commission into the science of water pollution.

At the ripe old age of sixteen, I visited Burnie in Tasmania as part of an ACT volleyball team. It was a good team; later that year, or perhaps it was the next, we won the Australian championship. So touring northern Tasmania and playing local teams was a bit of a doddle. In between games, we did a lot of unofficial team bonding, which consisted of drinking a lot of the local beer and various types of alcoholic cider. In one town, we sat on the roof of a house drinking beer after a game and one of our opponents fell off, breaking an arm. The 1970s were different like that. In Burnie, we did something of a pub-crawl, starting down near the harbour and making our way up the steep hill above the port. In those days, Burnie stank: the pulp mill filled the air with a pungent, organic odour, and it poured vast amounts of waste directly out into Bass Strait. It was said so much sulphur dioxide came out the smoke stacks that the acid rain etched the paintwork off cars. I remember looking back down the hill and being aghast at what I saw. A large red-orange stain pushed its way out into Bass Strait, as if the very land were bleeding out into the water. That was the paint factory, run by Tioxide Australia, pumping pigment directly into Bass Strait. Back then, Burnie had the reputation of being the most polluted city in Australia.

Thirty-five years later, I've come back to Burnie. The ferry from Melbourne docked at Devonport at 6.30 a.m., and I've driven the 50 kilometres in no time. The Bass Highway is a dual carriageway, boasting a 110–kilometre per hour speed limit. I recall another insight from that volleyball tour: the terminal at Launceston airport was larger and more impressive than that in Canberra, the national capital. Burnie and Launceston lie within the boundaries of Braddon and Bass, perennially two of the most marginal seats in federal parliament, and the decades of pork-barrelling show. But government largesse can only make up for so much. Burnie appears worn and disheartened as I drive into town past the derelict pulp and paper mill. The old factory looms over the main road, its paintwork starting to fade, many of its windows shattered. The Australian Pulp and Paper Mill, or the Pulp as it's referred to locally, stopped producing wood pulp in 1998, although paper production continued until just last year, relying on imported pulp. The last shipment came from Brazil. At its height, the Pulp employed 3500 workers. And yet Burnie is not dead yet. I look down at the town from a lookout on the same hill I must have staggered up in 1976. The air is clean and Bass Strait untainted, yet even from a distance it's evident that the harbour is busy. A large hillock of woodchips, ironic considering the town's history, awaits loading. Nearby, cranes busy themselves, tending the needs of a large container ship sporting the aquamarine livery of the Toll transport group. The company runs two ships, a nightly service each way between Melbourne and Tasmania. Burnie is Tasmania's busiest port, the fifth-largest container port in Australia.

Down in the town, businesses are beginning to open. Fortified by my second coffee for the day, I walk through the small CBD to where the harbour meets the beach. It's a lovely little beach, a few hundred metres long, cosseted between the protective walls of the harbour and a low headland. It's deserted in the early morning drizzle, its sand turned the same caramel colour as the beach at Point Ormond. A boardwalk, brand new and not yet complete, has been built above the dunes—part of plans to revitalise the old town, to make it more attractive to tourists and locals alike. More government largesse, no doubt. Near the far end of the boardwalk, up towards the main road, an impressive new building beckons. At first glance it looks like grey cement, but it's in fact clad with translucent grey-white plastic, allowing light to penetrate into the building's interior. This is the Makers' Workshop, part museum, part art and craft gallery, part tourist centre. It celebrates the city's past and explicitly outlines the city's marketing strategy: to portray Burnie as a place that still makes things. There are pamphlets promoting craft paper, mining machinery, whisky and cheese. Nowadays Burnie presents itself as a home to cottage industries, an environmentally conscious place where platypus and penguins can be seen in the wild.

I get talking to one of the volunteers. John is in his late sixties, with a bald head rimmed by a band of bright-orange hair. I ask him how Burnie is doing. He doesn't hold back, responding in staccato sentences. 'Very bad, like the rest of Tasmania. We're a basket case. And we always will be, because we always lose our young people. We lose our intelligentsia. I have two sons, both engineers. They don't live in Tasmania,' he tells me. John likes the platypus and penguins, and candidly concedes the dumping of paint pigments into Bass Strait was a disaster, but that doesn't mean he's convinced by the new clean, green Burnie, even if he's standing behind a counter promoting it. 'The environmentalists have been very successful in closing most things down in Tasmania. Twenty years ago we had a proposal to build a pulp mill at Wesley Vale here. But it was blocked by the Labor Party and the Greens at the time. Just like everything else. Like the last big power station they were going to build on the Gordon River. That was blocked with the support of that marvellous man Mister Bob Brown. Unfortunately, the Greens and Labor have gotten into bed, so we've virtually got a green government and the federals have too. We've lost our timber industry completely.'

I leave John to explain the hands-on paper-making experience to some curious Germans and head back outside to the start of the boardwalk. But instead of returning alongside the beach to the CBD, I turn the other way. A sign tells me there are little penguins. That would be something to see, within the boundaries of a town so recently decried for its industrial-scale pollution. Along the walkway at the viewing centre, there is a small group of people armed with clipboards, inspecting the place. It looks relatively new, a long wall with a sheltering roof, information panels and viewing slots. I peer out through one of the slots over some tussocks of grass and rocks to the waves of the ocean.

'You won't see any now', says a voice behind me. 'Wrong time of year. And they come in the evening.'

I turn to find a friendly looking fellow, small and dressed entirely in brown, from his shirt, jumper and corduroy pants to his deck shoes. He has a toothy grin, and seems a little agitated. In his agitation and his brownness, he invokes an image of a chipmunk. I don't need to ask questions—he tells me all about the penguins, how they are here mainly between November and April, and how their burrows near the viewing platform were cleverly hand-built by local volunteers. I thank him for the information, shake his hand and ask his name.

'Alvwyn Boyd', he says. 'I'm the town mayor.'

'How long have you been mayor?'

'About eleven years.'

'Really? Listen, this might seem strange, but I think you knew my father. Kevin Hammer.'

'Kevin? Yes, of course. You even look a bit like him. You know, he and your mother came here a few years ago, on a big cruise ship, and I was there greeting the people at the dock and I recognised him.'

'I know', I say. 'They told me all about it. They said you were there in your official regalia, that you whisked them away, gave them a private tour, had them over for lunch.' Then I tell Alvwyn about Dad's death.

'I'm sorry to hear that. He was a wonderful man. He taught me agriculture at Ringarooma, more than fifty years ago. I can still see him there, dressed in his khaki overalls.'

But Alvwyn can spare no more time for reminiscing. The people with the clipboards have questions. They're judges for the Tidy Towns competition, and the mayor is anxious to keep them happy. The lord mayors of Sydney and Melbourne may fawn over delegates from the Olympics and FIFA, but it's the arbiters of Keep Australia Beautiful that put the wind up leaders of our smaller communities. The clipboards stride back towards the Makers' Workshop, with Alvwyn in hot pursuit.

⌐⟋

'George Town', says the woman behind the information-centre counter, 'is the oldest town in Australia'.

'Really?' I say doubtfully. 'What about Sydney or Hobart?'

'No, they're cities. They don't count.'

'I see. So George Town is the third-oldest European settlement in Australia?'

'That's right. But we prefer oldest town. It sounds more impressive.'

I think of Parramatta, founded immediately after Sydney, and various other settlements in and around the New South Wales capital, but I don't argue. George Town's location has been both its biggest advantage and its biggest handicap. It sits snug just inside the mouth of the Tamar River, close to where it flows into Bass Strait. The Tamar is an atypical Australian river: it retains its depth and breadth for a considerable distance inland, remaining navigable for 45 kilometres, all the way to Launceston. Indeed the Tamar as far as Launceston is tidal—a saltwater estuary. The width of the river meant a bridge upstream from Launceston defied nineteenth-century engineers, and cross-river traffic relied on ferries until the Batman Bridge was constructed in 1968. So Launceston became the port and the railhead, at the junction where the westerly Bass Highway met the easterly Tasman Highway and the southerly Midlands Highway. George Town remained an outlier: a pilot station for ships entering the Tamar, a holiday village for Launceston and a signal station.

I find George Town rather bleak. On a wet winter's day its long main street, running down a ridgeline towards the sea, lies bare and exposed. There are few trees, fewer still that grow higher than the single-storey shopfronts. The rain has swept the street clean of people, so I drive to the nearby lookout on Mount George. Even with clouds dogging the horizon, the vantage point reveals a panorama encompassing Bass Strait in the north, the winding Tamar River valley and the distant highlands to the south. In colonial days, there was a semaphore station here, part of a relay that transmitted messages between Launceston, George Town and the Low Head lighthouse and pilot station. A replica semaphore has been built, but it's dwarfed by steel microwave and mobile-phone towers. At the lookout, one sign explains how the semaphore flags worked; another informs visitors that 'business is booming'. The sign explains that immediately after World War II, the population of George Town had dwindled to about three hundred, yet it now sits at over 4500. But, I wonder, how old is the sign? Among the booming businesses it lists is Carter Holt Harvey, a medium-density-fibreboard factory, which closed in 2006 after a disastrous fire, and the Beaconsfield gold mine, which closed the same year after a cave-in that killed one miner and trapped another two underground for a fortnight. Still, George Town has grown significantly since its post-war nadir. The town's renaissance can be attributed to the Batman Bridge and the development of Bell Bay, just south of George Town, as a major deepwater port capable of accommodating modern ships too large for Launceston. I drive down to the port, nestled in bushland and surrounded by nodes of major industry halfway between George Town and the Batman Bridge. Here you can find Comalco's aluminium smelter and BHP's ferroalloy plant, as well as the sawmill that has replaced the fibreboard plant. Bell Bay is also the site of Tasmania's only fossil-fuel-powered power station, fed by a natural-gas pipeline from Victoria. Bell Bay is linked across Bass Strait to the mainland electricity grid, allowing Tasmania to both import and export electricity. Nearby is another major industrial development: Gunns Limited's Tamar Valley Pulp Mill. The proposed mill is highly controversial, not just in Tasmania but throughout Australia. It has become symbolic of a larger debate over how much we value development and how much we value the natural environment.

I drive back into George Town. Beside the highway into town is a deserted factory. It's well maintained behind its security fence: lawns mowed and building painted. But all signage has been removed and its three flagpoles are bare. No indication remains of what was manufactured here. Spread along one wall is a huge black banner with white lettering: 'TASSIE SUPPORTS PULP MILL'.

⌒

Lucy Landon-Lane doesn't support the pulp mill. Nor do her neighbours. Little wonder—they live on the banks of the Tamar River opposite the site proposed for the fourth-largest mill in the world. Some have placards out on their fences, red writing on white: 'STOP THIS PULP MILL! PULP MILLS POISON LAND, AIR AND WATER.'

Lucy and her husband Chris grow organic walnuts. Nearby are four award-winning wineries, a fish farm, a truffle farm, peach and cherry orchards, and a dairy farm. In the lounge of Lucy's home a large feature window perfectly frames a curve of the river. 'Yeah, I'm a Nimby', says Lucy over a cup of tea in her kitchen. She's a compact woman, with clear blue eyes and a mad bird's nest of blond hair. 'I don't mind being called a Nimby. But I also don't just think of the Tamar as my backyard. I think of Tasmania as my backyard.'

Objections to the mill are many and varied. When it was first proposed, back in 2005, an immediate concern was that it would devour increasing amounts of native forest, including old-growth forest. The company behind the plan is Gunns, the largest woodchip exporter in the Southern Hemisphere, a company that has been logging Tasmania's native forests for more than a century. It's a company that environmentalists love to hate, and not without reason. In 1989, the chairman, Edmund Rouse, attempted to thwart the results of the state election. He tried bribing a Labor backbencher to cross the floor and support the pro-logging government of Liberal premier Robin Gray. Rouse was convicted and went to gaol. After leaving politics, Gray became a director of Gunns from 1996 until his retirement in 2010. He was on the board when it took legal action in 2005 against twenty prominent anti-logging individuals and groups, including Greens leader Bob Brown, as well as members of the Wilderness Society and the Huon Valley Environment Centre. The suit claimed the twenty had sullied the company's reputation. It was widely interpreted among environmentalists and civil libertarians as a 'gagging writ', a type of legal intimidation designed to curtail criticism. This background is important: any company would have had a hard time winning support for the mill, but Gunns was already seen by anti-logging activists as public enemy number one.

The forestry debate has driven a deep schism into Tasmanian society over several decades; no one on the environmental side of that debate believed the company's claims the mill would be world's best practice. They believed it even less when, in 2007, the Labor government of Paul Lennon passed the *Pulp Mill Assessment Act*, which set out special criteria for the assessment of the environmental impact of the mill, overruling existing industry standards. Among other changes, the Act removed the right of individuals and companies to seek redress if the mill damaged their health or their livelihoods. Now there is a real possibility that Gunns will be unable to get the financial backing to build the mill. Lucy says the company has only itself to blame.

'If it doesn't go ahead, the number-one reason would probably be Gunns's arrogance, presuming they could get away with whatever they wanted and not having any opposition. That somehow they could bulldoze it through. Number two, people power—people have been prepared to stand up and say no. And number three, a change in markets: people want products that are more ethically sound, including their paper. One of the reasons Gunns doesn't have a joint-venture partner is because they are known to be so deeply unpopular and [as having] no social licence. Södra, a Finnish company, were interested, but withdrew when they saw there was no social licence.'

In recent times, Gunns, led by a more progressive board, has attempted to make the mill more environmentally attractive. It would use an elemental chlorine free (ECF) process, greatly reducing the level of pollutants released into the environment. What's more, Gunns has promised the mill would no longer be fed by native forests and would instead rely entirely on plantation-grown feedstock. But that has not satisfied diehard opponents. For them, every concession made by Gunns is seen as evidence of initial duplicity. Lucy Landon-Lane says even with ECF and plantation feedstock, the mill presents numerous problems. She's concerned about air pollution, including fine particulate matter and rotten-egg smells. The plant would be powered by a wood-fired power station, increasing air pollution. Lucy says that winter fogs already plague the Tamar Valley and that the valley's temperature-inversion layer would trap smoke and other pollutants from the plant. She says Launceston, at the head of the valley, already has some of the highest air-pollution levels in the country. There are also concerns over the impact of the eucalyptus plantations. According to Lucy, aerial spraying with atrazine, a herbicide banned in the European Union, could pollute waterways, poisoning native plants and animals and threatening Tasmania's reputation as an exporter of clean, green food. Another concern is water. Pulp mills consume immense amounts of fresh water. Tasmania has the highest rainfall of any state south of the tropics, but it is not immune to drought. Then there is the effluent. The mill would pump 64 000 tonnes of wastewater into Bass Strait each and every day.

'Bass Strait is a big concern', says Lucy. 'It's very shallow and doesn't flush. The tides move the water back and forth, but it takes something like 160 days to flush water through the strait. So the effluent out there will just move and back and forth. It's not a big flushing system.

'The effluent contains a number of persistent organic pollutants: dioxins and furans. They're the main concerns. There is some commercial fishing that goes on out there and there is also a lot of recreational fishing. Migrating whales go through Bass Strait, and there is an important Australian fur seal colony that is about ten kilometres away from the effluent outflow point. There are bottlenose dolphins and all other kinds of sea life.

'The federal government told Gunns that they had to do hydrodynamic modelling of Bass Strait to see what was going to happen. The studies have only been done on federal waters. The effluent pipe actually stops short of federal waters. It's in state waters. There has been no proper assessment of what will happen in state waters, and there has been no assessment of what might happen in the Tamar, because the way the water moves, the effluent will flow back into the Tamar.'

Next day I venture out to find where the pipeline would enter the sea. I get as far as Bell Buoy Beach, where the road ends. From there I walk along the sand towards Five Mile Bluff. It's a foul day, the wind coming in off Bass Strait mixing rain and sea spray and throwing it into my face. I persist for a while, then retreat to the car, defeated by the elements. The coastline is rugged, inaccessible. The proposed effluent pipeline will push out under the sea—out of sight, out of mind. This is not the twenty-first-century equivalent of the Elwood Canal or the Burnie paint works. Here, the effluent wouldn't be visible, but 64 000 tonnes of wastewater pumped into

Bass Strait each day would be a lot. The impact would be be under the waves.

⟲

I drive through the rain towards Launceston. Lucy has put me in contact with Jon Bryan, a professional scuba diver with an abiding interest in Bass Strait. I find him living in a ramshackle house in suburban Launceston. Air tanks, wetsuits, flippers and other diving paraphernalia fill the house, giving the impression that time spent on land is merely an interregnum for Jon. We sit in the kitchen and talk, while an insistent tabby cat shuffles from one lap to the other, trying to draw warmth from each of us in turn. Jon is a big bloke, fifty years old, dressed in shorts and boots despite the day's cold dampness. He recounts his history as a professional diver, making thousands of dives off every continent save Africa. I figure anyone who goes scuba diving in Antarctica must be keen. His demeanour is low-key and practical, yet his voice comes alive as he talks of the sea.

'There's amazing underwater environments all across southern Australia. Tasmania has some of the most spectacular. Bass Strait has it's own character compared to the rest of Tasmania. It has its own unique fish and marine plant life and invertebrate life. It's a nice place to go diving to see pretty amazing things. The highlights are the shallow rocky reefs, which have lots of colourful fish on them.

'Another highlight is the seal colony at Tenth Island. It's an amazing colony. I've dived with seals all over the world. Leopard seals in Antarctica, steller seals in Canada, grey seals and harbour seals in the United Kingdom and Ireland, and of course Australian fur seals and New Zealand fur seals and sea lions across southern Australia. And this colony is the best colony I've ever experienced.

'The seals are very interested in divers. It's very shallow; there's no big drop offs where sharks can lurk. On a nice day, it's quite sheltered and calm and the visibility is usually good. They mightn't have ever seen a human being before, but they'll still come up and check you out, to the point where they'll pull your flippers or your fingers or stick their face in your face. They are very interactive animals. I've dived with whales and dolphins and lots of other big animals, but seals are the most curious about humans. If you dive at a seal colony where they feel confident, they're great fun. If you like big, playful dogs, then you'll like seals.'

I'm not so sure myself. Australian fur seals are big. Males grow to 2.5 metres and weigh 500 kilograms. But Jon tells me their future is uncertain. 'Their colony on Tenth Island lies just 12 kilometres from the proposed effluent outfall. Every day it would put 64 000 tonnes of effluent into the Bass Strait. The effluent is not tertiary treated and it can contain a whole range of toxic materials. The most concerning are the persistent organic pollutants like dioxins, which can bio-accumulate.

'The problem is that there doesn't appear to be any sort of third-party monitoring. The monitoring program that is being put in place doesn't deal with the types of organisms that are most likely to be impacted. That's bottlenose dolphins and the Australian fur seal. The seal colony at Tenth Island is a breeding colony, and seal pups are particularly vulnerable to this type of toxic effect, because seals are top-order predators, which feed regularly in the area of the effluent outfall, the pollution plume. They eat fish that eat smaller fish that eat organisms that pick up the dioxins. So that bio-accumulates and the mothers then give it to their pups through milk.

'Now, I find that quite unacceptable. We have a situation where monitoring of dioxin levels in seals is not going to be done. Instead they are going to look at eggs of fairy penguins at the mouth of the Tamar. The pollution plume is at the edge of the range of those penguins, so they are not going to feed as regularly in that plume as dolphins and seals do. Also, little blue penguins have shorter life spans and, being birds, they don't have as much fat as seals.'

Jon is concerned both by the content of the effluent and by the location of the outfall just 3 kilometres offshore. 'The key thing is that it is not in Commonwealth waters, but it's not right close to the shore. If they were putting it into Commonwealth waters, then there wouldn't be much chance of it getting the go-ahead. If I were designing it, I would put the pipe 20 kilometres out, to get it right out where it will disperse quickly. It appears to me that there is a cynical attempt to put it into an area that will allow the Commonwealth to wash its hands of the situation. Gunns is relying on a compliant state government not to cause any problems.

'I think there is a different perception of waste going into the sea. It's out of sight, out of mind to some extent. When people think of wilderness in Tasmania, it is of the forests and the mountains. That's really understandable. But very few people are aware of the marine environment, and our marine wildernesses are just stunning.'

The road out of Launceston is steep. Just minutes after leaving the CBD, I'm in farmland—neither a house in sight nor another car on the road. Just the rain to keep me company. It's a reminder of just how sparsely Tasmania is populated. Just 500 000 people, not that many more than Canberra. The Tasman Highway climbs up and up into the clouds, open fields giving way to eucalyptus plantations and then to native forest. The road winds this way and that, giant green ferns emerging out of the fog at the feet of towering trees, tops hidden in the mist. I'm on my way to Scottsdale, to hear the other side of the pulp mill story, not from some company flak, but from one of the forestry contractors whose livelihood is on the line. The couple had offered to meet me in Launceston, but when I learnt where they lived, I decided to make the one-hour drive, even if Scottsdale is far from the coast. My parents once resided in the town, the first place they lived after they were married. My elder sister and brother were born there, but I've never been there. I want to see it for myself.

The road begins to descend from the cloud. I stop at a lookout. On a clear day, the view across the valley to Scottsdale would be spectacular, but today there is low visibility. The road takes me down into a valley so green that, with its folding hills, it could be the Yorkshire Dales. I get to the edge of Scottsdale and my attention is caught by an unusual building, shaped like a barrel that has sunk, listing, two-thirds of the way into the ground. It is the Forest Eco Centre. Intrigued by the prospect of an 'eco' centre in a logging town, I spare a few minutes to explore. Inside, I find there is not much eco about it. The building is an innovative low-energy design, but it houses the offices of Forestry Tasmania, the government agency that administers state forests. The display area presents a pro-logging story cast in a pro-environment light. It's not the first place I've found on my journey that has appropriated the new environmental consciousness to turn a dollar, win an argument or titivate the mundane. There was the Eco Village in Mission Beach, eco tours in Eden and, my personal favourite, the EnviroDog Grooming Salon in Burnie. The coast of Australia is littered with claims of environmental sensibility, some genuine, some duplicitous. Who was it that said, 'We're all environmentalists now'?

I check my coordinates and head out of town along North Scottsdale Road. I don't get far. I'm arrested by a collection of weatherboard buildings, painted in telltale heritage colours: cream walls, russet corrugated roofs and a fading sign that reads, 'Scottsdale District School Farm. Est. 1929.' There can be little doubt my father once taught here. He was employed as an agriculture extension officer, helping to bring modern farming methods to the soldier-settlers of the northeast. There is no one about, no sign of any students, but the buildings are well maintained, with equipment hanging in sheds, and seed beds already set out for spring. A couple of poddy lambs lie on a path outside a cottage, curious of this interloper. There is smoke drifting from the chimney. I knock on the door. It's answered by a young bloke, hair in a ponytail and dressed in overalls. His daughter looks out at me cautiously from around the doorjamb. I tell him my story. He says he's just renting the cottage and knows nothing of its history, but says I'm welcome to look around. And so I do. It's not hard to imagine my father there, young and vigorous, evangelical about the new farming methods transforming agriculture, back in an era when to question the veracity of science was close to heresy.

The house of Karen and Ken Hall sits beside the road a few kilometres further along the road. It's a big place, testament to Ken's success in his thirty-five years as a logging contractor. Karen, a young-looking fifty-six, greets me. She makes apologies for Ken, who is ill in bed, and leads me through to the open-plan kitchen-dining area. A couple of Karen's grandkids are crawling round on the floor, gurgling with pleasure. Karen offers me the mandatory cup of tea, and we sit at the table and discuss the rise and fall of the forestry industry.

'Ken started as a hand feller, a bushman. He started straight from school, worked for Forestry Tas, assessing forests around the state. Then there came an opportunity, after we were married eight or nine years: a logging contracting business became available, so we bought that. I think in about 1984. That had one truck loader plus one employee plus Ken. So that was when we started logging in native forests.'

But Ken Hall stopped logging native forest years ago. In the late 1980s he saw the future was in plantation timber and tailored his business accordingly, investing up to $750 000 each for mechanical harvesting machines. He and Karen also started planting trees on their own land. But now there is little or no work. For decades, Ken has been aligned with Gunns, and Gunns is no longer exporting woodchips.

'A couple of years ago, when the downturn started to hit us in Tasmania, there were ten contractors who worked for the Gunns company in this area alone, and between us we employed 150 people', explains Karen. 'Now there are maybe five contractors left, working at less than 30 per cent capacity. And the workforce? There's probably barely fifty left, about a third of what it was. There are probably forty contractors in the state who are waiting for the financiers to foreclose. Some have already foreclosed. So, there are a lot of businesses who will be gone within the next couple of months.'

Karen says a number of factors have combined to cause the downfall. She cites the high Australian dollar, the impact of the Greens, Gunns's poor public image and the delay in building the pulp mill. She says that the Japanese pulp and paper factories that once bought woodchips from Gunns started sourcing chips from elsewhere once the company announced plans to build its own pulp mill. Scottsdale has been hard hit. The town used to have two softwood sawmills, but they were bought out by Gunns, which then closed them down when the concession to the state-owned pine forests was won by a competitor. The competitor built a new mill at Bell Bay. Gunns bought out the competitor, but the mill is now up for sale.

'I think it is more crucial than ever before that the pulp mill is built. Tasmania has little shops and little businesses and we do things in little ways, so I think it's frightening to some people, who think it might be a bit big. The economic modelling for our region and for the whole of the state has shown the impact is going to be massive. Economically and socially I'd hate to think where we are going to in this state if we don't have the mill. Businesses like ours, and our community, have lost so much already. It is just going to have a devastating effect if it doesn't go ahead.

'It splits families when there isn't enough work here for our young people. A lot of older people are moving to Tasmania, but they don't create businesses like younger people do. The fear that our young people will move away is a huge factor.'

As I stand to leave, the clouds part. Out of the lounge-room windows a vista reveals itself, stretching out across the emerald valley to Bridport on the coast 20 kilometres away, and beyond that, Bass Strait. Not so far away after all.

⌒⌐

The sun is out at last, bringing with it the promise of spring, still two weeks away. I walk through Launceston's City Park towards the centre of town. It is a grand Victorian park, complete with cast-iron gates, deciduous trees and carefully laid-out paths bisecting lawns like green felt. I pass statues of cast bronze, an elegant conservatory, a duck pond, a rotunda, a monkey house and a drinking fountain. The fountain is set beneath a small iron-lace cupola bearing a bas-relief profile of the Queen herself and the inscription 'Erected on Her Majesty's Diamond Jubilee 20 June 1897'. The structure is entirely covered in caramel and cream paint.

The park pours me out into the city centre, a small-scale CBD. Launceston may boast a population of only 100 000 people, roughly equal to Albury-Wodonga, but it has the air of a nascent capital. The neoclassical town hall, pillared and glowing cream in the morning light, could serve as the parliament of an Australian state or a small Baltic country. It bears its own coat of arms: a heraldic shield supported by two Tasmanian tigers rampant. The thylacines are constrained by blue linked chains. The coat of arms bears the city's motto: Progress with Prudence. One feels the tigers would have preferred a bit more prudence. Down by the harbour another neoclassical edifice, the customs house, echoes the confidence of another time. Somewhere along the way, Launceston was left behind. Just as it was settled from, and quickly eclipsed, George Town, Launceston in turn became the springboard from which Melbourne was settled three decades later. Walk the city streets, with their grand Victorian buildings, and it's possible to imagine the two cities exchanging fates had the goldfields been discovered in the Tasmanian highlands instead of the Victorian hinterland. As it was, Melbourne became the richest city on earth and the second largest in the British Empire, while Launceston drifted into relative obscurity. Lumber and fine wool can't compete with the allure of gold. Now it's Perth that shimmers with the aura of mineral wealth.

Tasmania is periodically called a mendicant state. Many Australians wouldn't know the definition of mendicant—begging or living on alms—but Tasmanians do. They hear it often enough, thrown at them by mainlanders and internal critics alike. West Australian premier Colin Barnett used the term most recently, comparing his state's willingness to set aside environmental concerns and develop a natural-gas processing hub on the Kimberley coast to Tasmanians' reluctance to support the Gunns pulp mill. Barnett believes Tasmania should do more to hold its own, rather than relying on continued subsidies from the mainland states. It's not unusual to hear critics closer to home say that Tasmania is in danger of becoming an aged-care facility surrounded by a national park.

I live in Canberra, a town that knows a thing or two about living off the wealth of others. Yet even the Australian Capital Territory looks relatively thrifty compared with the island state. The ACT, with a population of 350 000, is governed by a seventeen-member micro-parliament that combines the roles of state government and local council. It has an executive consisting of five ministers. Federally, the ACT has two members of the House of Representatives and two senators—twenty-one full-time politicians in all. Tasmania, with a population of 500 000, has five members of the House of

Representatives, twelve senators and forty state parliamentarians—fifty-seven full-time politicians, one for every 5750 voters. And they're augmented by twenty-nine local councils and a state public service of 25 000. I can see what Colin Barnett is complaining about, but what is the alternative? How can Tasmania build a viable economy without exploiting and polluting the natural environment?

On the top floor of an elegantly designed passive-solar office building I find John Pitt. John is an engineer, a hands-on fellow, a practical man. He looks fit and lean, and carries himself with the self-assurance exuded by the very successful. He's the managing director of Pitt & Sherry, an engineering firm based in Launceston. The company's motto is 'sustainable thinking' and John is an advocate of moving towards an environmentally sustainable economy. He's also an outspoken supporter of the Gunns pulp mill. We sit in the company's boardroom as John explains why the two aren't mutually exclusive.

'I've been really interested in all the work around the world that has been done on prosperity and defining prosperity. Most of the research demonstrates it is no longer about money, but a whole lot of intangible issues. In parallel with that, a purely growth-focused approach to economic development is doomed to failure. We can't grow and grow forever, because we live in a finite world. A lot of the things we see in society today, like income inequality and social disruption, can be attributed to too strong a focus on economic growth as opposed to prosperity growth.'

John has, however, concluded that Tasmania still needs to grow its economy if it is to reach a level providing sufficient prosperity. He says that in recent years manufacturing, as well as forestry, has gone into decline, and that no new value-adding industries have emerged to replace them. 'I asked myself, if you take an environmental and social perspective, what are the limits on growth? How much of our natural resources can we consume and moneterise to create the economic growth to be prosperous at a minimum level? It's about balancing those things. I came to the view that we want industries in this state that can deliver growth but be sustainable. I think the easy ones to get hold of are the ones that use renewable resources. Forestry and forest products are the prime example, together with renewable energy applications, of how you can use a resource that is naturally renewable to generate economic value but replace itself. Provided you control the environmental impacts of the by-products of that process, like the effluent and atmospheric discharges, you should have something that is very compatible with a natural setting like we've got here in Tasmania.'

Such issues came into sharp focus for Pitt & Sherry when the opportunity arose to work on the pulp mill. John says his firm tried to be rational, attempting to set aside the emotion that so characterises environmental debates in Tasmania. 'When this project came up, as we've done with a number of other contentious projects, we held what we call a conscience session, to test how our people thought about us getting involved. There's a difference between something being contentious and something being sustainable. Because we are technical people, we recognise those differences. So we like to place our opinions on objective evidence rather than belief.

'We tested this from a number of aspects. We did some internal surveys and discussions; we sent two of our key people ... to look at some of the current generation of technology in South America— Uruguay and Brazil and Chile—and they spent two or three weeks investigating those plants, looking at how compatible they are with those receiving environments and what would be the impact of building one of those plants here. They came back with very positive reports. Given that this mill was being set up around next-generation technology, particularly around emission control and wastewater treatments, we were really confident that the impacts would be acceptable and that this mill would be compatible.'

I ask about the effluent and the dangers posed by dioxin. John looks slightly annoyed. Not at me asking the question, I suspect, but rather because the issue persists. 'It's totally overstated. If you look at the papers to get the exact quantity, the amount of dioxin emitted per year is some fraction of the size of a pinhead, so we're talking of that scale. There is a lot alarmism surrounding the project that from a scientific perspective just isn't warranted. The effluent, which is directed through an ocean outfall into Bass Strait, is a fairly saline effluent because of the nature of the process, but aside from that, it's pretty benign. The expectation was that, despite the high volume discharge, it would be quite acceptable in terms of its impact and that is what the studies have projected.'

I recall Jon Bryan's point: if the effluent was so benign, why not discharge it deeper and further out to sea, in Commonwealth waters, where it would be dispersed more effectively? But I haven't come to quiz John on technical issues. Instead, I'm interested in his insights into Tasmanian mentality. I ask him where the state is headed.

'It's at a discontinuity in its history, where it can make some really good, clear decisions about where its future lies and bring the population together behind a common vision and progress it. Or it can continue to wallow in introspection and social disharmony. The forestry debate has been a real community splitter here because it has been adversarial. We haven't moved forward. It's so very divisive. There is real need to galvanise the community behind a common vision.'

Yeah, good luck. I think it, but I don't say it.

On the most perfect of days, cloudless and windless, the winter sky an intense blue dome, I take one last drive, along Victoria's Great Ocean Road. I head down through Anglesea and Aireys Inlet and have breakfast by the beach at Lorne. I'm going west, along the winding cliff tops of one of the world's most dramatic coastlines, bush-clad cliffs plunging down into Bass Strait, on this day a deep and sonorous blue. Occasional houses, hoisted by wealth above the bush, hold their breath at the view. Road signs request slower drivers, presumably those mesmerised by the beauty, to pull aside and let less besotted traffic pass. Other signs advise: 'drive on left in Australia'. In summer, the cars along this stretch must be as thick as bush flies, but today I am far from the madding crowd. So I follow the road, stopping here and there to breathe in the expanse. On such a day, in such a place, it's like having a backstage pass to heaven.

I stop at Mount Defiance, where the escaped convict William Buckley set up camp. Buckley evaded the authorities for more than thirty years, living with the Wauthorong people before re-entering

European society. He may or may not have inspired the Aust-ralianism 'Buckley's chance', meaning not much chance at all. He escaped near the present site of Melbourne en route to Van Diemen's Land in 1803, before the settlement of George Town across the strait. By the time he emerged from the wilderness in 1835, Launceston was a bustling port, and John Batman had come to establish Melbourne.

The road carries me west, leaving the coast after Apollo Bay to climb up, then down, through the forests of the Otway National Park, before rejoining the coast above the cliffs east of Port Campbell. These are real cliffs, sheer, 70 metres high, stretching unbroken for kilometre after kilometre, bathed in grandeur. This is the coast of the Twelve Apostles, of Loch Ard Gorge, of London Bridge; it's possibly the most celebrated section of Australia's much-celebrated coastline. The apostles are vertical islands of sandstone, as high as the cliffs themselves, carved from the mainland by the relentless Southern Ocean. Originally called the Sow and Piglets, some clever rebranding elevated them towards the holy—so the Twelve Apostles they are. They may be a disciple or two short of a dozen, but there is something in their grandeur that suggests divine ordination. The name fits.

A constant stream of tourists, cameras gorging, file along the ramparts connecting the cliff-top lookouts. A plethora of languages—German, Chinese, Thai, Swedish, Italian, Hindi—form a cheery melange. A couple from one hemisphere photographs a couple from another, before exchanging cameras and having the favour reciprocated. It's midday, but the winter sun is low enough to provide perfectly angled light.

Further along the road at Loch Ard Gorge I find myself suddenly alone, left to consider the cliffs and the ocean in temporary solitude. In 1878, the clipper ship the *Loch Ard*, three months into a voyage from London, shipwrecked here, the captain disoriented by heavy fog. Of the fifty-four people aboard, just two survived: a ship's apprentice, Tom Pearce, and a woman passenger, Eva Carmichael. Tom swam out and helped Eva ashore. Both were aged eighteen. The public were gripped by the romance of it all; Tom and Eva were gripped by the horror of it all. Afterwards, they went their separate ways.

Even on this most benign of days, it is not difficult to discern the power nature exerts in this place. Despite the complete lack of wind, the breakers roll in on the swell from the Southern Ocean, foaming white against the base of the cliffs. The rock walls themselves stand high and imperious, dwarfing human vanities. The gorge is a perfect horseshoe shape, and the sandstone cliffs honey-coloured in the midday sun, the glowing walls of a continent. Within the bay, two rock islands rise from the water, sides vertical, their flat tops covered in the same green stubble of vegetation as the cliffs of the mainland. The islands are doomed. The sea is cutting away at them at a rate of 2 centimetres a year. They are monumental, but mortal. One of the Twelve Apostles, the largest in fact, simply crumbled into the ocean one day in July 2005. The London Bridge, a two-arched peninsula, became a one-arched island when it partly collapsed in January 1990, leaving a couple of astounded tourists marooned. The islands before me in Loch Ard Gorge were joined by an archway until just two years ago, when it dissolved into the sea. The resulting islands were predictably christened Tom and Eva. One day they too will crumble and fall. But the sea also works away at the cliffs and peninsulas and promontories of the mainland, carving archways, which narrow to mere umbilicals before they too collapse, spawning new islands. Islands yield to the sea; new islands are born.

I think of my father. I wish he were here. I wish he were waiting in Canberra to hear of my adventures over a bottle of wine. I still feel as if he's simply voyaging somewhere, soon to return. I feel I should at least be able to email him, send him a text or upload some photo of this remarkable place.

I contemplate the ocean, so vast and yet, as we now know, so finite. The era of three-month sea voyages is gone; no longer can someone walk west from Melbourne into wilderness and disappear for three decades. The world is suddenly grown small; in our minds the atmosphere and the oceans have become shrunken, vulnerable and exposed. Threats encroach from all directions: rising sea levels, coral bleaching and acidification, bigger and more frequent cyclones, over-crowded cities, endangered species, beach erosion, overfishing and pollution. I feel myself growing old, as the world grows old. There is less time, less space.

Yet looking out across Loch Ard Gorge, with the warmth of the sun and the promise of spring in the air, the ravages of climate change feel remote, a storm beyond the horizon, and I enjoy simply being part of this grand and alluring landscape. I sit for long moments, long enough for the sun to begin its westward tilt. A group of young backpackers arrive and swarm around me, rambunctious and flirtatious, engrossed in their own world, ignoring me as they might a rock or a tree. It's time to go. I gather my ill-disciplined thoughts, repack my contemplations and begin the long drive home.

Acknowledgements

There are many people who deserve my thanks and my gratitude. First is my family: my wife Tomoko and our two children Cameron and Elena. They encouraged my travels, supported my writing and tolerated my absences. Second is the wonderful team at Melbourne University Publishing including Louise Adler, Colette Vella, Penelope White, Lily Keil and Terri King. Third are my friends and fellow writers, who offer encouragement, exchange ideas and offer insights. They know who they are. Last are the wonderful people I met in my travels—those who are mentioned in the book and those who are not. Without them, I would have no story to tell. So my thanks go out to all of those who spared the time to talk to me and share their insights, beliefs and hopes.